Circuit Complexity and Neural Networks

Foundations of Computing
Michael Garey and Albert Meyer, editors

Circuit Complexity and Neural Networks

Ian Parberry

The MIT Press
Cambridge, Massachusetts
London, England

This book was set in Computer Modern by the author and was printed and bound in the United States of America.

Library of Congress Cataloging-in-Publication Data

Parberry, Ian.
Circuit complexity and neural networks / Ian Parberry.
    p.   cm. — (Foundations of computing)
  Includes bibliographical references and index.
  ISBN 0-262-16148-6
  1. Neural networks (Computer science) 2. Computational
complexity. 3. Logic circuits. I. Title. II. Series
QA76.87.P38 1994
006.3—dc20   94-7955
                          CIP

Contents

QA
76.87
P38
1994

List of Figures

List of Tables

List of Theorems

List of Symbols

Sets

R	the set of real numbers
R$^+$	the set of positive reals
Z	the set of integers
N	the set of natural numbers
B	the Boolean set
U	the Boolean set using signs
F	the set of all functions
Σ	the set of all linear functions
Θ	the set of linear threshold functions
$\{x \mid P(x)\}$	the set of x such that property P holds on x
$[x, y]$	$\{z \in \mathbf{R} \mid x \leq z \leq y\}$
(x, y)	$\{z \in \mathbf{R} \mid x < z < y\}$

Functions

$f: A \rightarrow B$	the function f with domain A and range B
$\log n$	the logarithm to base 2 of n
$\log^k n$	$(\log n)^k$
$\ln n$	the natural logarithm of n
$\lceil x \rceil$	the smallest integer not less than $x \in \mathbf{R}^+$
$\lfloor x \rfloor$	the largest integer not exceeding $x \in \mathbf{R}^+$
$\lvert x \rvert, \mathrm{abs}(x)$	absolute value (magnitude) of $x \in \mathbf{R}$
$\lvert M \rvert$	determinant of matrix M
$\lVert x \rVert$	size of mathematical object x
$\sigma_n(w_1, \ldots, w_n)$	$\sigma_n(w_1, \ldots, w_n) : \mathbf{R}^n \rightarrow \mathbf{R}$, defined on p. 51
$\vartheta_n(w_1, \ldots, w_n, h)$	$\vartheta_n(w_1, \ldots, w_n, h) : \mathbf{R}^n \rightarrow \mathbf{B}$, defined on p. 52
$\theta_n(w_1, \ldots, w_n, h)$	$\vartheta_n(w_1, \ldots, w_n, h)$ restricted to the Boolean domain
$B(m, n, p)$	The probability of at least m failures in n independent Bernoulli trials, each with probability p of failure

Operations and Relations

$\binom{n}{r}$	the number of ways of choosing r things out of n, without replacement
$\leq_p$	reduces to in polynomial size
$\leq_c$	reduces to in polynomial size and polylog depth
$\wedge$	Boolean AND sign
$\vee$	Boolean OR sign
$\triangledown$	bitwise OR sign
$\oplus$	Boolean parity sign
$\neg$	Boolean complement sign
$\overline{x}$	Boolean complement of $x \in \mathbf{B}$
$x[b]$	$\overline{x}$ if $b = 0$, x if $b = 1$
IP	Boolean inner product
$\langle x, y \rangle$	integer inner product of x and y
$[x, y]$	pointwise product of x and y
$\mathcal{L}(C)$	language of C
$\subseteq$	is a subset of (or equal to)
$\subset$	is a proper subset of
$A \cup B$	set union, $\{x \mid x \in A \text{ or } x \in B\}$
$A \cap B$	set intersection, $\{x \mid x \in A \text{ and } x \in B\}$
$A \backslash B$	set difference, $\{x \mid x \in A \text{ and } x \notin B\}$
$A \triangle B$	symmetric set difference, $(A \cup B) \backslash (A \cap B)$
$\text{int}(x)$	integer of string x, defined on p. 4.3
$\text{str}(x)$	string of integer x, defined on p. 4.3
$\text{syn}(x)$	set of synonyms of string x, defined on p. 85
$\text{ant}(x)$	set of antonyms of string x, defined on p. 85
$\text{sim}(x)$	set of strings similar to x, $\text{syn}(x) \cup \text{ant}(x)$

Language Classes

$\mathcal{NP}$	the class of existential decision problems verifiable in polynomial size
$\mathcal{P}$	the class of decision problems computable in polynomial size

The following classes consist of languages recognized in polynomial size and polylog depth by the indicated circuit types. If present, a superscript of k means depth $\log^k n$ and a superscript of zero means depth $O(1)$.

$\mathcal{AC}$ alternating circuit
$\mathcal{NC}$ classical circuit
$\mathcal{MC}$ unit-weight threshold circuit
$\mathcal{RTC}$ randomized threshold circuit
$\mathcal{TC}$ small-weight threshold circuit
$\mathcal{WC}$ threshold circuit

Series Foreword

Theoretical computer science has now undergone several decades of development. The "classical" topics of automata theory, formal languages, and computational complexity have become firmly established, and their importance to other theoretical work and to practice is widely recognized. Stimulated by technological advances, theoreticians have been rapidly expanding the areas under study, and the time delay between theoretical progress and its practical impact has been decreasing dramatically. Much publicity has been given recently to breakthroughs in cryptography and linear programming, and steady progress is being made on programming language semantics, computational geometry, and efficient data structures. Newer, more speculative, areas of study include relational databases, VLSI theory, and parallel and distributed computation. As this list of topics continues expanding, it is becoming more and more difficult to stay abreast of the progress that is being made and increasingly important that the most significant work be distilled and communicated in a manner that will facilitate further research and application of this work. By publishing comprehensive books and specialized monographs on the theoretical aspects of computer science, the series on Foundations of Computing provides a forum in which important research topics can be presented in their entirety and placed in perspective for researchers, students, and practitioners alike.

Michael R. Garey
Albert R. Meyer

Preface

One of the basic problems with neural networks is that they do not always scale well. Early research has shown that they work adequately on small problems (those with a small amount of input data), but when they are scaled up to larger problems they often need more neurons than current technology can provide or take more time than users are willing to wait. The standard defense against this criticism is that technology is constantly improving, so it will eventually catch up with our needs. However, our needs are not static: as time progresses we will want to solve larger and larger problems. The important question is how *well* neural networks scale, that is, *how fast* does the computation time and number of neurons grow as the problem size increases? If they grow too fast, then it may not be feasible to expect that advances in technology can keep pace.

The number of neurons and running time of neural networks are examples of computational *resources*. Others include memory and hardware in conventional computers. The study of how the demand for computational resources scales with problem size dates from the 1960's with the seminal paper of Hartmanis and Stearns [58]. This area of research is called *computational complexity theory*, and is one of the richest fields of theoretical computer science. The aim of this book is the examination of how neural networks scale using, for the most part, a branch of computational complexity theory known as *circuit complexity*.

The reader will notice that the majority of the material in this book is on *computation* by neural networks as opposed to *learning*, which is slightly unusual since the balance in the technical literature is tipped in the other direction. Neural network computation is a necessary part of the foundations of neural network learning. Just as a child cannot learn to perform a task unless he or she is physically capable of performing it, a neural network cannot learn to compute a function unless it is physically capable of computing it. "Physically capable" in this context means "possessing sufficient resources", in particular, enough neurons and time.

Although this book is aimed at an audience interested in neural networks, some of it consists of background material about computational complexity theory as it applies to conventional computers. This is included because one of the aims of this book is to make a comparison between the complexity of neural networks and the complexity of conventional computers. This comparison is meaningless unless the reader knows something about the latter. I have attempted to present the background in as palatable a form as possible for neural networkers. For example, I have avoided all talk of Turing machines and nondeterminism. Instead, circuit complexity has been used throughout as a unifying theme.

A major part of this book consists of mathematical theorems and their proofs. I have attempted to write them in a modular fashion, with later proofs built upon earlier ones. Since this will involve the reader in a certain amount of hunting in previous chapters, I have numbered the Lemmas, Theorems, and Corollaries consecutively within each section (so, for example, the Corollary immediately following Theorem 3.2.4 is numbered Corollary 3.2.5), and provided a List of Theorems at the front of the book in addition to the more traditional List of Figures and List of Tables.

Most of the proofs in this book can be found in journals or conference proceedings. I have provided some bibliographic notes at the end of each chapter for those readers interested in reading the original research. The reader will, however, find some differences between those proofs and the proofs in this book. I have attempted wherever possible to simplify, rectify, complete, illuminate, integrate, and improve upon them.

Papers in the refereed literature typically contain gaps and elisions that can be filled easily or with a small amount of work by a trained researcher. I have kept in mind that this book may be consulted by members of other scientific communities, and that these readers will not possess the necessary technical skills. In order to reach this audience I have provided more technical details than a theoretical computer scientist would find strictly necessary. At the same time, I have attempted to make the proofs as structured as possible so that theoretical computer scientists can get the flavour of the argument without necessarily reading all of the details. The reader who is more interested in concepts can, of course, skip the proofs entirely. It is very difficult to write a book with these three disparate audiences in mind, and I will undoubtedly find critics amongst all of them. Nonetheless, I hope I have been able to make most of the readers happy most of the time.

I have used earlier drafts of this manuscript to teach a Ph.D. level seminar course on the complexity of neural networks at the University of North Texas since 1990. The background of the students varied from year to year, but in general they had very little exposure to theoretical computer science with the possible exception of a little algorithm analysis and elementary $\mathcal{NP}$-completeness. All of the material in the book can be covered in approximately twenty-eight 80-minute lectures, although there is sufficient material for up to 33 such lectures if each section is to be covered in depth. The relevant parts of Chapter 1 can be taught in a single 80-minute lecture. Chapter 2 can be taught in 1–3 lectures, depending on background of the students. Chapter 3 can be taught in 2–3 lectures. Each section thereafter generally takes a single lecture, with the following exceptions. Sections 4.3 and 4.4 can take two lectures each if covered in great detail. Section 6.3 can be added to the end of the lecture on Section 6.2. Sections 10.2 and 10.3 can be taught in a single lecture.

Since it includes a significant amount of background material on conventional complex-ity theory, this book can be used to teach a traditional course on computational com-plexity theory with an emphasis on circuit complexity. If this is the case, I recommend supplementing it with material from standard texts such as Garey and Johnson [46], Balcázar, Díaz, and Gabarró [11, 12], or Wagner and Wechsung [145]. This is not a general text on neural networks. If the reader wishes to learn more about the main-stream of research in neural networks, he or she should consult a text such as Caudill and Butler [24, 23], Diederich [37], Hertz, Krogh, and Palmer [59], Mehra and Wah [84], Rumelhart *et al.* [117, 118], Vemuri [141, 142], or Zurada [153].

For those who are interested in typesetting details, this book was produced from camera-ready copy provided by the author using LaTeX version 2.09 (based on TeX C Ver-sion 3.14t3), using macros provided by MIT Press. The List of Theorems was compiled by a simple shell-script hacked together by the author using `awk` and `sed`. The Bibliog-raphy was created by BibTeX. The index was produced using the program `makeindex`. The figures were prepared in encapsulated Postscript form using `idraw`, and the graphs using `xgraph`. These were included in the camera-ready copy produced by LaTeX using the `epsf` macros. The `dvi` file produced by LaTeX was translated into Postscript using `dvips`.

A list of errata for this book is available by anonymous `ftp` from `ftp.unt.edu` (IP address 129.120.1.1), in the directory `ian/ccnn`. Further errata can be sent by electronic mail to the author at `ian@ponder.csci.unt.edu`.

Acknowledgments

Many errors and mis-statements in early drafts of this manuscript were found by students who took my class on the complexity of neural networks at UNT from 1990 to 1992: Sonny Butler, Lonny McMichael, George Mobus, Itrel Monroe, Marcos Novaes, David Raymond, Hung-Li Tseng, Terry Tuck, and Ruojia Zhang. Thanks also to Keith Dean and Patrik Floreen for carefully reading parts of the draft manuscript and pointing out important flaws. I am grateful to David Tam of the Department of Biology and Center for Network Neuroscience at the University of North Texas for clearing up some of the misperceptions that I had about the biology of the neuron. Any remaining misperceptions in Section 3.1 are the product of the author's imagination. I am also grateful to my wife, Virginia Holt, for proof-reading the bulk of this manuscript. Thanks to Bob Prior and Beth LaFortune Gies at MIT Press for handling the editorial process with professionalism and grace. Particular thanks go to Teresa Ehling of MIT Press and Patrick O'Donnell of the MIT AI lab for assistance in dealing with the MIT Press LaTeX macros. The research described here was supported by the National Science Foundation under grant number CCR–9302917, and by the Air Force Office of Scientific Research, Air Force Systems Command, USAF, under grant number F49620–93–1–0100.

Circuit Complexity and Neural Networks

1 Introduction

Although computers are faster than brains for many tasks, they are significantly slower for everyday tasks such as visual pattern matching, voice recognition, and conversing in a natural language. Why is this so? One conjecture is that it is because brains have 10^{10} neurons, each of which has complicated behaviour and interact in complicated ways, whereas computers have 10^8 transistors, each of which have simple behaviour and interact in simple ways. Some scientists believe that the best way to design faster computers is to make them more brain-like. How is this to be done? This is the subject of much research. The generic term for the many competing models of brain-like computation is a *neural network*. The study of computation speed (and other computational resources such as memory and hardware) is called *computational complexity theory*. This chapter introduces computational complexity theory in high-level terms using two examples from Artificial Intelligence (Searle's Chinese Room, and computer intelligence through simulation), and describes how complexity theory is applicable to neural networks.

The philosopher John Searle has claimed that no computational device can ever rival the brain in one aspect: the ability to support intelligence. We examine his claim in Section 1.1 from the perspective of computational complexity theory, and conclude that his main evidence, the Chinese Room, requires too much memory to be practical. We further examine in Section 1.2 the possibility that intelligent machines can be designed by having a computer perform a neuron-by-neuron simulation of the human brain. While skeptical of Searle's claims this is philosophically untenable, we conclude that such a simulation requires too much hardware to be practical.

Much of the large and growing body of research in neural networks is concerned with experiments on small systems with tens or hundreds of artificial neurons. In Section 1.3 we address the problems of scaling up these experiments to brain-scale computations, in particular the possibility that time and hardware requirements grow too fast to be realized by any forseeable technology. This section sets the scene for the remainder of the book, which is summarized in Section 1.4. Finally, Section 1.5 describes some mathematical tools and techniques that should be mastered by the aspiring reader, and recommends some references for preliminary reading.

1.1 The Chinese Room

In 1980, the distinguished philosopher John Searle published a critique of Artificial Intelligence that almost immediately caused a flurry of debate and commentary in academic circles. The paper distinguishes between *weak AI*, which uses the computer as a tool to understand cognition, and *strong AI*, which has as its main goal the recreation of cognition in a computer by means of a formal symbol-processing program. Searle professes to prove by thought-experiment, analogy, and introspection that no formal program can think, and thus deduces that strong AI is misguided.

Despite the flood of criticism and counter-criticism that has been published, Searle seems to have changed his opinions little over the past decade. However, Searle's arguments are not necessarily convincing to a theoretical computer scientist. The three main weapons that Searle uses against strong AI are introspection, reasoning by analogy, and *Gedankenexperiment* ("thought experiment"). Introspection can be highly unstable pedagogical ground, since in using the mind to observe and reason about itself, one risks running afoul of the Heisenberg Uncertainty Principle: the process of self-analysis may change the mind to the extent that any conclusions are cast into serious doubt. Nonetheless, we should be prepared to allow introspection within certain bounds: we will allow Searle to look within himself and state that he understands English and does not understand Chinese.

One must be a little suspicious of reasoning by analogy primarily because one needs little experience in the realities of everyday life to realize that an analogy can be inappropriate if not properly subjected to the scrutiny of logic. Similarly, the *Gedankenexperiment*, despite its illustrious history, can be seriously misguided. Since a *Gedankenexperiment* is carried out purely in the mind, the conductor of the experiment is free to construct a fictional world in which reality does not apply, and hence runs the risk of coming to conclusions that have no basis in the real world. This is a fundamental flaw in Searle's reasoning: he carries out his *Gedankenexperiment* in an imaginary world where computation costs nothing.

Searle, like many academics not trained in Computer Science who like to publish papers about computation, appears to suffer from the misguided belief that Computer Science is a shallow discipline (if nothing else, because it has the word "Science" in its name). He ignores the paradigm shifts that have occurred in Computer Science over the last two decades. His arguments are limited to the theoretical computer science before the 1970's, which is based on the concept of *computability*, and the Church-Turing thesis that all models of symbolic computation are essentially the same.

Such a computational model assumes that computation is free. Unfortunately, just because a function is computable in the Church-Turing sense does not automatically mean that it is computable in the real world. Computation consumes resources, including time, memory, hardware, and power. A theory of computation, called *computational complexity theory*[1] has grown from this apparently simple observation. The prime tenet

---

[1] Computational complexity theory should not be the confused with the more recent science of complexity popularized by physicists.

of this extremely technical field is that some computational problems intrinsically require more resources than others. The resource usage of a computation is measured as a function of the size of the problem being solved, with the assumption that we can solve small problems with the computers available to us now, and we will wish to *scale up* to larger problems as larger and faster computers become available.

The crux of Searle's argument is the following: just because a computer can compute something does not imply that it understands it. This is a reasonable hypothesis in the light of 1950's Computer Science: a function being computable is not sufficient reason to believe that something that computes it truly understands it. According to Searle, proponents of strong AI, in contrast, believe the opposite. The Turing test pits a human being against a computer: if an independent observer cannot tell in conversation with the two via some anonymous medium such as a teletype which is the computer and which is the human being, then the computer is said by proponents of strong AI to be "intelligent".

Searle's *Gedankenexperiment* consists of the following. Program a computer to converse in a natural language by providing it with a table of all possible inputs and their corresponding outputs. When given an input, the computer looks up the correct response in the table, and outputs that response. He reasons that this passes the Turing test, but cannot be said to really *understand* what it is doing. He justifies the latter observation with an analogy. A human being can be given such a look-up table for a natural language that he or she does not understand, for example, Chinese. This person can pass the Turing test in Chinese, *despite the fact that they do not understand Chinese*. This is, despite some arguments to the contrary, a valid line of argument. It is not unreasonable to concede that a computer programmed in this manner does not understand what it is doing in any reasonable sense of the word "understand". However, Searle has missed an important point early in his argument. He has assumed that such a computer program is *possible*. Such a program is *not* possible for the simple reason that it requires too much in the way of resources.

Since the number of legal utterances in a natural language is uncountable, it is impossible to compile a complete look-up table of a language such as English or Chinese. However, this is not a serious barrier to the experiment. It would be sufficient for the purposes of passing the Turing test to compile a table of commonly used statements and legitimate responses. While the number of commonly used questions and statements is a matter of some debate, a conservative lower bound is easy to obtain by considering questions of a particular form.

Consider queries of the form

"Which is the largest, a <noun>$_1$, a <noun>$_2$, a <noun>$_3$, a <noun>$_4$, a <noun>$_5$,

aardvark	crocodile	guinea pig	orang-utan	shark
ant	deer	hamster	ostrich	sheep
antelope	dog	horse	otter	shrimp
bear	dolphin	hummingbird	owl	skunk
beaver	donkey	hyena	panda	slug
bee	duck	jaguar	panther	snail
beetle	eagle	jellyfish	penguin	snake
buffalo	eel	kangaroo	pig	spider
butterfly	ferret	koala	possum	squirrel
cat	finch	lion	puma	starfish
caterpillar	fly	lizard	rabbit	swan
centipede	fox	llama	raccoon	tiger
chicken	frog	lobster	rat	toad
chimpanzee	gerbil	marmoset	rhinoceros	tortoise
chipmunk	gibbon	monkey	salamander	turtle
cicada	giraffe	mosquito	sardine	wasp
cockroach	gnat	moth	scorpion	weasel
cow	goat	mouse	sea lion	whale
coyote	goose	newt	seahorse	wolf
cricket	gorilla	octopus	seal	zebra

Figure 1.1
100 animals.

a <noun>$_6$, or a <noun>$_7$?",

where <noun> denotes any commonly used noun. How many queries are there of this form? There is little difficulty in constructing a list of 100 commonly known animals (see, for example, Figure 1.1). Therefore, there are 100 choices for the first noun, 99 for the second, etc., giving a total of $100 \cdot 99 \cdot 98 \cdot 97 \cdot 96 \cdot 95 \cdot 94 = 8 \times 10^{13}$ queries based on Figure 1.1 alone.

This is a very large number that requires grounding in everyday experience. The *Science Citation Index*[2] is a publication that approaches the human limit for usable information crammed into the smallest amount of space. Each page contains approximately 275 lines of 215 characters, and each inch thickness of paper contains 1000 pages (over 5.9×10^7 characters). Assuming we could fit two queries of the above form and their responses on each line, each inch of paper would contain 5.5×10^5 queries. Therefore, if a look-up table for queries of the above form were constructed, and all the pages were stacked up, they would be 1.45×10^8 inches, that is, $2,300$ miles high. This would require a volume of paper almost 200 feet long, 200 feet wide, and 200 feet high. In contrast, the Great Pyramid of Cheops was (at the time of construction) over approximately 760 feet square and 480 feet high (see Figure 1.2). This is only part of the look-up table: with

---

[2] Published by the Institute for Scientific Information.

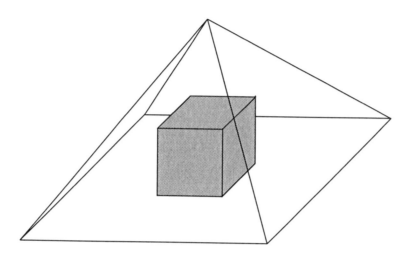

Figure 1.2
The Great Pyramid of Cheops and the look-up table.

merely 1000 nouns and 26 adjectives the stack of paper would be over a light-year[3] high, and the volume of paper would be 24.2 miles on a side.

Therefore, we can safely conclude that it is not possible to pass the Turing test by using a look-up table. Where does this leave Searle's Chinese Room *Gedankenexperiment*? One interpretation is that a look-up table contains *knowledge*, but no *understanding*. Searle's *Gedankenexperiment* illustrates that understanding enables us to perform computations with a reasonable amount of resource usage; certainly less memory than is required to store a look-up table, and less time than is required to access one. This is not in itself a definition of understanding, but it is a fundamental property that must be a part of any useful theory of cognition.

Naturally, understanding is not a Boolean trait; one can have a little understanding, rather than being limited to *no understanding* or *complete understanding*. With a little understanding of the concept of size, one can reduce the look-up table for the example queries to the size of Figure 1.1, simply by sorting the list of animals in increasing order of size. We appear to understand such things not by memorizing lists of facts, but by grounding the abstract concepts of the animals involved in everyday experience, from which information we compute facts such as their relative size. Perhaps understanding evolved as the most efficient way of storing, cross-referencing, and reasoning about large

---

[3] The distance that light travels in a year, approximately 5.88×10^{12} miles.

quantities of environmental data (that is, the most efficient way that can be realized within the design parameters of evolution).

The problem is that the size of Searle's look-up table grows exponentially in the size of the queries; a query schema such as the one we developed above with n adjectives in it requires space proportional to c^n, where c is the number of concrete nouns in everyday use. The prime axiom of computational complexity theory is that resource usage that grows exponentially (with the size of the input) is not of any use in the real world, whilst resource usage that grows subexponentially (for example, polynomially) with the size of the input is more practical. While it is true that some polynomials are smaller than exponential functions for small enough input size (see Figure 1.3), and therefore algorithms with exponential resource usage are sometimes useful in everyday life, this is not often the case. It is clear that it certainly is not the case for Searle's Chinese room.

1.2   Brain Simulation

Searle agrees that a digital computer can, *in principle*, simulate a human brain. The electrical behaviour of a single neuron is far from being well understood, but it would be surprising if it could only be described using continuous mathematics. Our first objection is on general principle: most phenomena in the Universe appear to be discrete, although in many cases the quanta are so small that continuous mathematics is a good approximation to reality. Our second objection comes from the experimental observation that the brain often continues to function when large numbers of neurons are damaged, and under conditions in which a large number of them misfire. It is difficult to believe that this robustness would be possible if it were *essential* that every neuron compute a real value to infinite precision. Fixed precision is almost certainly enough, and probably not too large a precision. Any fixed precision computation can be realized by a discrete computation.

Searle feels uncomfortable with the consequences of the Church-Turing thesis. Computers can be realized with any medium that can represent Boolean values and compute binary conjunction and complement, including water pipes. In principle, a plumber could devise a sewer system that can simulate a human brain. Searle finds this absurd, but not for the same reasons that we do. There is far too much computational power in the brain to implement it as a sewer system.

Can we make a rough guess as to how much computational power is contained in the human brain? It is difficult to obtain reliable estimates of the number of neurons in the human brain, but 10^{10} is probably a conservative figure. We assume that the bulk of the information passed from one neuron to another passes through the synapses; the

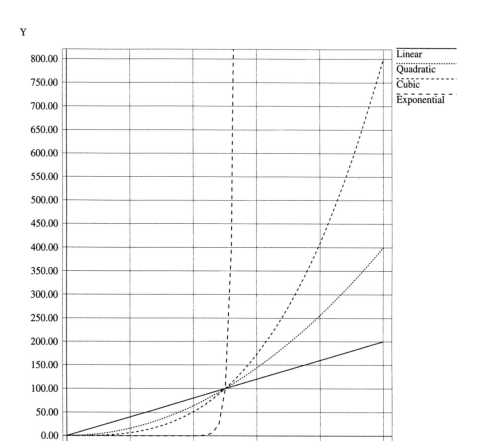

Figure 1.3
Some polynomial and exponential functions.

number of such connections per neuron varies with the type of neuron in question, and is somewhat difficult to estimate. Figures of around 10^6 to 10^8 synapses per neuron have been claimed, but 10^3 is a more conservative estimate. It is probably optimistic to assume that a pair of inputs to a neuron can be combined using a single floating point operation; even so, this implies that each neuron computes the equivalent of 10^3 floating point operations to combine the information input to it across its synapses. Combining these naive estimates with a firing time of 10^{-2} seconds per neuron, we see that the brain appears to have a processing power equivalent to at least 10^{15} floating point operations per second.

Searle's water-pipe brain simulator is clearly something that can be imagined, but not constructed. Even under high pressure, water would flow so slowly in the pipes that in order to achieve 10^{15} floating point operations per second it would require on the order of 10^{15} floating point operations to be computed simultaneously at different parts of the sewer. Even if these results could be combined in a meaningful way in a fast enough manner, the sheer size of the system make it so unreliable that it would stand little hope of passing the Turing test. For that matter, could a computer do a better job? Current supercomputers can execute 10^{10} floating point operations per second, and it is estimated that we might reach 10^{12} by 1994. The brain appears to have more available computational power than a thousand of these hypothetical supercomputers.

Our current technological weaknesses aside, is a neuron-by-neuron simulation of the brain plausible? Probably not. The concept of one computer model simulating another is a key one in the theory of computational complexity theory. The Church-Turing thesis states that any reasonable model of computation can simulate any other one. Computational complexity theory has similar theses that state that these simulations can be carried out with a fairly small overhead in resource use. Nonetheless, each simulation requires an overhead in either hardware or time, often by as much as a quadratic in amount of that resource used by the machine being simulated. Therefore, any computer doing a neuron-by-neuron simulation of the brain need not only be as computationally powerful as the brain, but dramatically more so. For example, contrast our figures on raw computing power above with experimental figures on simulating synaptic weight updates in current neuron models (summarized in Table 1.1). The reason why the computer figures are so poor (capable of simulating neural capacity somewhere between a worm and a fly, see Table 1.2) is that the raw computing power figures that we gave earlier completely ignored the extra overhead involved in the simulation. This is the real reason that we should abandon any hope of simulating cognition at a neuron-by-neuron level, rather than any philosophical or pedagogical objection.

In summary, it is reasonable to hypothesize that cognition can *in principle* be obtained by executing the appropriate formal symbol manipulation program, but that there may

Computer	Synapses	Updates
PC/AT	1.0×10^5	2.5×10^4
Symbolics	1.0×10^7	3.5×10^4
VAX	3.2×10^7	1.0×10^5
SUN 3	2.5×10^5	2.5×10^5
MARK III, V	1.0×10^6	5.0×10^5
CM-2 (64K)	6.4×10^7	1.3×10^6
Butterfly (64)	6.0×10^7	8.0×10^6
WARP (10)	3.2×10^5	1.0×10^7
Odyssey	2.6×10^5	2.0×10^7
CRAY XMP 1-2	2.0×10^6	5.0×10^7
MX-1/16	5.0×10^7	1.3×10^8

Table 1.1
Number of synapses, and synaptic weight updates per second for some common computers to simulate a neural network. The measurements for the MX-1/16 are projected performance only.

Creature	Synapses	Updates
Leech	7×10^2	2×10^4
Worm	5×10^4	2×10^5
Fly	8×10^7	1×10^9
Aplysia	2×10^8	2×10^{10}
Cockroach	9×10^8	3×10^{10}
Bee	3×10^9	5×10^{11}
Man	1×10^{14}	1×10^{16}

Table 1.2
Number of synapses, and synaptic weight updates per second for some common creatures.

be other barriers that prevent cognition from being realized that way in practice. To draw an analogy, the *Principia Mathematica* reduces mathematics to symbol manipulation, yet this is not how mathematicians do mathematics. While they freely acknowledge that it is a necessary condition for any "proof" to be *in principle* expressable in formal logic, it is not necessary that it be so expressed. Mathematicians reason informally for the purposes of communication: a human being simply cannot understand a proof of any great depth and difficulty if it is expressed in symbolic logic. In the same sense, the mind can *in principle* be reduced to a symbol manipulation program, but the program may be far too long and complicated for human beings to understand, and that the reason why we do not see thinking beings that are "mere symbol processors" is that the mind reduced to a symbol processing program may be too greedy of resources to be realized in the physical world.

1.3   Neural Networks and Scalability

We must face the fact that it may not be possible to build a computer that matches the brain in speed, size, reliability, portability, power consumption, and ease of fabrication. It may be, as some biologists believe, that biology is the only way to achieve these goals simultaneously. But perhaps not. Perhaps the brain is the only way that such a computational device could *evolve*. It is an open question whether we can devise one ourselves, independent of the constraints of evolution. It is still an open question as to whether we could make such a device sentient. It does not seem to be possible given our current state of technology and current state of knowledge about cognition, but Searle's arguments that such a thing is in principle impossible are unconvincing.

Many believe that neural networks adequately refute Searle's Chinese Room *Gedankenexperiment*. Searle dismisses neural networks and parallel computation as not bringing anything new to the concept of computation as it applies to cognition. In a sense he is right; they bring nothing new to the 1950's style of computability theory that he uses to bolster his arguments. However, parallel computers are faster and more hardware-efficient at solving some problems than sequential computers are.

The prime contribution of neural networks is not their mode of computation. The fact that they use a computational paradigm that differs from the traditional Church-Turing one is self-evident in some cases, but this is not the death-knell for Computer Science as many of the proponents of neural networks would have us believe. Theoretical computer science has dealt with unconventional modes of computation for decades, as we will see later in this book.

The prime contribution of neural networks is the capacity for efficient computation of certain problems. The first computers were created in rough analogy with the brain, or more correctly, in rough analogy with a carefully selected subset of what was known about the brain at the time. Although technology has advanced greatly in recent decades, modern computers are little different from their older counterparts. It is felt by some scientists that in order to produce better computers we must return to the brain for further inspiration.

It is important to determine which features of the brain are crucial to efficient computation, and which features are by-products or side-effects of these. It is not reasonable to believe that a computer that is comparable in computing power to the brain can be obtained by merely simulating its observed behaviour, simply because the overhead is too great. The general principles of brain computation must be understood before we try to implement an artificial system that exhibits them.

Computational complexity theory is a powerful technique that can be used to divine some of the general principles behind brain computation. However, the theory is in its infancy. Surprisingly, many apparently simple questions about efficient computation turn out to be difficult and deep. While computational complexity theorists equate exponential resource usage with intractability and polynomial resource usage with tractability, in real life any resource usage that grows faster than log-linear in problem size is probably too large to be of any real use. It remains to develop the tools that can make that fine-grained a distinction in resource requirements; for example, we cannot distinguish between problems with time requirements that intuitively grow exponentially with problem size from those that do not. Nonetheless, computational complexity theory often gives insights that may have profound philosophical ramifications.

The general framework used by neural network researchers is a finite network of simple computational devices wired together so that they interact and cooperate to perform a computation (see, for example, Figure 1.4). Yet there is little attention paid to how these finite networks scale to larger problems. When one designs a circuit to solve a given task, such as performing pattern recognition on an array of pixels, one typically starts with a small number of inputs, and eventually hopes to scale up the solution to real life situations. How the resources used by the circuit scale as the number of inputs increases is of prime importance. A good abstraction of this process is to imagine a potentially infinite series of circuits, one for each possible input size (see Figure 1.5), and to measure the increase in resources from one circuit in the series to the next.

The infinite family of circuits represents the advance of technology over time. Current technology allows us to build circuits with:

Inputs from sensors

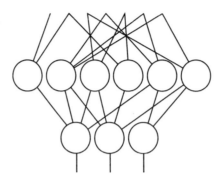

Outputs to affectors

Figure 1.4
A finite neural network with 9 nodes and 2 layers.

- on the order of 100 inputs
- on the order of 10^6 processing elements (which we will call *gates* or *processors*)
- processing elements that have 2 inputs (we will use the terminology *fan-in* 2), computing very simple functions (Boolean conjunction, disjunction, and complement).

Brain-style circuits appear to have:

- on the order of 10^7 inputs
- on the order of 10^{10} processing elements
- processing elements that have 10^3 inputs, computing apparently complicated functions.

It is likely that we will be able to proceed, if at all, by a series of technological jumps that allow us to increase some or all of these values at different points in time. That is, we will produce a family of circuits scaling from current technological limits up to brain-scale computations. Of course, our model scales beyond that point, but that is just for convenience.

We will be considering only scalable problems, that is, problems defined over arbitrary input sizes, such as sensor fusion over increasingly larger sets of sensors. The types of problems that we will consider are less grandiose than the type of computation that is typically exhibited as something that brains do well and computers do poorly. What we wish to see is how the resource usage of various circuit designs will scale up. Specifically,

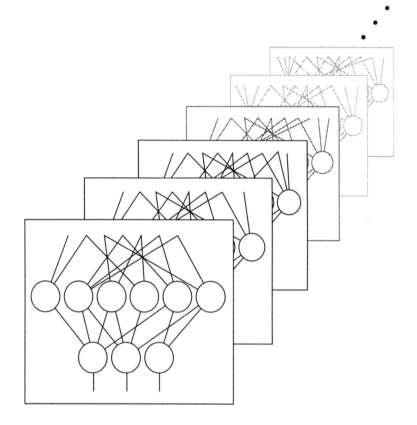

Figure 1.5
A neural network family.

we will investigate the consequences of scaling up two properties: the fan-in, and the functions computed by the processing elements.

1.4   Chapter and Section Breakdown

Although this book is about neural networks, not about computers, it is necessary to present some material about computers as background so that we can discuss neural networks in the proper context. Chapter 2 deals with the current generation of computers and standard models of computation. It is divided into four sections. Section 2.1 explores the concept of an an algorithm, and what it means for a function to be computable. In Section 2.2 a standard model of computation, the RAM, is introduced, and it is noted that a function is computable by an algorithm iff it is computable by a RAM. In Section 2.3 it is seen that the standard unit of modern circuit technology, the transistor, can be used to build *gates* that compute Boolean conjunction, disjunction, and complement. A model of computation called the *classical circuit family* is constructed from these gates. It is shown that complexity theory based on RAMs is very similar to complexity theory based on circuits, since RAMs and circuits can simulate one another with little increase in resources. This enables us to concentrate on a circuit-based model for the remainder of the book. Section 2.4 contains a discussion of some of the choices to be made in the design of a theoretical model of neural network computation.

Chapter 3 deals with a simple discrete model of neuron activity in which the inputs are real numbers and the output is a Boolean value. Each input is is labelled with a *weight*, and the neuron computes whether the weighted sum of its inputs exceeds a threshold value. Chapter 3 is divided into three sections. Section 3.1 discusses the biological motivation for this model of neuronal computation. Section 3.2 considers the case in which the input domain consists of arbitrary real numbers. function are closely related to one another. Section 3.3 considers the case in which the input domain is bounded above and below.

Chapter 4 deals with a restricted version of the neuron model discussed in Chapter 3 in which the input domain is the Boolean set. The functions computed by this type of neuron are collectively called *linear threshold functions*. Chapter 4 is divided into four sections. Section 4.1 contains some simple results on functions of this type. Section 4.2 contains some simple bounds on the size of integer weights. In Section 4.3 a function requiring large weights is described, and some preliminary results about it are derived. In Section 4.4 a lower bound on the weights of this function is proved.

Chapters 5–9 are devoted primarily to discovering exactly which functions can be computed (within certain size and depth bounds) by circuits with gates that compute certain types of linear threshold function. It should be pointed out that most neural network papers deal with the problem of learning, which is addressed in Chapter 10, whereas most of the chapters in this book are devoted to computation. It is important to determine the resources necessary for a neural network to compute a given function before one tackles the learning problem. If the architecture of the neural network has inadequate size or depth, then clearly no learning algorithm will enable that architecture to learn it.

Chapter 5 deals with a circuit model called the AND-OR circuit, which is based on Boolean conjunction, disjunction, and complement in which the fan-in is allowed to scale with size. Since these functions are linear threshold functions, this can be viewed as a restricted type of neural network. It has a node function set that is close to classical computers, but the key difference is that the fan-in is allowed to scale. Thus, alternating circuits can be looked upon as the first step along the road from classical circuits (which have fan-in 2), to more brain-like computation. We have simply abstracted one feature of brains, large fan-in, and incorporated it into our computational model. Naturally, we cannot expect to produce large fan-in gates with current technology, but we can expect fan-in to increase as technology advances. Chapter 5 is divided into four sections. Section 5.1 contains the formal definition of this AND-OR circuit model, and some simple and useful results. Section 5.2 contains results on computing with alternating circuits a simple kind of AND-OR circuit in which the gates are layered and alternate between AND and OR. This special type of AND-OR circuit will make some of our analyses easier. Section 5.3 is devoted to alternating circuits with exponential size. Although exponential size circuits cannot be considered scalable, we will find some of the results in this section useful when scaled down to small applications. Section 5.4 considers alternating circuits of polynomial size. The theory of $\mathcal{NP}$-completeness. is described using alternating circuits instead of the traditional Turing machine.

A key aspect of neural network research is that the depth of the circuits used is typically low. In Chapter 5, the depth was unrestricted, and hence could be a significant fraction of the size. Chapter 6 deals with alternating circuits with depth much smaller than size. Chapter 6 is divided into three sections. Section 6.1 considers alternating circuits with of polynomial size and polylog depth. This means that the depth is exponentially smaller than the size. The theory of $\mathcal{P}$-completeness. is described using alternating circuits instead of the traditional Turing machine. Section 6.2 is devoted to alternating circuits of polynomial size and bounded depth.

Chapter 7 deals with threshold circuits, which are a generalization of the alternating circuits of Chapters 5 and 6 obtained by allowing the functions computed by the processing elements to include the linear threshold functions from Chapter 4. This discrete neural network model is quite popular in the literature. Chapter 7 is divided into five sections. In Section 7.1 the weights are allowed to be arbitrary integers. In Section 7.2 the weights are restricted to ± 1. In Section 7.3 the weights are restricted to be polynomial. Section 7.4 considers relationships between threshold complexity classes. Section 7.5 is devoted to the curious fact that it is as yet unknown whether polynomial size threshold circuits of depth 3 are sufficient to solve every problem that can be solved in polynomial size and constant depth.

So far, we have dealt only with feedforward circuits. Chapter 8 deals with threshold circuits that have feedback loops. It is divided into three sections. Section 8.1 examines the relationship between these *cyclic networks* and the feedforward threshold circuits studied up to that point. Section 8.2 considers various problems related to the halting problem for cyclic networks. Perhaps not surprisingly, such questions are generally $\mathcal{NP}$-complete. Section 8.3 is devoted to a special kind of cyclic network called the *Hopfield network*, in which the weights are symmetric.

So far, we have dealt only with deterministic circuits. But there is evidence that the brain uses circuits that have an element of randomness. Chapter 9 deals with threshold circuits in which the gates exhibit random behaviour, and examines how they can be used to compute deterministic (as opposed to stochastic) functions. The random behaviour of the gates can be either independent, in which case it is found that such probabilism can actually reduce size and depth, or malicious, in which case the circuit must guard against frequent failure. Chapter 9 is divided into four sections. Section 9.1 considers a probabilistic neural network model obtained by adding to the threshold circuit model a special kind of gate that changes state at random with a certain fixed probability, and defines a notion of computation on such a circuit model to within an error probability that is less than 0.5. Section 9.2 considers randomized threshold circuit families in which the error probability may be bounded away from 0.5 by the multiplicative inverse of a polynomial. Section 9.3 introduces the *Boltzmann machine*, which has a completely different definition of probabilistic behaviour, yet is very close in resource requirements to threshold circuits. Section 9.4 considers threshold circuits with gates that behave unreliably.

Chapter 10 deals with the question of how neural networks can efficiently learn from experience. It is divided into three sections. Section 10.1 considers the *loading problem*, in which a neural network with a fixed architecture must learn a sequence of input-output pairs. It is found that this problem is $\mathcal{NP}$-complete even for quite simple architectures. This is an important result. It indicates that any universal learning algorithms such as backpropagation will take exponential time to converge in the worst case even for some innocent-looking learning tasks. Section 10.2 considers the problem of learning a presentation for a linear threshold function over a bounded domain. It is shown that the *perceptron learning algorithm* runs in time polynomial in the weight of the function being learned, even when the inputs are arbitrary reals. Section 10.3 considers the problem of learning a Boolean function over a large domain in which input-output pairs are presented at random according to an unknown probability distribution. An approximation to the function to be learned must be computed with high probability, regardless of the probability distribution. This is called *PAC learning*. It is proved that if the sample size is large enough, it is sufficient to construct hypotheses that are consistent with the data seen so far.

1.5 Mathematical Preliminaries

We assume in the remainder of this book that the reader is familiar with a certain amount of discrete mathematics that is typically taught to an undergraduate major in Computer Science. The reader can consult any one of the many good texts now available on the subject. The author particularly recommends Graham, Knuth, and Patashnik [54] and Rosen [115]. If the reader wishes to skip some of the more intricate technical details in this book, it is sufficient to merely gain a familiarity with the terms and notation in the following. If the reader wishes a full understanding of the material, however, it is necessary first to master these subjects:

- mathematical induction ([54, Chapter 1], [115, Chapter 3]),
- recurrence relations ([54, Chapter 7], [115, Sections 5.1–5.3]),
- the pigeonhole principle ([115, Section 4.2]),
- the principle of inclusion-exclusion ([115, Sections 5.4, 5.5]),
- floor and ceiling operators ([54, Chapter 3]), and
- graph terminology ([115, Sections 7.1, 7.2, 7.4]).

As is standard in theoretical computer science, we will use $\log n$ to denote the logarithm to base 2 of n. We will also make use of the popular "big-O notation": If $f, g : \mathbb{N} \to \mathbb{N}$, we say that $f(n)$ is $O(g(n))$ if there exists $c, n_0 \in \mathbb{N}$ such that for all $n \geq n_0$, $f(n) \leq c \cdot g(n)$. For convenience, we will follow the tradition of writing $f(n) = O(g(n))$. We say that $f(n)$ is $\Omega(g(n))$ if for all $c \in \mathbb{N}$, there exist infinitely many $n \in \mathbb{N}$ such that $f(n) \geq c \cdot g(n)$. If $f(n) = O(g(n))$ and $f(n) = \Omega(g(n))$, we say that $f(n) = \Theta(g(n))$. Finally, we say that $f(n) \sim g(n)$ if $\lim_{n \to \infty} f(n)/g(n) = 1$.

We will make use of two standard results from linear algebra. The first is *Cramer's rule* for the solution of simultaneous equations. Suppose we are given n simultaneous equations in n unknowns $x_1, \ldots, x_n$:

$$
\begin{array}{ccccccccc}
a_{1,1}x_1 & + & a_{1,2}x_2 & + & \cdots & + & a_{1,n}x_n & = & b_1 \\
a_{2,1}x_1 & + & a_{2,2}x_2 & + & \cdots & + & a_{2,n}x_n & = & b_2 \\
& & & & & & & \vdots & \\
a_{n,1}x_1 & + & a_{n,2}x_2 & + & \cdots & + & a_{n,n}x_n & = & b_n,
\end{array}
$$

where $a_{i,j}, b_i \in \mathbf{R}$ for $1 \leq i, j \leq n$, By Cramer's rule, the solution to these simultaneous equations (if there is one) is given by $x_i = \Delta_i/\Delta$ for $1 \leq i \leq n$, where

$$
\Delta = \begin{vmatrix}
a_{1,1} & a_{1,2} & \cdots & a_{1,n} \\
a_{2,1} & a_{2,2} & \cdots & a_{2,n} \\
& \vdots & & \\
a_{n,1} & a_{n,2} & \cdots & a_{n,n}
\end{vmatrix},
$$

and

$$
\Delta_i = \begin{vmatrix}
a_{1,1} & a_{1,2} & \cdots & a_{1,i-1} & b_1 & a_{1,i+1} & \cdots & a_{1,n} \\
a_{2,1} & a_{2,2} & \cdots & a_{2,i-1} & b_2 & a_{2,i+1} & \cdots & a_{2,n} \\
& & & & \vdots & & & \\
a_{n,1} & a_{n,2} & \cdots & a_{n,i-1} & b_n & a_{n,i+1} & \cdots & a_{n,n}
\end{vmatrix}.
$$

The equations have no solution iff $\Delta = 0$.

The second standard result from linear algebra is the *Hadamard inequality*, which states that the determinant of a square matrix is bounded above in magnitude by the product of the norms of its rows, that is, the absolute value of

$$
\begin{vmatrix}
m_{1,1} & m_{1,2} & \cdots & m_{1,n} \\
m_{2,1} & m_{2,2} & \cdots & m_{2,n} \\
& \vdots & & \\
m_{n,1} & m_{n,2} & \cdots & m_{n,n}
\end{vmatrix} \leq \prod_{i=1}^{n} \sqrt{\sum_{j=1}^{n} m_{i,j}^2}.
$$

1.6 Bibliographic Notes

Sections 1.1–1.3 are adapted from Parberry [96]. For other views on AI and neural networks couched in simple terms for nonspecialists, see Dretske [40] and Campbell [22, p. 109].

The debate about Searle's Chinese room shows little signs of abating. The impact that this has had on Searle's ideas can be guaged from comparing Searle's original article [122] with a more recent one [123]. Churchland and Churchland [31]) expound the neural network defense against Searle.

The British mathematician Alan Turing made fundamental contributions to both theoretical computer science and AI dating from before electronic computers were devised. This was no more than the ethos of the times: many early Computer Scientists were equally well versed in theory and AI. This versatility is not surprising in the light of the observation the two fields were at the time inexplicably intertwined by the fact that the only computational device upon which to model a computer was an intelligent one: the human brain. The well-known Turing test for intelligent computers comes from Turing [138]. Turing also in the same paper made an estimate of the computational power of the human brain, but one that is overly optimistic compared to the one in Section 1.2.

The observation that the number of legal utterances in a natural language is uncountable is due to Langendoen and Postal [76]. Seven nouns were chosen in our query schema rather than any other number since that appears to be the number of concepts that a typical human being can grasp simultaneously (Miller [85]).

Shepherd [125] estimates that the human cortex has a surface area of about 2,400 square centimeters, and Rockell, Hiorns, and Powell [114] report a uniform density of about 8×10^4 neuron per square millimeter, from which we can conclude that the number of neurons in the cortex alone is of the order of 10^{10}.

Estimates of current and future supercomputer performance are from Bell [15]. The estimates of computational performance for simple creatures and current computers in Tables 1.1 and 1.2 are from [36].

Computational complexity theory can be said to have come of age with the publications of the seminal paper of Hartmanis and Stearns [58]. Computational complexity theory has many theses that state that various machine simulations can be carried out with a fairly small overhead in resource use; there is the *sequential computation thesis* (Goldschlager and Lister [51]), the *parallel computation thesis* (Goldschlager [49, 50]), the *extended parallel computation thesis* (Dymond [41], and Dymond and Cook [42]), and the *generalized parallel computation thesis* (Parberry and Schnitger [101]).

The *Principia Mathematica* referred to in Section 1.2 is of course the groundbreaking work by Whitehead and Russell [148].

2 Computers and Computation

In order to compare and contrast neural networks with conventional computers, we must first define what we mean by a conventional computer. This chapter is divided into four major sections. Section 2.1 examines the concept of an algorithm, and what it means for a functions to be computable. Section 2.2 introduces a standard model of computation, the RAM, which in Section 2.3 is compared and contrasted with a second standard model of computation called a classical circuit family. The classical circuit is a formal model intended to capture the fundamental properties of current computer technology. It is found that the two standard models are closely related, in the sense that each can simulate the other with a small overhead in resources. Section 2.4 contains a discussion of some of the choices to be made in the design of a theoretical model of neural network computation.

2.1   Algorithms and Computability

Intuitively, an *algorithm* is a procedure for achieving a task. More formally, it is a set of explicit instructions for transforming one set of conditions into another. The initial conditions, or pre-conditions, are typically called the *input*, and the final conditions, or post-conditions are called the *output* of the algorithm. The following are familiar examples of algorithms:

- A recipe: the ingredients are the input, and food is the output.
- An automobile repair manual: the input is a non-functioning automobile, and the output is a correctly functioning one.
- An assembly manual: the input is a collection of parts, and the output is a useful appliance.

It is understood that algorithms are *general*, that is, they can be repeated on many different inputs, and give different outputs. For example, a recipe for a cake can be repeated on different occasions to produce different cakes.

The examples given above are all *concrete algorithms*, that is, they involve manipulating the physical universe. A second class of algorithms manipulates abstractions and ideas, and is called an *abstract algorithm*. For example, the following is an abstract algorithm for planning a murder mystery:

- Devise a cast of characters, their histories, skills, and behavioural characteristics, including a victim, a murderer, and a detective.
- Devise a setting for the action.
- Decide on a murder weapon, and a murder scenario.

- Decide on a motive for the murder.
- Devise a plot where the detective is able to solve a murder that seems insoluble, or the obvious solution of which is incorrect, making use only of logic, common knowledge, and information given to the reader in the course of the plot.
- Add red-herrings and ingenious sub-plots.

Since this book is about abstract algorithms, not concrete ones, we will often use the shorter term *algorithm* to mean *abstract algorithm*.

We will concentrate on a different type of abstract algorithm: one that manipulates mathematical objects. Mathematics is the backbone of our science and technology. Algorithms that manipulate mathematical objects are of great use in engineering and technical fields. For example, engineers manipulate numbers when designing bridges, and accountants manipulate them when computing tax returns. Later we will see algorithms that manipulate other, more complicated, mathematical objects.

One of the earliest algorithms learned by young school students is the algorithm for adding two natural numbers. First we learn the ten digits, how to add them, and the concept of a *carry* and how to compute it. Then, we learn that to add two arbitrary numbers, we do the following. First, we write them down one underneath the other, the digits right-justified and lined up. Starting with a zero carry, we work from the least to most significant digit. For each digit position, we add the current digit of the first number, the current digit of the second number and the carry, to obtain the current digit of the result, and the new carry. Later we learn, often by accident, that the algorithm is guaranteed to terminate, and that it is guaranteed to give the correct answer. At first we take it on faith, and later as we use the algorithm more and more often, and we see that it gives the correct answer, we gain more and more confidence in its correctness.

Our confidence in this algorithm can be analyzed using the rhetorical techniques established thousands of years ago in ancient Greece. The ancient Greek philosophers classified formal argument into three distinct classes:

- Ethos: Proof by authority. ("I am the teacher, and I *say* that it works.")
- Pathos: Proof by emotion. ("It would make me happy if you believe that it works.")
- Logos: Proof by logic. ("Here's how it works...")

Our initial confidence in the addition algorithm comes from the ethos or pathos of our teacher[1], and increases as experience verifies that it is indeed correct. Logos often comes much later, if at all.

---

[1] Preferably the former, but lamentably often the latter.

This book is dedicated to the logical analysis of how neural networks can be used to compute abstract algorithms. To do so, we will need a precise way of specifying abstract algorithms. We will use the following *algorithm description language*. The details of this language are not important, but a certain amount of precision is necessary. First, we need mathematical objects to manipulate. For now, we will content ourselves with numbers, the real numbers (denoted **R**), the integers (denoted **Z**), and the natural numbers[2] (denoted **N**). It is assumed that the reader is familiar with the elementary properties of these number systems, and the standard mathematical operations that can be performed upon them.

It is important to be able to *name* the mathematical objects that we are manipulating. In the abstract addition algorithm sketched above, we were able to use terms such as "the first number" and "the second number" without risk of confusion, but more complex algorithms will be clearer if we are able to refer to objects by name. For example, we want to be able to say "Call the first number x and the second number y. Add the current digit of x to the current digit of y...". We will sometimes use the term *identifier* for the name (which may be a string of alphabetic characters, with or without a superscript) of an object.

We also want to be able to carry out familiar operations on objects. For example, if x is a number, we want to be able to say "add 1 to x", which is at once an operation and a renaming, to be interpreted as "take the number named x, add 1 to it, and rename the result x" (the old value of x is lost). Wherever possible we will use standard mathematical notation for the operations, thus, for example, "$x + 1$" is short for "the number obtained by adding one to the number named x". We will use the symbol "$:=$", pronounced "becomes", for the naming and renaming operation. For example, "$x := x+1$" is the notation to be used for "add one to x". Each of the standard operations on mathematical objects is called a *statement*. The naming statement described above is called an *assignment statement*.

It is important to be able to ask simple questions about mathematical objects. We will allow in our abstract algorithms only specific questions that have a yes or no answer. Let **B** = {**false**, **true**} denote the Boolean set. To be more precise, a *Boolean expression* is a proposition about mathematical objects that is either true or false. We say that it has value **true** if it is true, and **false** otherwise. For example, if $x \in$ **R**, then "$x > 7$", "$x \in$ **Z**", and "x is a prime number" are all Boolean expressions. Boolean expressions can be combined with the normal logical connectives. For example "x or y" is a Boolean expression which is true iff either x is true or y is true, or both; "x and y" is a Boolean

---

[2]There is some ambiguity associated with the natural numbers; purists insist that **N** = $\{1, 2, 3, \ldots\}$, while it is often more convenient to take **N** = $\{0, 1, 2, \ldots\}$. We will use whichever is the most convenient. The purist will be able to tell whether $0 \in$ **N** from context.

expression which is true iff both x and y are true; "not x" is a Boolean expression which is true iff x is false. Boolean expressions can also be named. After the statement "$y := x > 0$" is executed, y has value **true** if at the time of execution x is positive, and **false** otherwise.

Statements can be combined in three basic ways to make an algorithm: *sequencing*, *selection*, and *iteration*. A sequence of statements, on different lines or on the same line separated by semicolons (or any combination of the two), is executed one statement at a time, in the order that the statements appear. Note that the value of an object cannot change once it is named; to change it requires a renaming operation. Thus, if $y = 6$ and the statement $x := y$ is executed, followed by the statement $y := 2$, then $x = 6$ and $y = 2$. That is, the operation on the right-hand side of the "$:=$" is evaluated (even if it is the identity operation), and the object resulting is given the name on the left-hand side of the assignment statement. The statement $x := y$ does not bind x to always be equal to y, but makes it equal to the value that y happens to have when the statement is executed. We will say that a sequence of statements is also a statement. To be more specific, we will call it a *compound statement*.

The second way of combining statements selects one of two statements according to the value of a Boolean expression. If S_1 and S_2 are statements and B is a Boolean expression, then a statement of the form

$$\textbf{if } B \textbf{ then } S_1 \textbf{ else } S_2$$

is called an *if-statement*. It is executed as follows. If the Boolean expression B is **true**, then S_1 is executed, otherwise S_2 is executed. S_2 may be the empty statement ("do nothing"), in which case the "**else**" is omitted.

There are two possible sources of ambiguity associated with if-statements, caused by the fact that both compound statements and if-statements are statements, and thus can be used for S_1 or S_2. Firstly, does

$$\textbf{if } B \textbf{ then } S_1; S_2$$

mean "If B is true then execute S_1 and S_2, else do nothing", or "If B is true then execute S_1 else do nothing, in either case execute S_2 next"? The normal convention is to take it to mean the latter. If the former is intended, some form of parenthesization is used, for example,

$$\textbf{if } B \textbf{ then begin } S_1; S_2 \textbf{ end.}$$

It is equally common to use indentation to resolve ambiguity, writing the former as (for example)

$$\textbf{if } B \textbf{ then}$$
$$S_1$$
$$S_2$$

or

$$\textbf{if } B \textbf{ then}$$
$$S_1; \ S_2$$

and the latter as

$$\textbf{if } B \textbf{ then}$$
$$S_1$$
$$S_2$$

or

$$\textbf{if } B \textbf{ then } S_1$$
$$S_2.$$

The second source of ambiguity caused by if-statements is called the *dangling else* problem If there are two nested if-statements with only one else clause (the other is an "else do nothing"), then to which **if** does the **else** belong? That is, if B_1 and B_2 are Boolean expressions and S_1, and S_2 are statements, then what does

$$\textbf{if } B_1 \textbf{ then if } B_2 \textbf{ then } S_1 \textbf{ else } S_2$$

mean? There are two possible interpretations. The first is that S_2 is done if B_1 is false, regardless of the value of B_2, and the second is that S_2 is done only if B_1 is true and B_2 is false. The standard solution is to attach the **else** to the closest unattached **if**, that is, the latter interpretation. If the former is meant, either some form of parenthesization or indentation is used, for example,

$$\textbf{if } B_1 \textbf{ then begin if } B_2 \textbf{ then } S_1 \textbf{ end else } S_2$$

or

$$\textbf{if } B_1 \textbf{ then}$$
$$\textbf{if } B_2 \textbf{ then } S_1$$
$$\textbf{else } S_2.$$

The third way of combining statements iterates a statement while a Boolean expression is true. If B is a Boolean expression and S is a statement, then the statement

$$\textbf{while } B \textbf{ do } S$$

is called a *while-statement*, or *while-loop*. It is executed as follows. The Boolean expression B is evaluated. If it is true, then S is executed, and then B is re-evaluated. If it is true, then S is executed once more. This process of execution and re-evaluation continues until B is false. Note that it is possible to write *infinite loops*, that is, while-statements that never terminate.

While while-loops are the only form of iteration that are necessary, it is often convenient to use two other forms of iteration. The *repeat-loop*

$$\textbf{repeat } S \textbf{ until } B$$

is equivalent to

$$S; \textbf{ while } \text{not } B \textbf{ do } S.$$

If n is an integer, then the *for-loop*

$$\textbf{for } i := 1 \textbf{ to } n \textbf{ do } S$$

is equivalent to

$$i := 1;$$
$$\textbf{while } i \leq n \textbf{ do}$$
$$S; \ i := i + 1.$$

We will also name statements. If N is a name, S is a statement, and P is a comma-separated list of names of mathematical objects, then we give S the name N by writing

$$\textbf{procedure } N(P); S$$

We call this a *declaration* rather than a statement, since it does not itself perform any mathematical operations. Rather, it associates a name with some operations to be performed later. The names P are called *formal parameters*. If S is a compound statement, it is usually delimited by using either parenthesization or indentation. The names P are not bound to any objects until N is actually executed. N is executed using a statement of the form

$$N(x_1, \ldots, x_n)$$

where $P = (P_1, \ldots, P_n)$ for some $n \in \mathbb{N}$, and $x_1, \ldots, x_n$ are the names of n mathematical objects (called *actual parameters*). This statement is called a *procedure call*. It has the effect of executing the statement S with all instances of P_i in S replaced[3] with x_i, for $1 \leq i \leq n$. S is called the *procedure body*.

---

[3]For those who are familiar with modern high-level programming languages, this is call-by-name. We will not use any of the tricks associated with call-by-name, so no harm will be done by thinking of it as call-by-reference.

A **function** is a special form of procedure. There are two properties which distinguish it from a regular procedure. The first concerns the parameters. Instead of replacing each instance of P_i with x_i, the statement $P_i := x_i$ is executed immediately before the function is executed, for $1 \le i \le n$. Thus, any change to formal parameters in the procedure body has no effect on the actual parameter (although changes will affect subsequent statements in S). The second concerns the way that a function is used. Unlike a procedure call, which is a statement, a function call is a mathematical object (which may therefore be used in operations and Boolean expressions). The body of the function must contain at least one *return* statement, which is a special statement of the form **return**(x), where x is a mathematical object. This has the effect of terminating the execution of the function, and the function call is effectively replaced by the object returned.

For example, the following function adds the two natural numbers x and y by using a binary version of the naive addition algorithm described earlier. It is convenient to think of $\mathbf{B} \subset \mathbf{N}$, taking $\mathtt{true} = 1$ and $\mathtt{false} = 0$. We will use either form of $\mathbf{B}$, as appropriate. If $x, y \in \mathbf{B}$, then one can define Boolean disjunction, conjunction, and exclusive-or by $x \vee y = x + y - xy$, $x \wedge y = xy$, $x \oplus y = x + y - 2xy$, respectively, where "+" and "−" denote integer addition and subtraction respectively, and concatenation denotes integer multiplication. Let "$\triangledown$" denote the bitwise OR operation. That is, if $x, y, z \in \mathbf{N}$, then $z = x \triangledown y$ is defined as follows. Suppose the binary representation of x is $x_1 x_2 \cdots x_n$, the binary representation of y is $y_1 y_2 \cdots y_n$, and the binary representation of z is $z_1 z_2 \cdots z_{n+1}$. Thus, for example,

$$x = \sum_{i=1}^{n} x_i 2^{n-i}.$$

Then, for $1 \le i \le n$, $z_i = x_i \vee y_i$.

```
1.   function add(y, z)
2.       x := 0; c := 0; d := 1;
3.       while (y > 0) ∨ (z > 0) ∨ (c > 0) do
4.           a := y mod 2; b := z mod 2;
5.           if a ⊕ b ⊕ c then x := x ▽ d;
6.           c := (a ∧ b) ∨ (b ∧ c) ∨ (a ∧ c);
7.           d := 2d; y := ⌊y/2⌋; z := ⌊z/2⌋;
8.       return(x)
```

How can we convince ourselves that this addition algorithm is correct using the techniques of *logos*, rather than *ethos* ("if it's in a book then it must be right") or *pathos* ("you'd better believe it's right or I won't sell many copies of this book")?

We claim that if a and b are natural numbers, then add(a, b) returns the value $a + b$. It is sufficient to prove that when line 8 is executed, $x = a + b$. For each of the identifiers used in function add, we will use a subscript i to denote the value of the identifier after the ith iteration of the while-loop on lines 3–7, for $i \geq 0$, with $i = 0$ meaning the time immediately before the while-loop is entered and immediately after the statement on line 2 is executed.

We will make frequent use of the following identity (which follows immediately from the definition of division and remaindering): For all natural numbers n,

$$2\lfloor n/2 \rfloor + (n \bmod 2) = n. \tag{2.1.1}$$

By examining the algorithm in detail, we can see that:

$$
\begin{align}
y_{j+1} &= \lfloor y_j/2 \rfloor \tag{2.1.2}\\
z_{j+1} &= \lfloor z_j/2 \rfloor \tag{2.1.3}\\
d_{j+1} &= 2d_j \tag{2.1.4}\\
c_{j+1} &= \lfloor (y_j \bmod 2 + z_j \bmod 2 + c_j)/2 \rfloor \tag{2.1.5}\\
x_{j+1} &= x_j + d_j((y_j \bmod 2 + z_j \bmod 2 + c_j) \bmod 2). \tag{2.1.6}
\end{align}
$$

(Equation (2.1.5) is a little difficult to see – to verify that it is correct, try all 8 possible combinations of the three Boolean values.)

LEMMA 2.1.1 For all natural numbers $j \geq 0$, $(y_j + z_j + c_j)d_j + x_j = y_0 + z_0$.

PROOF: The proof is by induction on j. The base of the induction, $j = 0$, is trivial, since $c_0 = 0$, $d_0 = 1$, and $x_0 = 0$. Suppose

$$(y_j + z_j + c_j)d_j + x_j = y_0 + z_0. \tag{2.1.7}$$

We are required to prove that

$$(y_{j+1} + z_{j+1} + c_{j+1})d_{j+1} + x_{j+1} = y_0 + z_0.$$

By Equations (2.1.2), (2.1.3), (2.1.4), (2.1.5), and (2.1.6),

$$
\begin{aligned}
(y_{j+1} + z_{j+1} + c_{j+1})d_{j+1} + x_{j+1} = \\
(\lfloor y_j/2 \rfloor + \lfloor z_j/2 \rfloor + \lfloor (y_j \bmod 2 + z_j \bmod 2 + c_j)/2 \rfloor)2d_j + \\
x_j + d_j((y_j \bmod 2 + z_j \bmod 2 + c_j) \bmod 2).
\end{aligned}
$$

Therefore, by Equation (2.1.1),

$$(y_{j+1}+z_{j+1}+c_{j+1})d_{j+1}+x_{j+1} = (\lfloor y_j/2 \rfloor + \lfloor z_j/2 \rfloor)2d_j + x_j + d_j(y_j \bmod 2 + z_j \bmod 2 + c_j).$$

Applying Equation (2.1.1) twice more, we see that

$$(y_{j+1} + z_{j+1} + c_{j+1})d_{j+1} + x_{j+1} = (y_j + z_j + c_j)d_j + x_j.$$

Therefore, by the induction hypothesis (2.1.7),

$$(y_{j+1} + z_{j+1} + c_{j+1})d_{j+1} + x_{j+1} = y_0 + z_0.$$

$\square$

THEOREM 2.1.2 The algorithm terminates with x containing the sum of y and z.

PROOF: It is clear that the algorithm terminates, since on every iteration of the loop, the values of y and z are halved (rounding down if they are odd). Therefore, they will eventually both have value zero, and will retain that value on subsequent iterations. At the first point at which $y = z = 0$, either c will equal zero, or c will be assigned zero on the next iteration of the loop. Therefore, eventually $y = z = c = 0$, at which point the loop terminates.

Suppose the loop terminates after t iterations, for some $t \geq 0$. By Lemma 2.1.1,

$$(y_t + z_t + c_t)d_t + x_t = y_0 + z_0.$$

Since $y_t = z_t = c_t = 0$, we see that $x_t = y_0 + z_0$. Therefore, the algorithm terminates with x containing the sum of the initial values of y and z. $\square$

Our addition example illustrates some important properties that algorithms should have if they are to be useful. The algorithm itself is finite, that is, it can be written down in a finite amount of space. Nonetheless, it is so general that it works for any pair of integers, no matter how large. This is important: the algorithm works for infinitely many inputs, yet it has finite length. Another way to perform integer addition would be to have a look-up table of all possible natural numbers and their sums. One might object that such a list would have infinite length, and thus would take infinite time to construct. However, a pragmatist would repond that it is sufficient to have a look-up table of only the *commonly used* numbers and their sums. Unfortunately, there are so many commonly-used integers that such a list would be prohibitively large to construct, carry around, and use[4]. It is easier to remember the finite and small algorithm for addition that we learned as children. Not only will it work for all numbers that we are likely to meet in practice; it will work for any numbers that we *can* ever meet.

---

[4]This may not be the case for some people, but it is certainly true for scientists and engineers.

We will use the term *algorithm* only for a *finite* sequence of statements and declarations. We will say that we have an algorithm that *computes* a function f iff we have a finite sequence of statements and declarations which for every input x, outputs $f(x)$. Another useful method for computing a function is to devise a table of outputs for all possible inputs that we are likely to meet in practice. Such a table can easily be encoded using our algorithmic notation. For example, we can store the sums of all pairs of natural numbers up to 10 with statements

$$T_{1,1} := 2$$
$$\vdots$$
$$T_{10,10} := 20.$$

We will say that we have a *nonuniform* algorithm that computes f iff for every finite set of inputs, there is an algorithm that computes f on those inputs. The intuition behind this definition is that the finite set of inputs are those that we are "likely to meet in practice". Realistically, we can only expect to meet inputs that are small. We can define a nonuniform algorithm to be an infinite sequence of algorithms, one for each input size, where the *size* of a mathematical object is intuitively defined to be the amount of space needed to describe it (for example, the size of a natural number could be the number of bits in its binary representation).

We will say that any function that has a finite algorithm is *computable*.

THEOREM 2.1.3 Not all functions are computable.

PROOF: It is clear that there are far more noncomputable functions than computable ones since there are *a priori* only a countable number of finite algorithms, whereas there are uncountably many functions: For a contradiction, suppose that there are a countable number of functions $f : \mathbb{N} \to \mathbb{N}$. Number the functions $f_1, f_2, \ldots$ Define $f : \mathbb{N} \to \mathbb{N}$ by $f(x) = f_x(x) + 1$. Since f is a perfectly good function, it must appear somewhere in our list of functions. Suppose $f = f_k$. But then $f_k(k) = f(k) = f_k(k) + 1$, which is a contradiction. Therefore, the functions cannot be enumerated, and so there are uncountably many functions. □

The above proof technique is called *diagonalization*.

Theorem 2.1.3 is not *constructive*, in the sense that it proves the existence of (an uncountably infinite number of) noncomputable functions, but does not provide an explicit example. It is not difficult to construct a function which is not computable. Let S be the set of all algorithms which compute functions with domain and range $\mathbb{N}$. Clearly S

is countable. Define $h : S \times \mathbb{N} \rightarrow \mathbb{B}$ (called the *halting function*) as follows:

$$h(x, y) = \mathbf{true} \text{ iff the } x\text{th algorithm halts on the } y\text{th input.}$$

THEOREM 2.1.4 The halting function is not computable.

PROOF: For a contradiction, suppose that the halting function h defined above is computable. Then, there exists an algorithm that computes it. Modify this algorithm to compute a second function $g : \mathbb{N} \rightarrow \mathbb{N}$ defined by $g(x) = h(x, x)$ for all $x \in \mathbb{N}$. Further modify this algorithm so that instead of returning the result "1", it enters an infinite loop (**while true do** $x := x$;). The new algorithm must appear in our enumerated list $p_1, p_2, \ldots$ of algorithms. Suppose that it is p_k for some $k \in \mathbb{N}$. But what does p_k do on input k? It goes into an infinite loop if p_k halts on input k, and it halts with result "0" if p_k does not halt on input k, a contradiction. Therefore, p_k cannot exist, which implies that there is no algorithm to compute the halting function, so the halting function is not computable. □

While the above proof is by diagonalization, the use of diagonalization is not strictly necessary.

Almost every definition of "algorithm" invented to date is equivalent to ours in the sense that exactly the same functions are "computable" under each definition. There are, of course, models which are strictly more powerful. For example, consider adding an oracle for the halting function to one of the standard models of computation (an oracle is a black-box that can "magically" evaluate a specific function). This augmented model is clearly more powerful than ours, but it is also clear where the power stems from: the added ability to compute a function which was previously not computable. This is regarded as cheating, since it does not give us any real idea of how to compute the halting function. Every *non-cheating* model of computation invented to date is equivalent to ours in the sense that the same set of functions are "computable" under each model. This observation is commonly called the *Church-Turing thesis* in honour of the contributions of Alan Turing and his Ph.D. adviser Alonzo Church, who were among the first to recognize this phenomenon.

2.2   The von Neumann Computer

In Section 2.1 we defined the notion of *computability*, but we did not mention computers. We shall now proceed to rectify this omission.

A *random-access machine*, abbreviated to RAM, consists of three parts, called the *central processing unit*, the *arithmetic-logic unit*, and the *memory* (see Figure 2.1). The

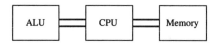

Figure 2.1
A random-access machine.

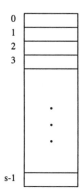

Figure 2.2
The memory of a random-access machine.

central processing unit and arithmetic-logic unit are abbreviated respectively to CPU and ALU. The memory consists of s *words*, each capable of holding an integer with absolute value less than 2^w, for some $s, w \in \mathbb{N}$, $w \geq \log s$. These words of memory are numbered consecutively, starting at 0 (see Figure 2.2). These numbers are called the *addresses* of their corresponding words.

An *address* has the form either $\#i$, i, or $@i$, where $i \in \mathbb{Z}$. These values have the following meaning:

$\#i$ The integer i
i The integer stored in word i
$@i$ The integer stored in the word with address stored in word i.

The first is called an *immediate value*, the second is called a *regular address*, and the third is called an *indirect address*.

A *program* for a RAM is a list of instructions. The instructions are numbered consecutively, starting at 0. A *computation instruction* has the form **INST i j**, where **INST** is the name of the instruction, i is a regular or indirect address, and j is an address. The

Instruction	Meaning
LOAD i j	Place a copy of j into i
LSHZ i j	Place 2j into i
LSHO i j	Place 2j + 1 into i
RSH i j	Place $\lfloor j/2 \rfloor$ into i
SEL i j	Place the remainder modulo 2 of j into i

Table 2.1
Computation instructions.

legal computation instructions are shown in Table 2.1. An *instruction* is either a computation instruction, or an instruction of the form GOTO i j, where i is an immediate value and j is an address, or a HALT instruction. Their effects will be described later.

A *computation* of a RAM on an input $x_1, \ldots, x_n \in \mathbf{B}^n$ is defined as follows. Time is divided into discrete intervals. Time 0 denotes the period immediately before the computation begins. At this time, the contents of word 0 is set to n, and the contents of word i is set to x_i for $1 \leq i \leq n$, and zero for $i > n$. The computation begins with the first instruction in the program. At each time interval, a single instruction from the program is executed. If it is a computation instruction, its effect is as described as above, and the next instruction to be executed is the next instruction in the program. If it is GOTO i j, then the next instruction to be executed is the ith instruction in the program (called the *target* of the GOTO instruction) if the contents of the word with address j is greater than zero, and is the next instruction otherwise. If it is HALT, then the computation ends. Suppose word 0 contains the value m at that time. Then, the *output* of the RAM is $(y_1, \ldots, y_m)$, where for $1 \leq i \leq m$, y_i is the contents of word i.

There are many things that can go wrong with a computation:

Arithmetic Overflow: The value in one of the words of memory exceeds $2^w - 1$.

Address Overflow: A word with address exceeding $s - 1$ is accessed.

Program Counter Overflow: Control passes to a non-existent instruction.[5]

Infinite Loop: The program never executes a HALT instruction.

A computation is said to be *valid* if none of the various overflow conditions occur. It is said to be *terminating* or *halting* if it does not go into an infinite loop.

---

[5] This can happen if the target of a GOTO instruction is larger than the number of instructions in the program, or the last instruction of the program is neither a HALT instruction, nor a GOTO instruction transferring control back into the program.

The RAM is a reasonable model of the current-generation digital computer. Although some of the architectural details differ from computer to computer, our description is close enough to the truth for most practical purposes. The model that we have described is called the *von Neumann computer* after one of the principal scientists involved in its design and implementation. Note that for any individual RAM the values of s and w are fixed. This corresponds to the situation in practice in which the amount of memory and the number of bits per word in any given computer is fixed at any given time. However, the amount of memory may be upgraded periodically but infrequently, and even less frequently the whole machine may be upgraded to one with larger word size. A RAM program is indeed an algorithm in the sense of Section 2.1, since it is finite and can be used to compute a function on all inputs (provided a large enough RAM can be found to execute it).

Note that although a RAM program can in principle be executed on any input, any given RAM can only be used to execute a given program on inputs up to a certain size (otherwise it runs out of memory). Let P be a RAM program which, when implemented on a RAM, halts on all inputs, and never experiences program counter overflow. For all $n \in \mathbb{N}$, let $W(n)$ be the minimum value of w such that P experiences no arithmetic overflow on any input $(x_1, \ldots, x_n) \in \mathbf{B}^n$ when executed on a RAM with $w = W(n)$, and let $S(n)$ be the minimum value of s such that P experiences no address overflow on any input $(x_1, \ldots, x_n) \in \mathbf{B}^n$ when executed on a RAM with $s = S(n)$. Then, the function $W : \mathbb{N} \to \mathbb{N}$ is called the *word size* bound of P, and the function $S : \mathbb{N} \to \mathbb{N}$ is called the *space* bound for P. Intuitively, the word size and space bounds are bounds on w and s for any RAM which is to execute P correctly on inputs of any given size. That is, they give information as to what extent any given RAM must be upgraded in order to compute inputs of greater size.

The word size and space bounds of a program are examples of *resources* used by a program. A third resource is that of *time*, which is a function $T : \mathbb{N} \to \mathbb{N}$ defined as follows: $T(n)$ is the maximum, over all inputs $x \in \mathbf{B}^n$, of the number of instructions executed by a RAM executing program P on input x. A RAM program is said to run in *polynomial time* if it runs in time $O(n^c)$ for some $c \in \mathbb{N}$.

It is clear that a RAM program is an abstract algorithm. However, it can also be demonstrated that every abstract algorithm can be implemented as a RAM program. The first step is to realize that every mathematical object can be encoded as an integer or series of integers, and every operation on them encoded as integer operations. The second step is to realize that every statement in our algorithm description language can be implemented as a sequence of RAM instructions. For example, the statement

$$\textbf{while } x > 0 \textbf{ do } x := x - 1$$

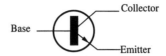

Figure 2.3
A transistor.

can be implemented by storing x in word number 54, and executing the following sequence
of instructions.

1.	GOTO	#3	54	(go to line 3 if $x > 0$)
2.	GOTO	#5	#1	(exit the while-loop otherwise)
3.	SUB	54	#1	(subtract 1 from x)
4.	GOTO	#1	#1	(go back to the top of the loop)

The details are too long to be described in detail here: suffice it to say that several
undergraduate courses in Computer Science are essentially devoted to them.

The observation of the duality between abstract algorithms and programs for computers is really just another corollary of the Church-Turing thesis. It was the observation
that one machine design (in our case the RAM) can execute any abstract algorithm (provided the RAM is large enough) that led von Neumann to design the first stored program
computer. Up until that point, all programs were "hard-wired" into the machine. A large
amount of research in computer science goes into bridging the gap between algorithm
description languages such as the one we have used, and instructions for execution on a
computer.

2.3 Transistors, Gates, and Circuits

The following description of transistors and gates is over-simplified, but contains the
essence of the true picture. The *transistor* is the basic building block for computers.
A transistor is basically a switch controlled by one of its inputs, called the *base*. The
base controls the flow of current from an input called the *collector* to an output called
the *emitter*. If a voltage is applied to the base, then current can flow from the collector
to the emitter. If no voltage is applied to the base, then no current can flow from the
collector to the emitter.

The Boolean value **true** is represented by a fixed current (typically at 0.5 volts). The
Boolean value **false** is represented by the lack of current, or in practice a very small
amount of current (small enough to be reliably distinguished from **true**). An AND-*gate*

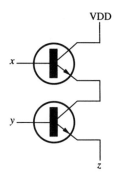

Figure 2.4
An AND-gate computing $z = x \wedge y$.

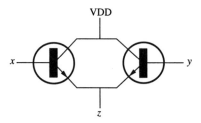

Figure 2.5
An OR-gate computing $z = x \vee y$.

is a circuit with two inputs that outputs **true** iff the two inputs are **true**. An OR-*gate* is a circuit with two inputs that outputs **true** iff at least one input is **true**. A NOT *gate* is a circuit with a single input that outputs **true** iff the input is **false**. It is easy to build AND and OR gates from transistors (see Figures 2.4 and 2.5 respectively), and a NOT gate can be built from a transistor and a resistor (see Figure 2.6). In each of the figures, VDD represents a source of current, and GND represents the ground, thus a connection from VDD to GND carries the Boolean value **true**. Figure 2.7 shows the symbols that we will use for AND, OR, and NOT gates.

It is reasonable to ask why we use the construction in Figure 2.4, since a transistor seems to act like an AND-gate (if there is current at the collector *and* the base, then there is current at the emitter, and otherwise there is not). The answer is that there is a small loss of current through each transistor, so that if many AND gates are cascaded together

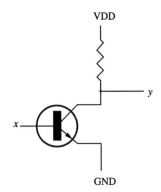

Figure 2.6
A NOT gate computing $y = \neg x$.

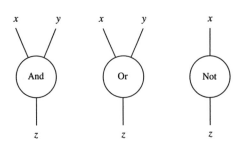

Figure 2.7
Symbols for AND, OR, and NOT gates.

in a circuit, the value of **true** at the end of the circuit may be indistinguishable from **false** unless the current is "refreshed" from VDD at each gate, as shown in Figure 2.4.

A *classical circuit* is a 5-tuple $C = (V, X, Y, E, \ell)$, where

> V is a finite ordered set
> $X \cap V = \emptyset$
> $Y \subseteq V$
> $(V \cup X, E)$ is a directed, acyclic graph with fan-in 2
> $\ell : V \rightarrow \{\text{AND}, \text{OR}, \text{NOT}, 0, 1\}$.

The set V represents a set of *gates*, each of which computes a Boolean function determined by the *node function assignment* ℓ. The range of ℓ is called the *node function set*. A gate

$g \in V$ will be referred to as an $\ell(g)$-gate. X represents a set of inputs, and Y represents a set of outputs. E represents the connections between the gates, the inputs, and the outputs. We call the graph $(V \cup X, E)$ the *interconnection graph* of C.

For example, Figure 2.8 shows a classical circuit $C = (V, X, Y, E, \ell)$, where

$$
\begin{aligned}
V &= \{g_1, g_2, g_3, g_4, g_5, g_6, g_7, g_8, g_9, g_{10}\} \\
X &= \{x_1, x_2, x_3, x_4\} \\
Y &= \{g_{10}\} \\
E &= \{(x_1, g_1), (x_2, g_1), (x_2, g_2), (x_3, g_2), (x_3, g_3), (x_4, g_3), (g_1, g_4), (g_2, g_7), \\
&\quad (g_2, g_5), (g_3, g_6), (g_4, g_7), (g_5, g_8), (g_6, g_8), (g_7, g_9), (g_8, g_9), (g_9, g_{10})\}
\end{aligned}
$$

$$
\begin{array}{lll}
\ell(g_1) = \text{AND} & \ell(g_5) = \text{NOT} & \ell(g_8) = \text{OR} \\
\ell(g_2) = \text{AND} & \ell(g_6) = \text{NOT} & \ell(g_9) = \text{AND} \\
\ell(g_3) = \text{OR} & \ell(g_7) = \text{OR} & \ell(g_{10}) = \text{NOT}. \\
\ell(g_4) = \text{NOT}
\end{array}
$$

C computes the function

$$
y = \neg((\neg(x_1 \wedge x_2) \vee (x_2 \wedge x_3)) \wedge (\neg(x_2 \wedge x_3) \vee \neg(x_3 \vee x_4))).
$$

Let $C = (V, X, Y, E, \ell)$ be a classical circuit, where $X = \{x_1, \ldots, x_n\}$ and $Y = \{y_1, \ldots, y_m\}$. For each $b_1, \ldots, b_n \in \mathbf{B}$, define $v_C(b_1, \ldots, b_n) : V \cup X \to \mathbf{B}$ as follows. If $g = x_i$ for some $1 \leq i \leq n$, define $v_C(b_1, \ldots, b_n)(g) = b_i$. If $g \in V$, and $(g_1, g), (g_2, g) \in E$, then if

$\ell(g) = \text{AND}$, then $v_C(b_1, \ldots, b_n)(g) = v_C(b_1, \ldots, b_n)(g_1) \wedge v_C(b_1, \ldots, b_n)(g_2)$;

$\ell(g) = \text{OR}$, then $v_C(b_1, \ldots, b_n)(g) = v_C(b_1, \ldots, b_n)(g_1) \vee v_C(b_1, \ldots, b_n)(g_2)$;

$\ell(g) = \text{NOT}$, then $v_C(b_1, \ldots, b_n)(g) = \neg v_C(b_1, \ldots, b_n)(g_1)$;

$\ell(g) = 0$, then $v_C(b_1, \ldots, b_n)(g) = 0$;

$\ell(g) = 1$, then $v_C(b_1, \ldots, b_n)(g) = 1$.

We will call $v_C(b_1, \ldots, b_n)(g)$ the *value* of gate g of circuit C on input $b_1, \ldots, b_n$. Where it is immediately apparent from context which circuit and which input is involved, we will write $v(g)$ instead of $v_C(b_1, \ldots, b_n)(g)$. The *output* of C on inputs $b_1, \ldots, b_n \in \mathbf{B}$ is defined to be $v_C(b_1, \ldots, b_n)(y_1), \ldots, v_C(b_1, \ldots, b_n)(y_m)$. An n-input classical circuit $C = (V, X, Y, E, \ell)$ is said to *compute* a Boolean function $f : \mathbf{B}^n \to \mathbf{B}^m$ if for all $b_1, \ldots, b_n \in \mathbf{B}$, the output of C on input $b_1, \ldots, b_n$ is $f(b_1, \ldots, b_n)$. Two classical circuits are said to be *equivalent* if they compute the same function.

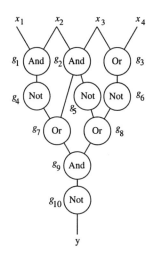

Figure 2.8
A classical circuit.

Classical circuits are an alternate model of computation to the RAM program. One obvious difference is that a RAM program will compute a function on an input of any size, whereas a classical circuit will compute a function on an input of a fixed size only. This can easily be redressed by considering a classical circuit *family* $C = (C_1, C_2, \ldots)$, where for $n \in \mathbb{N}$, C_n has n inputs.

THEOREM 2.3.1 Every Boolean function f can be computed by a classical circuit family.

PROOF: It is sufficient to consider a function $f : \mathbf{B}^n \to \mathbf{B}$. The proof is by induction on n. The Theorem is certainly true for $n = 1$ (in which case there are only four functions to consider, the always **true** function, the always **false** function, the identity function, and the complement function, each of which can be realized with at most one gate).

Suppose that every function on $n - 1$ inputs can be computed by a classical circuit. Define $f_0, f_1 : \mathbf{B}^{n-1} \to \mathbf{B}$ as follows:

$$f_0(x_1, \ldots, x_{n-1}) = f(x_1, \ldots, x_{n-1}, 0)$$
$$f_1(x_1, \ldots, x_{n-1}) = f(x_1, \ldots, x_{n-1}, 1)$$

Then,

$$f(x_1, \ldots, x_n) = (f_0(x_1, \ldots, x_{n-1}) \wedge (x_n = 0)) \vee (f_1(x_1, \ldots, x_{n-1}) \wedge (x_n = 1))$$
$$= (f_0(x_1, \ldots, x_{n-1}) \wedge \neg x_n) \vee (f_1(x_1, \ldots, x_{n-1}) \wedge x_n).$$

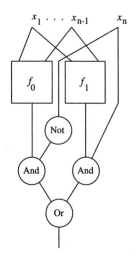

Figure 2.9
Circuit for computing f in the proof of Theorem 2.3.1.

Since f_0 and f_1 can be computed by a classical circuit (by the induction hypothesis), f can be computed by the classical circuit shown in Figure 2.9. □

We can conclude from Theorem 2.1.3 and Theorem 2.3.1 that classical circuit families are more powerful than abstract algorithms. Furthermore, they can do anything that a RAM can do.

It is clear from the comment following Theorem 2.3.1 that the simulation cannot be carried out in the opposite direction: there can be no RAM program that simulates circuit families. This implies that the Church-Turing thesis does not hold for classical circuit families. However, it is clear that the extra computing power of classical circuits comes from their ability to encode noncomputable functions in their interconnection graphs, since if we take that ability away from them, they are equivalent to RAMs. Define a *uniform* circuit family $(C_1, C_2, \ldots)$, where $C_n = (V_n, X_n, Y_n, E_n, \ell_n)$ to be a circuit family in which the interconnection graph (V_n, E_n) and the gate assignment function ℓ_n are computable by a RAM program. Uniform circuits and RAMs are closely related:

THEOREM 2.3.2 A Boolean function is computable iff it can be computed by a uniform classical circuit family.

PROOF: Suppose f can be computed by a uniform circuit family $C = (C_1, C_2, \ldots)$. A

RAM program that computes f on an input of n bits first computes the interconnection graph and gate assignment function of C_n, and then performs a gate-by-gate simulation. The details are left to the reader (see Problem 3).

Conversely, suppose f is computable. Then, f can be computed by a RAM program. For each $n \in \mathbf{N}$, construct a circuit C_n that simulates the action of a RAM on inputs of n bits. The details are left to the reader (see Problem 4). □

Therefore, uniform classical circuit families satisfy the Church-Turing thesis, whereas nonuniform ones (which can be thought of as a form of nonuniform algorithm) do not.

The *size* of a classical circuit $C = (V, X, Y, E, \ell)$ is defined to be $\|V\|$, the number of gates. The *depth* is defined to be the maximum number of gates in V on any path from an input to an output. The gates in a circuit of depth d can be partitioned in d *levels* or *layers*. The inputs X are said to be at *level* 0. A gate $v \in V$ is said to be at *level* $i > 0$ if

1. for all $u \in V \cup X$ such that $(u, v) \in E$, u is at a level less than i, and
2. there exists $u \in V \cup X$ at level $i - 1$ such that $(u, v) \in E$.

The *size* of a circuit family $C = (C_1, C_2, \ldots)$ is said to be $Z(n)$ if for all $n \in \mathbf{N}$, the size of C_n is at most $Z(n)$. The *depth* of C is said to be $D(n)$ if for all $n \in \mathbf{N}$, the depth of C_n is at most $D(n)$.

We say that a uniform circuit family is $\mathcal{P}$-*uniform* if there is a polynomial-time RAM program that computes its gate assignment function and interconnection graph. $\mathcal{P}$-uniform circuit families are very closely related to polynomial-time RAM programs:

THEOREM 2.3.3 A function f has a $\mathcal{P}$-uniform circuit family of polynomial size iff it can be computed by a RAM in polynomial time.

PROOF: The proof is similar to that of Theorem 2.3.2, and is left to the reader (see Problem 5). □

2.4   Choosing the Right Model

The RAM is widely accepted by theoretical computer scientists as being the right model for studying everyday computation. Theoretical computer scientists prefer to think of the RAM as having an infinite number of words, of infinite length. This models the intuition that one gets when using a computer for everyday tasks; the memory and word size are more than adequate for ordinary tasks, hence one very seldom thinks of them as being finite. Only when one is doing serious research, typically starting with small problems and building up to larger ones, does one run into problems of inadequate memory and over-long run times. When this occurs, one is forced to consider how one's algorithm scales with the size of the problem being solved. Although the theoretician's RAM has an infinite amount of resources at its disposal, it can only use a finite amount of those resources in any computation. Those resources are measured in much the same way that we have measured them, and the model is essentially identical to ours for all intents and purposes, except for the fact that we have not mentioned infinity at all. The mere mention of infinite memory is enough to discourage many inexperienced readers of theoretical texts, but the mental image of infinite computations can be exorcised by remembering that to a theoretical computer scientist, "infinite" is just a shorthand for "more than is needed".

What is the right model for neural networks? An infinite model is clearly inappropriate. All we can build now is small, finite classical circuits. However, it is reasonable to expect that as time progresses, we will be able to construct larger and larger circuits that can perform computations on more inputs. As we do so, we will need to keep track of how resource usage grows as a function of the number of inputs. For example, if the number of gates grows exponentially with the number of inputs, then we will not be able to construct circuits for any but the very smallest input sizes. The circuit family model is appropriate for this scenario.

Is the classical circuit model a reasonable model of a neural network? After all, its original design was loosely based on neuron function. It captures the observations that the brain is made up of an interconnected network of small units that compute simple discrete functions via electrical impulses. However, it is a gross simplification of what really occurs. In the remainder of this book we will make the model more complicated by adding other simple features of the brain, and we will compare how computations scale in this new model as compared to classical circuits.

Should a neural network model be uniform or nonuniform? This question is an important pedagogical one, but not one that has received a great deal of discussion in the literature. If we are indeed using a family of circuits to model human endeavour as we construct neural networks for larger and larger problems, the uniform circuits are perhaps more appropriate: most circuits constructed today are uniform since it is necessary to use computers to construct them. A circuit whose interconnection graph is not computable will run into severe problems at fabrication time. However, it seems that often the best circuits for some problems are nonuniform. While the brain exhibits some uniformity of construction at a high level, at a low level there is very little structure to be seen. The question of whether nonuniformity is necessary to brain function is a deep one that deserves further consideration.

2.5   Problems

1. Show how each statement of the addition algorithm add(y, z) described in Section 2.1 can be implemented as a RAM program (see Section 2.2). What is the running time of the addition program you obtain in this manner? Modify the program so that it runs in time $O(n)$.

2. Devise a subtraction algorithm for natural numbers that runs in time $O(n)$ when implemented as a RAM program. Extend this algorithm to perform addition and subtraction of integers.

3. Show that if f can be computed by a classical circuit family, then it can be computed by a RAM program. (see Theorem 2.3.2).

4. Show that if f can be computed by a RAM program, then it can be computed by a classical circuit family (see Theorem 2.3.2).

5. Show that a function f has a $\mathcal{P}$-uniform circuit family of polynomial size iff it can be computed by a RAM in polynomial time (Theorem 2.3.3).

2.6   Bibliographic Notes

The British mathematician Alan Turing was among the first to formalize the intuitive idea of a computable function. Theorem 2.1.4 is due to Turing [137]. There are many equivalent ways of defining computability, for example, Turing's *Turing machine* [137], Chomsky's *type-0 grammars* [29], Church's *λ-calculus* [30], Kleene's *recursive functions* [74], and Post's *production systems* [110]. The Random-Access Machine that we have used is based on that of Sheperdson and Sturgis [124].

The construction of AND, OR, and NOT gates from transistors in Section 2.3 is overly simplified. In practice, different implementations may have to be used. For more details on how to implement them in VLSI, see Mead and Conway [83]. Figure 2.6 is from Mead and Conway [83].

There are many recent books which cover the contents of this chapter in greater detail. Goldschlager and Lister [51] give more details on the transformation from abstract algorithms to programs, and the construction of computers from gates. For more in-depth information on the design and analysis of abstract algorithms, the reader can consult, for example, Aho, Hopcroft, and Ullman [3, 4], Harel [57], or Cormen, Leiserson, and Rivest [35].

Theorem 2.3.3 is after Borodin [20]. The question of whether uniform or nonuniform circuits are appropriate for neural networks was first raised by Parberry and Schnitger [100, 102].

3 The Discrete Neuron

Since neural networks are motivated by how brains compute, we open this chapter with a simplified account of how neurons work, in Section 3.1. A simple model of neuron activity, called a *linear threshold function* is introduced. Some properties of linear threshold functions are discovered in Section 3.2. In Section 3.3 it is argued that linear threshold functions with arbitrary real inputs are less useful than those with inputs draw from the real interval $[0, 1]$, and further properties of these functions are discovered.

3.1 Physiology of the Neuron

The following description of the physiology of a neuron is a simplification; the processes are actually much more complicated, and there are many exceptions to the structure and behaviour described. However, it is not too far from the truth.

The basic unit of the nervous system is a specialized type of cell called a *neuron* (see Figure 3.1). The neuron consists of a cell body, or *soma*, emanating from which are many filament-like *dendrites*, and an *axon*. The axon is typically very much longer than the dendrites. The dendrite and axon branch in a tree-like fashion. The point at which the axon joins the soma is called the *axon hillock*.

The neuron is bounded by a lipid membrane that is permeable to water, but impermeable to ions and various water-soluble molecules. This is useful for maintaining an internal environment that is different from the environment between the cells, for example, a typical neuron at rest will contain an internal concentration of the positive sodium ion that is 10 times greater than the external concentration. The concentrations of the important ions are shown in Table 3.1. A typical neuron at rest will, due to the different concentrations of ions across the membrane, have a potential of -70 mV. The concentrations of sodium and potassium ions are of particular importance (see Figure 3.2).

The impermeability of the cell membrane also means that the neuron must employ

Ion	Outside	Inside
Na^+	150	15
K^+	5	150
Cl^-	125	9
A^-	20	155

Table 3.1
Concentrations of important ions inside and outside a typical nerve cell. A^- represents large intracellular anions to which the cell membrane is impermeable. All concentrations are in mMole.

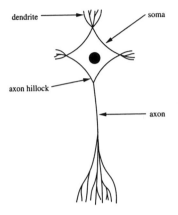

Figure 3.1
A neuron.

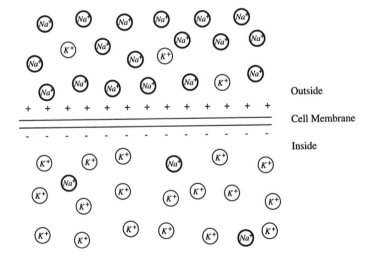

Figure 3.2
The neuronal membrane at rest.

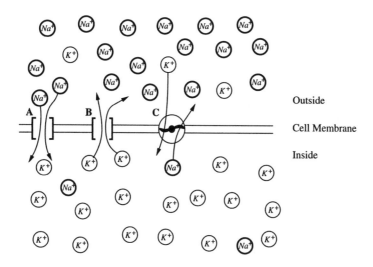

Figure 3.3
A sodium channel (A), potassium channel (B), and a sodium-potassium pump (C).

special mechanisms for transporting across the membrane ions and molecules that are essential for metabolic and functional purposes. These mechanisms are provided by proteins embedded in the membrane. They include (see Figure 3.3):

- the *sodium channel*, which when open allows sodium to pass through the membrane,
- the *potassium channel*, which when open allows potassium to pass through the membrane,
- and the *sodium-potassium pump*, which selectively moves potassium into, and sodium out of the neuron.

When the neuron is at rest, the sodium and potassium channels are closed. However, the channels and the membrane itself are not perfectly impermeable, so sodium and potassium can pass through the membrane by osmosis. The action of the sodium-potassium pump is therefore essential to the maintenance of the resting state as shown in Figure 3.2.

If the potential at the axon hillock exceeds a threshold value of around -55 mV, the sodium channels in the immediate vicinity open, allowing sodium to enter the membrane by osmotic pressure. The polarity of the membrane in that area actually reverses, and rises to approximately $+60$ mV, at about which time the potassium channels open, allowing potassium to leave the membrane also under osmotic pressure. The membrane is thus *hyperpolarized* to about -90 mV, and then returns gradually to its resting state.

The net result of the initial depolarization is thus the *action potential* shown in Figure 3.4.

The resulting action potential travels down the axon to the synapses in the following fashion: the opening of the sodium channels in one region results in an in-flow of sodium ions which depolarizes neighbouring regions of the membrane, which cause neighbouring sodium channels to open. Once a channel closes, however, it remains closed for a small *refractory period*. This ensures that an action potential generated at the axon hillock travels in one direction towards the synapses only, although travel in the opposite direction is in principle possible and can be produced *in vitro*. The size, shape, and amplitude of the action potential produced at the axon hillock are very nearly independent of the manner in which the membrane was initially depolarized, and remain invariant as it travels along the axon.

When an action potential reaches the synapse, it triggers the release of chemicals called *neurotransmitters*, which cross a small *synaptic gap* to bind with receptors in the dendrite or soma of a neighbouring neuron. This generates a potential in the membrane of that neuron which may be either positive (in which case the synapse is called *excitatory*) or negative (in which case the synapse is called *inhibitory*), and which may have a large or small amplitude, depending on the synapse in question. This potential is transmitted to the axon hillock via the soma, but in the absence of the active assistance provided to an action potential, it degrades exponentially over time. The resulting potentials accumulate at the axon hillock, and the entire process repeats itself.

The presence or absence of an action potential in the axon of a neuron can be modelled by the output of a Boolean value. The neurotransmitters crossing the synaptic gap can be modelled by the input of real numbers. The potential that arrives at the axon hillock as the result of the action of a single synapse is a multiple of this value, depending on the type of synapse and the distance from the synapse to the axon hillock. This can be modelled as a real-valued *synaptic weight* that is used to multiply the input. If the sum of the inputs times their respective weights exceeds the threshold value of the axon hillock, the neuron outputs `true`, otherwise it outputs `false`. The Boolean function computed by this simple neuron model is called a *linear threshold function*, and is the subject of the remainder of this chapter.

3.2   The Real Domain

A function $f : \mathbf{R}^n \to \mathbf{R}$ is called a *linear* function if it is linear in all parameters. That is, there exists $w_1, \ldots, w_n \in \mathbf{R}$ such that for all $x_1, \ldots, x_n \in \mathbf{R}$, $r \in \mathbf{R}$, and $1 \leq i \leq n$,

$$\frac{f(x_1, \ldots, x_n) - f(x_1, \ldots, x_{i-1}, r, x_{i+1}, \ldots, x_n)}{x_i - r} = w_i.$$

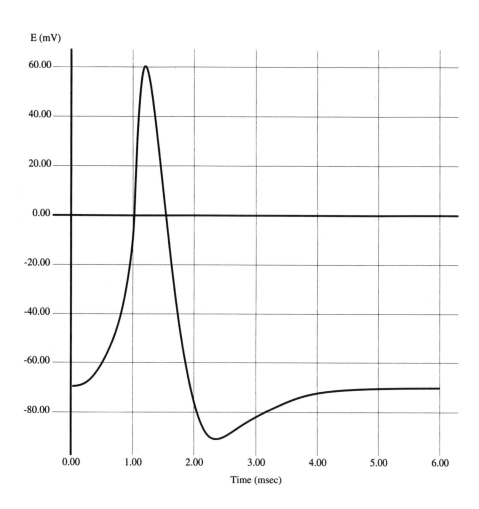

Figure 3.4
The action potential.

Linear functions are essentially weighted sums of their parameters:

THEOREM 3.2.1 A function $f : \mathbf{R}^n \to \mathbf{R}$ is linear iff there exists $w_1, \ldots, w_n \in \mathbf{R}$ such that for all $x_1, \ldots, x_n \in \mathbf{R}$,

$$f(x_1, \ldots, x_n) = \sum_{i=1}^{n} w_i x_i + f(\underbrace{0, \ldots, 0}_{n}).$$

PROOF: Suppose $f : \mathbf{R}^n \to \mathbf{R}$ is of the form

$$f(x_1, \ldots, x_n) = \sum_{i=1}^{n} w_i x_i + f(\underbrace{0, \ldots, 0}_{n})$$

for some $w_1, \ldots, w_n \in \mathbf{R}$. Then, for all $r \in \mathbf{R}$ and $1 \leq i \leq n$,

$$
\begin{aligned}
&f(x_1, \ldots, x_n) - f(x_1, \ldots, x_{i-1}, r, x_{i+1}, \ldots, x_n) \\
&= \sum_{j=1}^{n} w_j x_j - \left(\sum_{j=1}^{i-1} w_j x_j + w_i r + \sum_{j=i+1}^{n} w_j x_j \right) \\
&= w_i (x_i - r).
\end{aligned}
$$

That is, f is linear.

Conversely, suppose that f is linear. Then, there exists $w_1, \ldots, w_n \in \mathbf{R}$ such that for all $x_1, \ldots, x_n \in \mathbf{R}$, $r \in \mathbf{R}$, and $1 \leq i \leq n$,

$$\frac{f(x_1, \ldots, x_n) - f(x_1, \ldots, x_{i-1}, r, x_{i+1}, \ldots, x_n)}{x_i - r} = w_i. \tag{3.2.1}$$

We claim that for all $x_1, \ldots, x_n \in \mathbf{R}$,

$$f(x_1, \ldots, x_n) = \sum_{i=1}^{n} w_i x_i + f(\underbrace{0, \ldots, 0}_{n}).$$

The proof is by induction on n. If $n = 1$, by (3.2.1) there exists $w_1 \in \mathbf{R}$ such that for all $x_1 \in \mathbf{R}$,

$$\frac{f(x_1) - f(0)}{x_1 - 0} = w_1.$$

That is, $f(x_1) = w_1 x_1 + f(0)$, as required.

Now suppose that the hypothesis is true for all linear functions with domain $\mathbf{R}^{n-1}$. It is clear that the function $f_0 : \mathbf{R}^{n-1} \to \mathbf{R}$ defined by

$$f_0(x_1, \ldots, x_{n-1}) = f(x_1, \ldots, x_{n-1}, 0)$$

is also a linear function. Taking $i = n$ and $r = 0$ in (3.2.1), we see that for all $x_1, \ldots, x_n \in$
R,

$$f(x_1, \ldots, x_n) = f_0(x_1, \ldots, x_{n-1}) + w_n x_n.$$

Hence, by the induction hypothesis,

$$f(x_1, \ldots, x_n) = \sum_{i=1}^{n-1} w_i x_i + f_0(\underbrace{0, \ldots, 0}_{n-1}) + w_n x_n$$

$$= \sum_{i=1}^{n} w_i x_i + f(\underbrace{0, \ldots, 0}_{n}),$$

as required. $\square$

Let **B** denote the Boolean set $\{0, 1\}$. Intuitively, the integer 0 represents the logical
value `false`, and 1 represents the logical value `true`. A function $f : \mathbf{R}^n \to \mathbf{B}$ is called a
linear threshold function if there exists a linear function f_l such that for all $x \in \mathbf{R}^n$,
$f(x) = 1$ iff $f_l(x) \geq 0$. Intuitively, f is the function which, on input x, outputs the
truth or falsehood of the proposition $f_l(x) \geq 0$. More formally, $f(x) = 1$ iff there exists
$w_1, \ldots, w_n \in \mathbf{R}$ such that for all $x = (x_1, \ldots, x_n) \in \mathbf{R}^n$,

$$f(x) = 1 \text{ iff } \sum_{i=1}^{n} w_i x_i \geq -f_l(\underbrace{0, \ldots, 0}_{n}).$$

The constants $w_1, \ldots, w_n$ that define f_l are called *weights*, and the value

$$h = -f_l(\underbrace{0, \ldots, 0}_{n})$$

is called the *threshold* value. The sequence $(w_1, \ldots, w_n, h)$ is called a *presentation* of f.

In order to be precise, we will use a concise notation for the linear threshold function
with a given presentation. Let Σ denote the set of linear functions. Define $\sigma_n : \mathbf{R}^n \to \Sigma$
as follows: $\sigma_n(w_1, \ldots, w_n) : \mathbf{R}^n \to \mathbf{R}$, where

$$\sigma_n(w_1, \ldots, w_n)(x_1, \ldots, x_n) = \sum_{i=1}^{n} w_i x_i.$$

The function $\sigma_n(w_1, \ldots, w_n)$ is called an *excitation function*, and the value

$$\sigma_n(w_1, \ldots, w_n)(x_1, \ldots, x_n)$$

will be called the *excitation level* of the linear threshold function $\vartheta_n(w_1, \ldots, w_n, h)$ on input $(x_1, \ldots, x_n)$. Let Θ denote the set of linear threshold functions. Define $\vartheta_n : \mathbf{R}^{n+1} \to \Theta$ as follows: $\vartheta_n(w_1, \ldots, w_n, h) : \mathbf{R}^n \to \mathbf{B}$, where

$$\vartheta_n(w_1, \ldots, w_n, h)(x_1, \ldots, x_n) = 1 \text{ iff } \sigma_n(w_1, \ldots, w_n)(x_1, \ldots, x_n) \geq h.$$

A simple computational model of the neuron motivated by the observations of Section 3.1, is as follows. Neuron output is expressed as a Boolean value. Synaptic weights are real numbers, positive for an excitatory synapse, and negative for an inhibitory one. The activity of a neuron that has threshold value h, and n synaptic connections with synaptic weights $w_1, \ldots, w_n$ to neurons with excitation levels $x_1, \ldots, x_n$, respectively, is given by $\vartheta_n(w_1, \ldots, w_n, h)(x_1, \ldots, x_n)$. Linear threshold functions are a crude computational model of the neuron, with the weights playing the role of the synaptic weights, and the threshold value playing the role of the depolarization threshold of the axon hillock. This model is far too crude to be a good model of the neuron in the traditional scientific sense: its behaviour is not a good predictor of how a real neuron behaves. However, we will use it as an abstraction of certain features of neurons, and investigate in subsequent chapters how standard models of computation behave when this abstraction is added to them.

Although every presentation uniquely defines a linear threshold function, it is clear that every linear threshold function has infinitely many presentations. That is, for each linear threshold function $f : \mathbf{R}^n \to \mathbf{B}$ there are infinitely many choices of weights $w_1, \ldots, w_n$ and threshold h such that $f = \vartheta_n(w_1, \ldots, w_n, h)$. This observation is a corollary of the following elementary result:

LEMMA 3.2.2 For all $\mu \in \mathbf{R}^+$, $\vartheta_n(w_1, \ldots, w_n, h) = \vartheta_n(\mu w_1, \ldots, \mu w_n, \mu h)$.

PROOF: Suppose $\mu \in \mathbf{R}^+$, $h, w_1, \ldots, w_n \in \mathbf{R}$, $n \in \mathbf{N}$. Then, for all $x_1, \ldots, x_n \in \mathbf{R}^n$,

$$
\begin{aligned}
\vartheta_n(\mu w_1, \ldots, \mu w_n, \mu h)(x_1, \ldots, x_n) = 1 \quad &\Leftrightarrow \quad \sigma_n(\mu w_1, \ldots, \mu w_n)(x_1, \ldots, x_n) \geq \mu h \\
&\Leftrightarrow \quad \sum_{i=1}^{n} \mu w_i x_i \geq \mu h \\
&\Leftrightarrow \quad \sum_{i=1}^{n} w_i x_i \geq h \\
&\Leftrightarrow \quad \sigma_n(w_1, \ldots, w_n)(x_1, \ldots, x_n) \geq h \\
&\Leftrightarrow \quad \vartheta_n(w_1, \ldots, w_n, h)(x_1, \ldots, x_n) = 1.
\end{aligned}
$$

That is, $\vartheta_n(\mu w_1, \ldots, \mu w_n, \mu h) = \vartheta_n(w_1, \ldots, w_n, h)$. $\square$

A linear threshold function is said to be *degenerate* if it does not depend upon all of its inputs. More precisely, a linear threshold function $f : \mathbf{R}^n \to \mathbf{B}$ is *degenerate in the jth position* if for all $x_1, \ldots, x_n, y \in \mathbf{R}$,

$$f(x_1, \ldots, x_n) = f(x_1, \ldots, x_{j-1}, y, x_{j+1}, \ldots, x_n). \tag{3.2.2}$$

THEOREM 3.2.3 A linear threshold function is degenerate in the *jth* position iff for all presentations $(w_1, \ldots, w_n, h)$ of f, $w_j = 0$.

PROOF: Clearly, if $f = \vartheta_n(w_1, \ldots, w_{j-1}, 0, w_{j+1}, \ldots, w_n, h)$, then f is degenerate in the jth position. Conversely, suppose that f is a linear threshold function degenerate in the jth position.

Suppose $f = \vartheta_n(w_1, \ldots, w_n, h)$. Suppose there exists $x_1, \ldots, x_n \in \mathbf{R}$ such that $f(x_1, \ldots, x_n) = 0$ (we will return to the remaining case later). Suppose, for a contradiction, that $w_j \neq 0$. Set

$$y = (h - \sum_{i=1}^{j-1} w_i x_i - \sum_{i=j+1}^{n} w_i x_i)/w_j.$$

Then,

$$\sum_{i=1}^{j-1} w_i x_i + w_j y + \sum_{i=j+1}^{n} w_i x_i = h$$
$$\Rightarrow \quad \sigma_n(w_1, \ldots, w_n)(x_1, \ldots, x_{j-1}, y, x_{j+1}, \ldots, x_n) = h$$
$$\Rightarrow \quad \vartheta_n(w_1, \ldots, w_n, h)(x_1, \ldots, x_{j-1}, y, x_{j+1}, \ldots, x_n) = 1$$
$$\Rightarrow \quad f(x_1, \ldots, x_{j-1}, y, x_{j+1}, \ldots, x_n) = 1$$

But $f(x_1, \ldots, x_n) = 0$, which contradicts equation (3.2.2). Therefore, $w_j = 0$ as claimed.

If there does not exist $x_1, \ldots, x_n \in \mathbf{R}$ such that $f(x_1, \ldots, x_n) = 0$, (that is, f is the function which returns 1 on all inputs), a similar argument prevails (Problem 1). $\square$

Lemma 3.2.2 in fact uniquely characterizes the presentations of any nondegenerate linear threshold function:

THEOREM 3.2.4 If f is a nondegenerate linear threshold function, then

$$f = \vartheta_n(w_1, \ldots, w_n, h) = \vartheta_n(v_1, \ldots, v_n, r)$$

iff there exists $\mu \in \mathbf{R}$ such that $h = \mu r$ and $w_i = \mu v_i$ for $1 \leq i \leq n$.

PROOF: Suppose $f = \vartheta_n(w_1, \ldots, w_n, h) = \vartheta_n(v_1, \ldots, v_n, r)$. The "if" part of the hypothesis follows immediately by Lemma 3.2.2. It remains to prove the "only-if" part.

First, we claim that for all $1 \le i \le n$, there exists a unique $t_i \in \mathbf{R}$ such that

$$f(\underbrace{0, \ldots, 0}_{i-1}, x_i, \underbrace{0, \ldots, 0}_{n-i}) = 1 \text{ iff } x_i \ge t_i. \tag{3.2.3}$$

It is easy to see that t_i exists, for $1 \le i \le n$: if $(w_1, \ldots, w_n, h)$ is a presentation of f, then

$$t_i = h/w_i. \tag{3.2.4}$$

It is also clear that t_i is unique: for a contradiction, suppose there exists $s_i \in \mathbf{R}$, $s_i \ne t_i$, such that

$$f(\underbrace{0, \ldots, 0}_{i-1}, x_i, \underbrace{0, \ldots, 0}_{n-i}) = 1 \text{ iff } x_i \ge s_i. \tag{3.2.5}$$

Then, either $s_i < t_i$, or vice-versa. Without loss of generality, assume that $s_i < t_i$. By (3.2.3),

$$f(\underbrace{0, \ldots, 0}_{i-1}, s_i, \underbrace{0, \ldots, 0}_{n-i}) = 0, \tag{3.2.6}$$

and by (3.2.5),

$$f(\underbrace{0, \ldots, 0}_{i-1}, s_i, \underbrace{0, \ldots, 0}_{n-i}) = 1. \tag{3.2.7}$$

But (3.2.6) contradicts (3.2.7). Therefore, each t_i is unique, for $1 \le i \le n$.

Thus, the constants $t_1, \ldots, t_n$ are unique to the linear threshold function, that is, they are independent of presentation. Therefore, by (3.2.4), if $(v_1, \ldots, v_n, r)$ and $(w_1, \ldots, w_n, h)$ are presentations of f, then for all $1 \le i \le n$,

$$r/v_i = h/w_i. \tag{3.2.8}$$

There are two possible cases. If $h, r \ne 0$, then we can take $\mu = h/r$. Then, $h = \mu r$ and for all $1 \le i \le n$,

$$\begin{aligned} \mu v_i &= hv_i/r \quad \text{(by the definition of } \mu) \\ &= w_i \quad\quad \text{(by Equation (3.2.8)).} \end{aligned}$$

Alternatively, if one of h or r is equal to 0, then by Equation 3.2.8, $h = r = 0$. By a similar argument to the above, it can be shown that for all $1 \le i \le n-1$, there exists a unique $t_i \in \mathbf{R}$ such that

$$f(\underbrace{0, \ldots, 0}_{i-1}, x_i, \underbrace{0, \ldots, 0, -1}_{n-i}) = 1 \text{ iff } x_i \ge t_i, \tag{3.2.9}$$

and the result follows similarly (see Problem 2). □

COROLLARY 3.2.5 If f is a linear threshold function, then

$$f = \vartheta_n(w_1, \ldots, w_n, h) = \vartheta_n(v_1, \ldots, v_n, r)$$

iff there exists $\mu \in \mathbf{R}$ such that $h = \mu r$ and $w_i = \mu v_i$ for $1 \leq i \leq n$.

PROOF: This is an immediate consequence of Theorem 3.2.3 and Theorem 3.2.4. □

Of particular interest are linear functions with the property that

$$f(\underbrace{0, \ldots, 0}_{n}) = 0.$$

We will call functions with the latter property *zero-preserving* functions. A linear threshold function is said to have *zero threshold* iff it has a presentation with a threshold value of zero (which, by Corollary 3.2.5, implies that all of its presentations have a threshold value of zero). Note that linear threshold functions have a zero-preserving linear part iff they have a threshold value of zero. Although not every linear threshold function has a threshold of zero, their thresholds can be made zero with the addition of an extra input.

THEOREM 3.2.6 For every linear threshold function $f: \mathbf{R}^n \to \mathbf{B}$, there exists a zero-threshold linear threshold function $g: \mathbf{R}^{n+1} \to \mathbf{B}$ such that for all $x_1, \ldots, x_n \in \mathbf{B}$,

$$f(x_1, \ldots, x_n) = g(x_1, \ldots, x_n, 1).$$

PROOF: Let f be a linear threshold function. Suppose $(w_1, \ldots, w_n, h)$ is a presentation of f. Then, setting $w_{n+1} = -h$, we see that

$$
\begin{aligned}
f(x_1, \ldots, x_n) = 1 \quad &\Leftrightarrow \quad \vartheta_n(w_1, \ldots, w_n, h)(x_1, \ldots, x_n) = 1 \\
&\Leftrightarrow \quad \sigma_n(w_1, \ldots, w_n)(x_1, \ldots, x_n) \geq h \\
&\Leftrightarrow \quad \sum_{i=1}^{n} w_i x_i \geq h \\
&\Leftrightarrow \quad \sum_{i=1}^{n} w_i x_i - h \geq 0 \\
&\Leftrightarrow \quad \sigma_{n+1}(w_1, \ldots, w_{n+1})(x_1, \ldots, x_n, 1) \geq 0 \\
&\Leftrightarrow \quad \vartheta_{n+1}(w_1, \ldots, w_{n+1}, 0)(x_1, \ldots, x_n, 1) = 1.
\end{aligned}
$$

Therefore, setting $g = \vartheta_{n+1}(w_1, \ldots, w_{n+1}, 0)$ gives the required result. □

3.3   Bounded Domains

Rather than consider arbitrary linear threshold functions, it is more usual to limit their domain to be some proper subset of $\mathbf{R}^n$. For example, suppose we construct a neural network from neurons that compute linear threshold functions. Those neurons not directly in contact with the outside world (that is, those that receive their input purely from the output of other neurons) will have domain $\mathbf{B}^n$. Furthermore, practical considerations may require that each input to the neural network be scaled down to a limited interval $[-\alpha, \alpha]$ for some $\alpha \in \mathbf{R}$. In this case, the neurons in contact with the outside world will have domain a subset of $[-\alpha, \alpha]^n$. We will call a domain of this form a *bounded domain*. In other cases, the domain may be further reduced to a finite subset of $\mathbf{R}^n$.

Corollary 3.2.5 indicates that linear threshold functions over the real domain have very little scope for the selection of presentations. Linear threshold functions with limited domain have a much wider scope which will often allow the selection of presentations which are in some senses superior to others. Recall that a linear threshold function is the composition of a linear function with a threshold function. We will find that there is more leeway in choosing presentations if the portion of the range of the linear function below the threshold value is strictly bounded away from it. To be more specific, a presentation $(w_1, \ldots, w_n, h)$ is said to be *δ-separable* on domain $S \subseteq \mathbf{R}^n$, where $\delta \in \mathbf{R}^+$, iff for all $x_1, \ldots, x_n \in S$,

$$\vartheta_n(w_1, \ldots, w_n, h)(x_1, \ldots, x_n) = 0 \text{ iff } \sigma_n(w_1, \ldots, w_n)(x_1, \ldots, x_n) \leq h - \delta.$$

A linear threshold function is said to be *separable* on domain $S \subseteq \mathbf{R}^n$ iff it has a δ-separable presentation for some $\delta \in \mathbf{R}^+$.

The *weight* of a presentation $(w_1, \ldots, w_n, h)$ is defined to be

$$\max \{|w_i| \mid 1 \leq i \leq n\}.$$

LEMMA 3.3.1   For all $\delta \in \mathbf{R}^+$, $S \subseteq \mathbf{R}^n$, and all linear threshold functions f, if f has a weight w presentation that is λ-separable on S, then f has a weight $w\delta/\lambda$ presentation that is δ-separable on S.

PROOF: This is simply a stronger version of Lemma 3.2.2. Suppose f is a separable linear threshold function, $S \subseteq \mathbf{R}^n$, and $\delta \in \mathbf{R}^+$. By hypothesis, there exists a presentation $(w_1, \ldots, w_n, h)$ and $\lambda \in \mathbf{R}$ such that $f = \vartheta_n(w_1, \ldots, w_n, h)$, and

$$\vartheta_n(w_1, \ldots, w_n, h)(x_1, \ldots, x_n) = 0 \text{ iff } \sigma_n(w_1, \ldots, w_n)(x_1, \ldots, x_n) \leq h - \lambda.$$

Set $\mu = \delta/\lambda$. Then, by Lemma 3.2.2, $f = \vartheta_n(\mu w_1, \ldots, \mu w_n, \mu h)$, and furthermore,

$$\vartheta_n(\mu w_1, \ldots, \mu w_n, \mu h)(x_1, \ldots, x_n) = 0 \text{ iff } \sigma_n(\mu w_1, \ldots, \mu w_n)(x_1, \ldots, x_n) \leq \mu h - \delta.$$

That is, $(\mu w_1, \ldots, \mu w_n, \mu h)$ is a δ-separable presentation for f on S of weight $w\delta/\lambda$. $\square$

Note that Lemma 3.3.1 implies that whilst we are justified in quantifying the separability of presentations, we would not be justified in quantifying the separability of linear threshold functions:

COROLLARY 3.3.2 For all $\delta \in \mathbf{R}^+$, every separable linear threshold function has a δ-separable presentation.

It will sometimes make things easier to change the domain of a linear threshold function to a more convenient one. For example, it is sufficient for most purposes to limit discussion to domains which are a subset of $[0, 1]$, in the sense that most interesting results for those domains scale in a trivial fashion to arbitrary bounded domains. More formally:

THEOREM 3.3.3 For every nontrivial bounded domain $S \subseteq [-\alpha, \alpha]^n$ and every linear threshold function f over S, there exists a bounded domain $T \subseteq [0, 1]^n$ and a one-to-one correspondence $\phi : S \to T$ such that $f\phi^{-1}$ is a linear threshold function, and $(w_1, \ldots, w_n, h)$ is a presentation of f iff

$$(w_1, \ldots, w_n, (\textstyle\sum_{i=1}^{n} w_i + h/\alpha)/2)$$

is a presentation of $f\phi^{-1}$.

PROOF: Suppose $S \subseteq [-\alpha, \alpha]^n$ is a bounded domain, where $\alpha \in \mathbf{R}^+$, and f is a linear threshold function over S. Define $\ell : \mathbf{R} \to \mathbf{R}$ by $\ell(x) = (x/\alpha + 1)/2$, and $\phi : S \to [0, 1]^n$ by $\phi(x_1, \ldots, x_n) = (\ell(x_1), \ldots, \ell(x_n))$. Let T denote the range of ϕ.

Suppose $(w_1, \ldots, w_n, h)$ is a presentation of f. Then, for all $(x_1, \ldots, x_n) \in T$,

$$
\begin{aligned}
f\phi^{-1}(x_1, \ldots, x_n) = 1 \quad &\Leftrightarrow \quad f(\alpha(2x_1 - 1), \ldots, \alpha(2x_n - 1)) = 1 \\
&\Leftrightarrow \quad \vartheta_n(w_1, \ldots, w_n, h)(\alpha(2x_1 - 1), \ldots, \alpha(2x_n - 1)) = 1 \\
&\Leftrightarrow \quad \sigma_n(w_1, \ldots, w_n)(\alpha(2x_1 - 1), \ldots, \alpha(2x_n - 1)) \geq h \\
&\Leftrightarrow \quad \alpha \sum_{i=1}^{n} w_i(2x_i - 1) \geq h \\
&\Leftrightarrow \quad \sum_{i=1}^{n} w_i x_i \geq (h/\alpha + \sum_{i=1}^{n} w_i)/2 \\
&\Leftrightarrow \quad \sigma_n(w_1, \ldots, w_n)(x_1, \ldots, x_n) \geq (h/\alpha + \sum_{i=1}^{n} w_i)/2
\end{aligned}
$$

$$\Leftrightarrow \quad \vartheta_n(w_1, \ldots, w_n, (h/\alpha + \sum_{i=1}^{n} w_i)/2)(x_1, \ldots, x_n) = 1.$$

That is, $f\phi^{-1}$ is a linear threshold function over T with presentation

$$(w_1, \ldots, w_n, (\sum_{i=1}^{n} w_i + h/\alpha)/2).$$

Conversely, if $(w_1, \ldots, w_n, h)$ is a presentation of $f\phi^{-1}$, then one can show similarly that for all $(x_1, \ldots, x_n) \in S$,

$$f(x_1, \ldots, x_n) = 1 \Leftrightarrow \vartheta_n(w_1, \ldots, w_n, \alpha(2h - \sum_{i=1}^{n} w_i))(x_1, \ldots, x_n) = 1,$$

that is, $(w_1, \ldots, w_n, \alpha(2h - \sum_{i=1}^{n} w_i))$ is a presentation of f over S. $\square$

The intuition behind Theorem 3.3.3 is as follows. If we wish to prove a result about the weights of a linear threshold function over domain $S \subseteq [-\alpha, \alpha]^n$, we simply use Theorem 3.3.3 to change domains, and prove a theorem about the weights of $f\phi^{-1}$. Since for every presentation of $f\phi^{-1}$ there is a presentation of f with the same weights, the result also applies to the weights of f. In order to simplify matters, we will for the remainder of this chapter restrict our interest to domains that are a subset of $[0, 1]^n$. Readers who are interested in larger bounded domains can use Theorem 3.3.3 before applying the relevant result.

We can, when appropriate, further simplify matters by restricting ourselves to presentations with positive weights.

THEOREM 3.3.4 For every bounded domain $S \subseteq [0, 1]^n$, every linear threshold function f over S, and every m with $1 \leq m \leq n$, there exists a bounded domain $T \subseteq [0, 1]^n$ and a one-to-one correspondence $\phi: S \to T$ such that $f\phi^{-1}$ is a linear threshold function, and $(w_1, \ldots, w_n, h)$ is a presentation of f iff

$$(w_1, \ldots, w_{m-1}, -w_m, w_{m+1}, \ldots, w_n, h - w_m)$$

is a presentation of $f\phi^{-1}$.

PROOF: Suppose $S \subseteq [0, 1]^n$ is a bounded domain, f is a linear threshold function over S, and $1 \leq m \leq n$. Define $\phi: S \to [0, 1]^n$ by

$$\phi(x_1, \ldots, x_n) = (x_1, \ldots, x_{m-1}, 1 - x_m, x_{m+1}, \ldots, x_n).$$

Let T be the range of ϕ.

Suppose $(w_1, \ldots, w_n, h)$ is a presentation of f over S. Then, for all $(x_1, \ldots, x_n) \in T$,

$$f\phi^{-1}(x_1, \ldots, x_n) = 1$$
$$\Leftrightarrow \quad f(x_1, \ldots, x_{m-1}, 1 - x_m, x_{m+1}, \ldots, x_n) = 1$$
$$\Leftrightarrow \quad \vartheta_n(w_1, \ldots, w_n, h)(x_1, \ldots, x_{m-1}, 1 - x_m, x_{m+1}, \ldots, x_n) = 1$$
$$\Leftrightarrow \quad \sigma_n(w_1, \ldots, w_n)(x_1, \ldots, x_{m-1}, 1 - x_m, x_{m+1}, \ldots, x_n)) \geq h$$
$$\Leftrightarrow \quad \sum_{i=1}^{m-1} w_i x_i - w_m x_m + \sum_{i=m+1}^{n} w_i x_i \geq h - w_m$$
$$\Leftrightarrow \quad \sigma_n(w_1, \ldots, w_{m-1}, -w_m, w_{m+1}, \ldots, w_n)(x_1, \ldots, x_n) \geq h - w_m$$
$$\Leftrightarrow \quad \vartheta_n(w_1, \ldots, w_{m-1}, -w_m, w_{m+1}, \ldots, w_n, h - w_m)(x_1, \ldots, x_n) = 1.$$

That is, $f\phi^{-1}$ is a linear threshold function over T with presentation

$$(w_1, \ldots, w_{m-1}, -w_m, w_{m+1}, \ldots, w_n, h - w_m).$$

Conversely, if $(w_1, \ldots, w_n, h)$ is a presentation of $f\phi^{-1}$ over T, then one can show similarly that for all $(x_1, \ldots, x_n) \in S$,

$$f(x_1, \ldots, x_n) = 1 \Leftrightarrow \vartheta_n(w_1, \ldots, w_{m-1}, -w_m, w_{m+1}, \ldots, w_n, h - w_m)(x_1, \ldots, x_n) = 1,$$

that is,

$$(w_1, \ldots, w_{m-1}, -w_m, w_{m+1}, \ldots, w_n, h - w_m)$$

is a presentation of f over S. $\square$

It would be unreasonable to expect that natural or artificial neurons are able to realize every linear threshold function. In particular, the requirement that the weights be real numbers represented to infinite precision is not realistic. Fortunately, it is possible to limit the precision of weights of linear threshold functions that are separable on a bounded domain. We will measure precision by restricting weights to be integers (which we can do without loss of generality), and then measuring the size of the integers needed.

A presentation $(w_1, \ldots, w_n, h)$ is said to be an *integer presentation* if $h \in \mathbf{Z}$ and for $1 \leq i \leq n$, $w_i \in \mathbf{Z}$. Note that it is sufficient to limit the weights to be integers, since the threshold then can be rounded up to the nearest integer without harm. The existence of integer presentations is intrinsically of some interest, since it is an indication that it is enough to implement weights using fixed precision. This is a useful piece of knowledge, since one would imagine that small weights accurate to an arbitrarily large number of decimal places will be difficult to realize in practice. We will demonstrate that integer presentations exist, and furthermore, we will be able to derive an upper bound on their weight. By Lemma 3.2.2, the maximum weight of an integer presentation also provides an upper bound on the total number of bits to which real weights must be stored, whether or not they be integers. The following result states that the weight of an *integer* presentation of a separable linear threshold function over a bounded domain is bounded above by the product of the number of inputs and the ratio of the weight to the separability of an arbitrary *real* presentation.

THEOREM 3.3.5 Every linear threshold function over a bounded domain $S \subseteq [0, 1]^n$ with a weight w, δ-separable presentation has an integer presentation of weight at most nw/δ.

PROOF: Let f be a linear threshold function with a weight w, δ-separable presentation over a bounded domain $S \subseteq [0, 1]^n$. There exists (by Lemma 3.3.1) a weight nw/δ, n-separable presentation $(w_1, \ldots, w_n, h)$ of f over S. We will assume without loss of generality that $w_i \geq 0$ for $1 \leq i \leq n$, since if any of the weights are negative, we can apply Theorem 3.3.4 (as many times as necessary) to transform the domain, the threshold function, and the presentation so that the latter has non-negative weights, apply the proof as below, and then use Theorem 3.3.4 (again) to obtain an integer presentation of the original function.

Suppose $w_i - 1 \leq v_i < w_i$ for $1 \leq i \leq n$. We claim that $(v_1, \ldots, v_n, h - n)$ is a presentation of f over S. Suppose $(x_1, \ldots, x_n) \in S$. There are two cases to consider.

Firstly, suppose $f(x_1, \ldots, x_n) = 1$. Since $(w_1, \ldots, w_n, h)$ is a presentation of f over S,

$$\vartheta_n(w_1, \ldots, w_n, h)(x_1, \ldots, x_n) = 1,$$

and therefore,

$$\sigma_n(w_1, \ldots, w_n)(x_1, \ldots, x_n) \geq h,$$

that is,

$$\sum_{i=1}^n w_i x_i \geq h.$$

Since $v_i \geq w_i - 1$ for $1 \leq i \leq n$, this implies that

$$\sum_{i=1}^n v_i x_i \geq h - \sum_{i=1}^n x_i,$$

which, since $x_i \in [0, 1]$ implies that

$$\sum_{i=1}^n v_i x_i \geq h - n.$$

That is,
$$\sigma_n(v_1, \ldots, v_n)(x_1, \ldots, x_n) \geq h - n,$$
and so
$$\vartheta_n(v_1, \ldots, v_n, h - n)(x_1, \ldots, x_n) = 1.$$

Secondly, suppose $f(x_1, \ldots, x_n) = 0$. Since $(w_1, \ldots, w_n, h)$ is an n-separable presentation of f over S,
$$\vartheta_n(w_1, \ldots, w_n, h)(x_1, \ldots, x_n) = 0,$$
and therefore,
$$\sigma_n(w_1, \ldots, w_n)(x_1, \ldots, x_n) \leq h - n,$$
that is,
$$\sum_{i=1}^{n} w_i x_i \leq h - n.$$
Since $v_i < w_i$ for $1 \leq i \leq n$, this implies that
$$\sum_{i=1}^{n} v_i x_i < h - n.$$
That is,
$$\sigma_n(v_1, \ldots, v_n)(x_1, \ldots, x_n) < h - n,$$
and so
$$\vartheta_n(v_1, \ldots, v_n, h - n)(x_1, \ldots, x_n) = 0.$$

Therefore, for all $(x_1, \ldots, x_n)$, $f(x_1, \ldots, x_n) = \vartheta_n(v_1, \ldots, v_n, h - n)(x_1, \ldots, x_n)$, that is, $(v_1, \ldots, v_n, h - n)$ is a presentation of f over S. Thus, our claim has been proven.

Now, for $1 \leq i \leq n$ there is an integer u_i such that $w_i - 1 \leq u_i < w_i$. By the above claim, $(u_1, \ldots, u_n, h - n)$ is a presentation of f over S. Since $u_i \leq w_i$ and $w_i \geq 0$ for $1 \leq i \leq n$, $(u_1, \ldots, u_n, h - n)$ has weight no greater than that of $(w_1, \ldots, w_n, h)$, which is nw/δ. □

COROLLARY 3.3.6 Every linear threshold function separable on a bounded domain has an integer presentation.

PROOF: This is an immediate consequence of Corollary 3.3.2 and Theorem 3.3.5. □

It remains for us to find an upper bound on the weight of a δ-separable presentation of a linear threshold function over a finite domain. In this case, separability is no longer an issue:

THEOREM 3.3.7 Every linear threshold function over a finite domain is separable.

PROOF: Suppose f is a linear threshold function over a finite domain S. Suppose $(w_1, \ldots, w_n, h)$ is a presentation of f. Define

$$\delta = h - \max\left\{\sigma_n(w_1, \ldots, w_n)(x_1, \ldots, x_n) \mid (x_1, \ldots, x_n) \in S, \; f(x_1, \ldots, x_n) = 0\right\}.$$

Since S is a finite domain, δ is well-defined. Clearly $(w_1, \ldots, w_n, h)$ is δ-separable. $\square$

If f is a linear threshold function over a bounded domain S, $K \subseteq S$ is said to be a *kernel* of f over S if $\|K\| = n + 1$ and there is a presentation $(w_1, \ldots, w_n, h)$ of f over S such that for all $x_1, \ldots, x_n \in K$, $\sigma_n(w_1, \ldots, w_n)(x_1, \ldots, x_n) \in \{h - 1, h\}$.

THEOREM 3.3.8 Every nondegenerate linear threshold function over a finite domain has a kernel.

PROOF: Suppose $S \subset [0, 1]^n$ is a finite domain and f is a linear threshold function on S. Consider the following inequalities in unknowns $w_1, \ldots, w_n, h$, one for each $s = (s_1, \ldots, s_n) \in S$. If $f(s) = 0$, the inequality corresponding to s is

$$\sigma_n(w_1, \ldots, w_n)(s_1, \ldots, s_n) \leq h - 1. \tag{3.3.10}$$

If $f(s) = 1$, the inequality corresponding to s is

$$\sigma_n(w_1, \ldots, w_n)(s_1, \ldots, s_n) \geq h. \tag{3.3.11}$$

The inequalities of the form (3.3.10) and (3.3.11) define a convex polytope in $\mathbf{R}^{n+1}$ whose interior and surface points are 1-separable presentations of f. This polytope must be nontrivial, since by Theorem 3.3.7, f is separable, and so by Corollary 3.3.2 it has a 1-separable presentation.

Since f is nondegenerate, there is a point on the hypersurface of the polytope which meets exactly $n+1$ hyperfaces (see Problem 3). This point satisfies $n+1$ of the inequalities (3.3.10), (3.3.11) in exact equality. Therefore, there are $n + 1$ equations in $w_1, \ldots, w_n, h$,

$$
\begin{aligned}
s_{1,1}w_1 &+ s_{1,2}w_2 + \cdots + s_{1,n}w_n - h = t_1 \\
s_{2,1}w_1 &+ s_{2,2}w_2 + \cdots + s_{2,n}w_n - h = t_2 \\
&\quad\vdots \\
s_{n+1,1}w_1 &+ s_{n+1,2}w_2 + \cdots + s_{n+1,n}w_n - h = t_{n+1},
\end{aligned}
$$

where $s_i = (s_{i,1}, \ldots, s_{i,n}) \in S$ for $1 \leq i \leq n + 1$, $t_i \in \{0, -1\}$, whose solution is a 1-separable presentation of f. The set $\{s_i \mid 1 \leq i \leq n + 1\}$ is thus a kernel of f over S. $\square$

If $S \subseteq [0,1]$, and K is a kernel of f over S, the *volume* of K is defined to be the volume of a parallelpiped in $\mathbf{R}^{n+1}$ whose sides are vectors from the origin to points which are obtained from members of $K \subseteq [0,1]^n$ by adding a co-ordinate of unity in the $(n+1)$th dimension. That is, if $K = \{s_i \mid 1 \leq i \leq n+1\}$ where $s_i = (s_{i,1}, \ldots, s_{i,n})$, then the volume of K is given by the absolute value of the determinant

$$\begin{vmatrix} s_{1,1} & s_{1,2} & \cdots & s_{1,n} & 1 \\ s_{2,1} & s_{2,2} & \cdots & s_{2,n} & 1 \\ & & & \vdots & \\ s_{n+1,1} & s_{n+1,2} & \cdots & s_{n+1,n} & 1 \end{vmatrix}.$$

The *volume* of a linear threshold function f over S is defined to be the maximum volume of all kernels of f.

THEOREM 3.3.9 Every linear threshold function f over a finite domain $S \subset [0,1]^n$ of volume V has a 1-separable presentation of weight at most $(n+1)^{(n+1)/2}/V$.

PROOF: Suppose f is a nondegenerate linear threshold function of volume V over a finite domain $S \subset [0,1]^n$. By Theorem 3.3.8, f has a kernel of volume V over S. Therefore, there is a 1-separable presentation $(w_1, \ldots, w_n, h)$ which satisfies the $n+1$ simultaneous equations

$$\begin{aligned} s_{1,1}w_1 &+& s_{1,2}w_2 &+& \cdots &+& s_{1,n}w_n &-& h &=& t_1 \\ s_{2,1}w_1 &+& s_{2,2}w_2 &+& \cdots &+& s_{2,n}w_n &-& h &=& t_2 \\ & & & & & & & & & \vdots & \\ s_{n+1,1}w_1 &+& s_{n+1,2}w_2 &+& \cdots &+& s_{n+1,n}w_n &-& h &=& t_{n+1}, \end{aligned}$$

where $s_{i,j} \in [0,1]$, $t_i \in \{0,-1\}$.

By Cramer's rule, the solution to these simultaneous equations is given by $w_i = \Delta_i/\Delta$ for $1 \leq i \leq n$, and $h = \Delta_{n+1}/\Delta$, where

$$\Delta = \begin{vmatrix} s_{1,1} & s_{1,2} & \cdots & s_{1,n} & -1 \\ s_{2,1} & s_{2,2} & \cdots & s_{2,n} & -1 \\ & & & \vdots & \\ s_{n+1,1} & s_{n+1,2} & \cdots & s_{n+1,n} & -1 \end{vmatrix},$$

and

$$\Delta_i = \begin{vmatrix} s_{1,1} & s_{1,2} & \cdots & s_{1,i-1} & t_1 & s_{1,i+1} & \cdots & s_{1,n} & -1 \\ s_{2,1} & s_{2,2} & \cdots & s_{2,i-1} & t_2 & s_{2,i+1} & \cdots & s_{2,n} & -1 \\ & & & & \vdots & & & & \\ s_{n+1,1} & s_{n+1,2} & \cdots & s_{n+1,i-1} & t_{n+1} & s_{n+1,i+1} & \cdots & s_{n+1,n} & -1 \end{vmatrix}.$$

Therefore, w_i is bounded above by the maximum determinant of an $(n + 1) \times (n + 1)$ matrix over $[-1, 1]$ divided by V. By the Hadamard inequality, the determinant of an $(n + 1) \times (n + 1)$ matrix over $[0, 1]$ is bounded above in magnitude by $(n + 1)^{(n+1)/2}$. Thus, we deduce that $w_i \leq (n + 1)^{(n+1)/2}/V$.

If f is a degenerate linear threshold function, then a similar argument follows (Problem 4). $\square$

We can now define the *weight* of a linear threshold function over a finite domain to be the minimum weight of an integer presentation of that function.

3.4   Problems

1. Complete the proof of Theorem 3.2.3 in the case when there does not exist $x_1, \ldots, x_n \in$ **R** such that $f(x_1, \ldots, x_n) = 0$.

2. Complete the proof of Theorem 3.2.4 in the case where one of $h, r = 0$.

3. Show, in the proof of Theorem 3.3.8, that if there is no point on the hypersurface of the polytope which meets exactly $n + 1$ hyperfaces, then f must be degenerate.

4. Complete the proof of Theorem 3.3.9 in the case in which f is degenerate.

3.5   Bibliographic Notes

The neuron model discussed in this chapter is often called the *McCulloch-Pitts neuron*, after McCulloch and Pitts [82]. The reader who is unsatisfied with the physiological sketch of the neuron in Section 3.1 can consult standard textbooks such as Shepherd [125], or survey articles such as Stevens [135] and Fischbach [43]. Table 3.1 is taken from Tam [136].

Sections 3.3 and 3.3 are from Parberry [98]. Many of the results in Section 3.3 are the obvious generalization of results which are well-known for the Boolean domain. Theorem 3.3.6 for the Boolean domain appears in Minsky and Papert [86]. The technique used in Theorem 3.3.9 is a slight generalization of the technique used in Muroga, Toda, and Takasu [89].

4 The Boolean Neuron

Chapter 3 examined linear threshold functions with real inputs, which may be an appropriate model for artificial neurons that receive inputs from receptors. However, since the output of each of these neurons is a Boolean value, it follows that neurons that are internal to a circuit receive only Boolean inputs. These neurons are said to compute *Boolean linear threshold functions*, which are the subject of this chapter. Section 4.1 begins with some simple properties of Boolean linear threshold functions.

The remainder of this chapter is devoted to the derivation of upper and lower bounds on the synaptic weights necessary to realize all Boolean linear threshold functions. This is an interesting question, since if we are to develop a new technology capable of implementing gates that compute Boolean linear threshold functions, it would be useful to know beforehand exactly how large the weights need to be. Section 4.2 contains some simple upper and lower bounds. Sections 4.3 and 4.4 contain the proof of a more difficult lower bound. The former defines the function that requires large weights, and proves some preliminary results about it. The latter contains the remainder of the proof. These require a certain amount of mathematical ability, and so we recommend that the less sophisticated reader skip directly from Section 4.2 to Chapter 5 (preferably pausing to read the statement of Corollary 4.4.10 on p. 98, and the brief statement following its proof, *en passant*).

4.1 Threshold Logic

As was mentioned in Section 3.3, neurons which are internal to a neural network (that is, those which obtain their inputs from the outputs of other neurons rather than from the external world) have domain $\mathbf{B}^n$, which we will call the *Boolean domain*. It may also be reasonable to restrict the inputs to the neural network to be Boolean, since it is unlikely that the inputs will be accurate to more than a few decimal places, and, in addition, devices that clip the inputs and encode them in binary are cheap and readily available. A linear threshold function with Boolean domain (that is, one of the form $f: \mathbf{B}^n \to \mathbf{B}$ for some $n \in \mathbb{N}$) will be called a *Boolean linear threshold function*.

Define θ_n to be ϑ_n with range restricted to Boolean linear threshold functions. That is, $\theta_n(w_1, \ldots, w_n, h): \mathbf{B}^n \to \mathbf{B}$, where for all $x_1, \ldots, x_n \in \mathbf{B}$,

$$\theta_n(w_1, \ldots, w_n, h)(x_1, \ldots, x_n) = \vartheta_n(w_1, \ldots, w_n, h)(x_1, \ldots, x_n).$$

We will depict an abstract discrete neuron with a circle representing the soma, lines extending upwards representing the dendrites, and a line extending downwards representing the axon; each "dendrite" line will be labelled with the appropriate synaptic

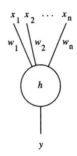

Figure 4.1
A gate computing $y = \theta_n(w_1, \ldots, w_n, h)(x_1, \ldots, x_n)$.

weight (see Figure 4.1). A synapse will be indicated by attaching one of the "dendrites" to the "axon" of the appropriate neuron.

If $x, y \in \mathbf{B}$, let $x \wedge y$ denote the Boolean conjunction of x and y, that is, $x \wedge y \in \mathbf{B}$, and $x \wedge y = 1$ iff $x = 1$ and $y = 1$. Let $x \vee y$ denote the Boolean disjunction of x and y, that is, $x \vee y \in \mathbf{B}$, and $x \vee y = 1$ iff $x = 1$ or $y = 1$ or $x = y = 1$. Let $x \oplus y$ denote the Boolean parity of x and y, that is, $x \oplus y \in \mathbf{B}$, and $x \oplus y = 1$ iff $x = 1$ or $y = 1$, but $x \neq y$. Let $\overline{x}$ denote the Boolean complement of x, that is, $\overline{x} \in \mathbf{B}$, and $\overline{x} = 1$ iff $x = 0$. Define the *conjunction* function $\mathrm{AND}: \mathbf{B}^n \to \mathbf{B}$, the *disjunction* function $\mathrm{OR}: \mathbf{B}^n \to \mathbf{B}$, the *parity* function $\mathrm{XOR}: \mathbf{B}^n \to \mathbf{B}$, and the *complement* function $\mathrm{NOT}: \mathbf{B} \to \mathbf{B}$, as follows:

$$
\begin{aligned}
\mathrm{AND}(x_1, \ldots, x_n) &= x_1 \wedge x_2 \wedge \cdots \wedge x_n \\
\mathrm{OR}(x_1, \ldots, x_n) &= x_1 \vee x_2 \vee \cdots \vee x_n \\
\mathrm{XOR}(x_1, \ldots, x_n) &= x_1 \oplus x_2 \oplus \cdots \oplus x_n \\
\mathrm{NOT}(x) &= \neg x.
\end{aligned}
$$

Further, the *majority*, or *consensus* function $\mathrm{MAJORITY}: \mathbf{B}^n \to \mathbf{B}$, is defined as follows:

$$
\mathrm{MAJORITY}(x_1, \ldots, x_n) = 1 \text{ iff } \|\{x_i \mid x_i = 1,\ 1 \le i \le n\}\| \ge n/2.
$$

It is easy to see that conjunction, disjunction, complement, and majority are Boolean linear threshold functions, since

$$
\mathrm{AND} = \theta_n(\underbrace{1, \ldots, 1}_{n}, n) \tag{4.1.1}
$$

$$
\mathrm{OR} = \theta_n(\underbrace{1, \ldots, 1}_{n}, 1) \tag{4.1.2}
$$

$$
\begin{aligned}
\text{NOT} &= \theta_n(-1, 0) & (4.1.3)\\
\text{MAJORITY} &= \theta_n(\underbrace{1, \ldots, 1}_{n}, n/2). & (4.1.4)
\end{aligned}
$$

However, it is also easy to see that the parity function is not a Boolean linear threshold function.

THEOREM 4.1.1 For $n \geq 2$, the parity function on n inputs is not a linear threshold function.

PROOF: The proof follows easily by induction on $n \geq 2$. Suppose $n = 2$. For a contradiction, suppose the two-input parity function is a linear threshold function. Then, there exists a presentation (w_1, w_2, h) such that for all $x_1, x_2 \in \mathbf{B}$,

$$
\text{XOR}(x_1, x_2) = \theta_2(w_1, w_2, h)(x_1, x_2),
$$

that is,

$$
x_1 \oplus x_2 = 1 \text{ iff } w_1 x_1 + w_2 x_2 \geq h.
$$

Therefore, by considering the output of the parity function on inputs $(0, 0)$, $(0, 1)$, $(1, 0)$, and $(1, 1)$ respectively, we see that

$$
\begin{aligned}
h &> 0 & (4.1.5)\\
w_1 &\geq h & (4.1.6)\\
w_2 &\geq h & (4.1.7)\\
w_1 + w_2 &< h. & (4.1.8)
\end{aligned}
$$

But (4.1.6) and (4.1.7) imply that $w_1 + w_2 \geq 2h$, which with (4.1.8) implies $h < 0$, contradicting (4.1.5). We conclude that the two-input parity function cannot be a linear threshold function.

Now suppose $n > 2$, and that the parity function on $n - 1$ inputs is not a linear threshold function. For a contradiction, suppose the n-input parity function is a linear threshold function, with presentation $(w_1, \ldots, w_n, h)$. Then, for all $x_1, \ldots, x_{n-1} \in \mathbf{B}$,

$$
\begin{aligned}
\text{XOR}(x_1, \ldots, x_{n-1}) = 1 \quad &\Leftrightarrow \quad \text{XOR}(x_1, \ldots, x_{n-1}, 0) = 1\\
&\Leftrightarrow \quad \theta_n(w_1, \ldots, w_n, h)(x_1, \ldots, x_{n-1}, 0) = 1\\
&\Leftrightarrow \quad \sigma_n(w_1, \ldots, w_n)(x_1, \ldots, x_{n-1}, 0) \geq h\\
&\Leftrightarrow \quad \sum_{i=1}^{n-1} w_i x_i \geq h\\
&\Leftrightarrow \quad \sigma_{n-1}(w_1, \ldots, w_{n-1})(x_1, \ldots, x_{n-1}) \geq h\\
&\Leftrightarrow \quad \theta_{n-1}(w_1, \ldots, w_{n-1}, h)(x_1, \ldots, x_{n-1}) = 1.
\end{aligned}
$$

That is, $(w_1, \ldots, w_{n-1}, h)$ is a presentation of the parity function on $n - 1$ inputs, which implies that the latter is a linear threshold function, contradicting the induction hypothesis. We conclude that the n-input parity function cannot be a linear threshold function. $\square$

Note also that the complement function is a linear threshold function, since for all $x \in \mathbf{B}$, $\overline{x} = \theta_1(-1, 0)(x)$. The complement function also interacts with linear threshold functions in useful ways. For all Boolean functions $f : \mathbf{B}^n \to \mathbf{B}$, let $\overline{f}$ denote the Boolean complement of f, defined by

$$\overline{f}(x_1, \ldots, x_n) = \overline{f(x_1, \ldots, x_n)}$$

for all $x_1, \ldots, x_n \in \mathbf{B}$. The complement of a linear threshold function is also a linear threshold function.

LEMMA 4.1.2 The complement of a Boolean linear threshold function with integer presentation $(w_1, \ldots, w_n, h)$ is a Boolean linear threshold function with integer presentation $(-w_1, \ldots, -w_n, 1 - h)$.

PROOF: Let f be a linear threshold function with an integer presentation $(w_1, \ldots, w_n, h)$. For all $x_1, \ldots, x_n \in \mathbf{B}$,

$$
\begin{aligned}
\overline{f}(x_1, \ldots, x_n) = 1 \quad &\Leftrightarrow \quad \theta_n(w_1, \ldots, w_n, h)(x_1, \ldots, x_n) = 0 \\
&\Leftrightarrow \quad \sigma_n(w_1, \ldots, w_n)(x_1, \ldots, x_n) < h \\
&\Leftrightarrow \quad \sigma_n(w_1, \ldots, w_n)(x_1, \ldots, x_n) \leq h - 1 \\
&\Leftrightarrow \quad \sum_{i=1}^{n} w_i x_i \leq h - 1 \\
&\Leftrightarrow \quad \sum_{i=1}^{n} -w_i x_i \geq 1 - h \\
&\Leftrightarrow \quad \sigma_n(-w_1, \ldots, -w_n)(x_1, \ldots, x_n) \geq 1 - h \\
&\Leftrightarrow \quad \theta_n(-w_1, \ldots, -w_n, 1 - h)(x_1, \ldots, x_n) = 1.
\end{aligned}
$$

Thus, $(-w_1, \ldots, -w_n, 1 - h)$ is a presentation of $\overline{f}$. $\square$

Note that by Theorem 3.3.6 and Lemma 4.1.2, the complement of a Boolean linear threshold function is a Boolean linear threshold function. It also remains a linear threshold function when one complements its inputs.

LEMMA 4.1.3 For all $1 \leq m \leq n$, a Boolean linear threshold function with presentation $(w_1, \ldots, w_n, h)$ and inputs $x_1, \ldots, x_n$ is a Boolean linear threshold function of $x_1, \ldots, x_{m-1}, \overline{x}_m, x_{m+1}, \ldots, x_n$ with presentation

$$(w_1, \ldots, w_{m-1}, -w_m, w_{m+1}, \ldots, w_n, h - w_m).$$

PROOF: The proof is almost identical to that of Theorem 3.3.4. The function ϕ complements the mth weight. $\square$

LEMMA 4.1.4 A Boolean linear threshold function with presentation $(w_1, \ldots, w_n, h)$ is a Boolean linear threshold function of the complements of its inputs with presentation

$$(-w_1, \ldots, -w_n, h - \sum_{i=1}^{n} w_i).$$

PROOF: Apply Lemma 4.1.3 with $m = 1, 2, \ldots, n$. $\square$

An interesting observation can be made by combining Lemma 4.1.2 and Lemma 4.1.4: the complement of a linear threshold function f has a presentation with exactly the same weights as any integer presentation of f.

THEOREM 4.1.5 The complement of a Boolean linear threshold function with integer presentation $(w_1, \ldots, w_n, h)$ is a Boolean linear threshold function of the complements of its inputs with presentation

$$(w_1, \ldots, w_n, 1 - h + \sum_{i=1}^{n} w_i).$$

PROOF: This is an immediate consequence of Lemma 4.1.2 and Lemma 4.1.4. $\square$

Theorem 4.1.5 is particularly interesting when applied to the Boolean linear threshold functions conjunction, disjunction and majority.

COROLLARY 4.1.6 (De Morgan's Laws) For all $x_1, \ldots, x_n \in \mathbf{B}$,

$$\overline{\mathrm{AND}}(x_1, \ldots, x_n) = \mathrm{OR}(\overline{x}_1, \ldots, \overline{x}_n)$$
$$\overline{\mathrm{OR}}(x_1, \ldots, x_n) = \mathrm{AND}(\overline{x}_1, \ldots, \overline{x}_n).$$

PROOF: This is an immediate consequence of Theorem 4.1.5 and Equations (4.1.1) and (4.1.2), respectively. $\square$

COROLLARY 4.1.7 For every odd n and for all $x_1, \ldots, x_n \in \mathbf{B}$,

$$\overline{\mathrm{MAJORITY}}(x_1, \ldots, x_n) = \mathrm{MAJORITY}(\overline{x}_1, \ldots, \overline{x}_n).$$

PROOF: By Equation (4.1.4),

$$\mathrm{MAJORITY}(x_1, \ldots, x_n) = \theta_n(\underbrace{1, \ldots, 1}_{n}, n/2)(x_1, \ldots, x_n).$$

Therefore, since n is odd,

$$\mathrm{MAJORITY}(x_1, \ldots, x_n) = \theta_n(\underbrace{1, \ldots, 1}_{n}, (n+1)/2)(x_1, \ldots, x_n).$$

Finally, by Theorem 4.1.5, this implies that

$$\overline{\mathrm{MAJORITY}}(x_1, \ldots, x_n) = \mathrm{MAJORITY}(\overline{x}_1, \ldots, \overline{x}_n).$$

$\square$

An alternate formalism for linear threshold functions uses the integers -1 and 1 to represent the logical values `false` and `true`, respectively. This is often called *bipolar* logic. This is clearly equivalent to the formalism that we have used (Problem 1), by Theorem 3.3.3.

It is sometimes convenient to use only presentations that ensure that the excitation level never exactly matches the threshold value. Such presentations will be called *decisive*. It is easy to prove the following:

THEOREM 4.1.8 Every Boolean linear threshold function that has an integer presentation of weight w has a decisive integer presentation of weight $2w$.

The proof is left to the reader (see Problem 2).

4.2 Simple Weight Bounds

We can use the results of Section 3.3 to obtain an upper bound on the weight of integer presentations of Boolean linear threshold functions. Some things are simpler in the Boolean domain, for example, since the Boolean domain is finite, Boolean linear threshold functions are always separable (by Theorem 3.3.7). Furthermore, Boolean linear threshold functions have volume at least one, since the determinant of any matrix over the integers is an integer, and hence any non-zero determinant is at least one in magnitude. Therefore, by Theorem 3.3.9, any Boolean linear threshold function has an integer presentation of weight at most $(n + 1)^{(n+3)/2}$. However, by being more careful we can obtain a slightly better bound:

THEOREM 4.2.1 Every Boolean linear threshold function f has an integer presentation of weight at most $(n + 1)^{(n+1)/2}/2^n$.

PROOF: Suppose f is a Boolean linear threshold function. As in the proof of Theorem 3.3.9, we will assume without loss of generality that f is nondegenerate. By Theorem 3.3.8, f has a kernel over S. Therefore, there is a 1-separable presentation $(w_1, \ldots, w_n, h)$ which satisfies the $n + 1$ simultaneous equations

$$
\begin{aligned}
w_1 s_{1,1} &+ w_2 s_{1,2} + \cdots + w_n s_{1,n} - h = t_1 \\
w_1 s_{2,1} &+ w_2 s_{2,2} + \cdots + w_n s_{2,n} - h = t_2 \\
&\phantom{+ w_2 s_{2,2} + \cdots + w_n s_{2,n} - h =} \vdots \\
w_1 s_{n+1,1} &+ w_2 s_{n+1,2} + \cdots + w_n s_{n+1,n} - h = t_{n+1},
\end{aligned}
$$

where $s_{i,j} \in \{0, 1\}$, $t_i \in \{0, -1\}$.

By Cramer's rule, the solution to these simultaneous equations is given by $w_i = \Delta_i/\Delta$ for $1 \le i \le n$, and $h = \Delta_{n+1}/\Delta$, where

$$
\Delta = \begin{vmatrix}
s_{1,1} & s_{1,2} & \cdots & s_{1,n} & -1 \\
s_{2,1} & s_{2,2} & \cdots & s_{2,n} & -1 \\
& & \vdots & & \\
s_{n+1,1} & s_{n+1,2} & \cdots & s_{n+1,n} & -1
\end{vmatrix},
$$

and

$$
\Delta_i = \begin{vmatrix}
s_{1,1} & s_{1,2} & \cdots & s_{1,i-1} & a_1 & s_{1,i+1} & \cdots & s_{1,n} & -1 \\
s_{2,1} & s_{2,2} & \cdots & s_{2,i-1} & a_2 & s_{2,i+1} & \cdots & s_{2,n} & -1 \\
& & & & \vdots & & & & \\
s_{n+1,1} & s_{n+1,2} & \cdots & s_{n+1,i-1} & a_{n+1} & s_{n+1,i+1} & \cdots & s_{n+1,n} & -1
\end{vmatrix}
$$

for $1 \le i \le n$, where $s_{j,k} \in \{0, 1\}$, $a_j \in \{0, -1\}$, for $1 \le j \le n + 1$, $1 \le k \le n$.

Clearly, by construction $(w_1, \ldots, w_n, h)$ is a presentation of f. By Lemma 3.2.2 with $\mu = |\Delta|$, there is a presentation $(v_1, \ldots, v_n, g)$ of f with

$$
|v_i| = \text{abs} \begin{vmatrix}
s_{1,1} & s_{1,2} & \cdots & s_{1,i-1} & a_1 & s_{1,i+1} & \cdots & s_{1,n} & -1 \\
s_{2,1} & s_{2,2} & \cdots & s_{2,i-1} & a_2 & s_{2,i+1} & \cdots & s_{2,n} & -1 \\
& & & & \vdots & & & & \\
s_{n+1,1} & s_{n+1,2} & \cdots & s_{n+1,i-1} & a_{n+1} & s_{n+1,i+1} & \cdots & s_{n+1,n} & -1
\end{vmatrix}
$$

for $1 \leq i \leq n$, where $s_{j,k} \in \{0,1\}$, $a_j \in \{0,-1\}$, for $1 \leq j \leq n+1$, $1 \leq k \leq n$. Since an integer determinant is always an integer, $(v_1, \ldots, v_n, g)$ is an integer presentation.

Negating column i of this determinant, multiplying each of the first n columns by 2 and adding column $n+1$ to each of them, we find that

$$2^n \, |v_i| = \text{abs} \begin{vmatrix} t_{1,1} & t_{1,2} & \cdots & t_{1,i-1} & b_1 & t_{1,i+1} & \cdots & t_{1,n} & -1 \\ t_{2,1} & t_{2,2} & \cdots & t_{2,i-1} & b_2 & t_{2,i+1} & \cdots & t_{2,n} & -1 \\ & & & & \vdots & & & & \\ t_{n+1,1} & t_{n+1,2} & \cdots & t_{n+1,i-1} & b_{n+1} & t_{n+1,i+1} & \cdots & t_{n+1,n} & -1 \end{vmatrix}$$

for $1 \leq i \leq n$, where $t_{j,k} = 2s_{j,k} - 1 \in \{-1,1\}$, $b_j = -2a_j - 1 \in \{-1,1\}$, for $1 \leq j \leq n+1$, $1 \leq k \leq n$.

By the Hadamard inequality, the determinant of an $(n+1) \times (n+1)$ matrix over $\{-1,1\}$ is bounded above in magnitude by $(n+1)^{(n+1)/2}$. Thus, we deduce that $|v_i| \leq (n+1)^{(n+1)/2}/2^n$. $\square$

It is useful to obtain bounds on the number of n-input Boolean linear threshold functions.

THEOREM 4.2.2 There are at least $2^{n(n-1)/2}$ Boolean linear threshold functions with n inputs.

PROOF: Let $C(n)$ be the number of n-input Boolean linear threshold functions with zero threshold. Then, $C(1) = 2$, and we claim that for $n > 1$,

$$C(n) \geq (2^{n-1} + 1)C(n-1).$$

Let $f = \theta_n(w_1, \ldots, w_n, 0)$ be a Boolean linear threshold function. We will count the number of ways that the weights $w_1, \ldots, w_n$ can be chosen to give different functions f. Partition the domain $\mathbf{B}^n$ of f into two sets

$$\mathbf{B}_0^n = \{(x_1, \ldots, x_{n-1}, 0) \mid x_i \in \mathbf{B} \text{ for } 1 \leq i < n\}$$

and

$$\mathbf{B}_1^n = \{(x_1, \ldots, x_{n-1}, 1) \mid x_i \in \mathbf{B} \text{ for } 1 \leq i < n\}.$$

Since there are exactly as many choices for f restricted to domain $\mathbf{B}_0^n$ as there are $(n-1)$-input Boolean linear threshold functions with zero threshold, the weights $w_1, \ldots, w_{n-1}$ can be chosen in $C(n-1)$ different ways, each of which makes f have a different output for some $x \in \mathbf{B}_0^n$. This choice of the first $n-1$ weights fixes the relative order of $\sigma_n(w_1, \ldots, w_n)(x)$ for all $x \in \mathbf{B}_1^n$ (which values we can easily make distinct, see Problem 3), regardless of the choice of w_n. Then, w_n can be chosen to make $\sigma_n(w_1, \ldots, w_n)(x) < 0$ for the first i of the $x \in \mathbf{B}_1^n$ in this order, for $0 \leq i \leq 2^{n-1}$. Therefore, $C(n) \geq (2^{n-1} + 1)C(n-1)$, as claimed.

Therefore, by induction on n,

$$C(n) \geq \prod_{i=0}^{n-1}(2^i + 1) > 2^{n(n-1)/2}.$$

□

It is reasonable to ask whether the lower bound in Theorem 4.2.2 is tight. It can be matched to within a polynomial, as follows. We can conclude from these two results that there are $2^{\Theta(n^2)}$ Boolean linear threshold functions.

THEOREM 4.2.3 There are less than 2^{n^2} nondegenerate Boolean linear threshold functions with n inputs.

PROOF: By the argument used in the proof of Theorem 3.3.8, each nondegenerate linear threshold function with n inputs corresponds to at least one point at the intersection of $n+1$ hyperplanes in $(n+1)$-dimensional space. There are 2^n such hyperplanes (one for each Boolean input), and hence at most

$$\binom{2^n}{n+1} < \frac{2^{n(n+1)}}{(n+1)!} < 2^{n^2}$$

possible points of intersection. Therefore, there are less than 2^{n^2} nondegenerate Boolean linear threshold functions with n inputs. □

We can deduce from Theorem 4.2.2 that there are n-input Boolean linear threshold functions with weight at least $2^{(n-1)/2}$, since if all Boolean linear threshold functions have weights strictly less than this value, then there would be less than $2^{n(n-1)/2}$ Boolean linear threshold functions. This counting argument is a little unsatisfactory, since it does not give any specific Boolean linear threshold functions with weights this large. A specific example is relatively easy to find:

THEOREM 4.2.4 If n is odd, $w_i = 2^{\lfloor (i-1)/2 \rfloor}$ for $1 \leq i \leq n$, and $h = 2^{(n-1)/2}$, the Boolean linear threshold function $\theta_n(w_1, \ldots, w_n, h)$ has weight $2^{(n-1)/2}$.

PROOF: Suppose n is odd. Let $k = (n-1)/2$. It is easier to permute the inputs and consider instead the Boolean linear threshold function

$$f = \theta_n(1, 2, 4, \ldots, 2^{k-1}, 2^k, 2^{k-1}, \ldots, 4, 2, 1, 2^k).$$

We are required to prove that there is no integer presentation of f with weights smaller in magnitude than 2^k. Suppose $(w_1, \ldots, w_n, h)$ is an arbitrary presentation of f. We will without loss of generality assume that it is a positive presentation (that is, a presentation in which all weights are positive), by Theorem 3.3.4. It is sufficient to prove that $w_{k+1} \geq 2^k$.

For $1 \leq i \leq k$, define $u_i, v_i \in \mathbf{B}^n$ as follows:

$$u_i = (\overbrace{\underbrace{0, \ldots, 0}_{i}, 1, 0, \ldots, 0}^{k+1}, \overbrace{1, \ldots, 1, \underbrace{0, \ldots, 0}_{i}}^{k})$$

$$v_i = (\overbrace{\underbrace{1, \ldots, 1}_{i}, 0, 0, \ldots, 0}^{k+1}, \overbrace{1, \ldots, 1, \underbrace{0, \ldots, 0}_{i}}^{k}).$$

Then,

$$\sigma_n(1, 2, 4, \ldots, 2^{k-1}, 2^k, 2^{k-1}, \ldots, 4, 2, 1, 2^k)(u_i) = 2^i + (2^k - 1 - \sum_{j=0}^{i-1} 2^j)$$
$$= 2^k,$$

and

$$\sigma_n(1, 2, 4, \ldots, 2^{k-1}, 2^k, 2^{k-1}, \ldots, 4, 2, 1, 2^k)(v_i) = \sum_{j=0}^{i-1} 2^j + (2^k - 1 - \sum_{j=0}^{i-1} 2^j)$$
$$= 2^k - 1,$$

so $f(u_i) = 1$ and $f(v_i) = 0$ for $1 \leq i \leq k$. Therefore, $\sigma_n(w_1, \ldots, w_n)(u_i) \geq h$, that is,

$$w_{i+1} + \sum_{j=k+2}^{2k+1-i} w_j \geq h, \tag{4.2.9}$$

and $\sigma_n(w_1, \ldots, w_n)(v_i) < h$, that is,

$$\sum_{j=1}^{i} w_j + \sum_{j=k+2}^{2k+1-i} w_j < h. \tag{4.2.10}$$

Inequalities (4.2.9) and (4.2.10) imply that

$$w_{i+1} \geq \sum_{j=1}^{i} w_j,$$

for $1 \leq i \leq k$. Therefore, by induction on i, $w_{i+1} \geq 2^i$ for $1 \leq i \leq k$. In particular $w_{k+1} \geq 2^k$. $\square$

It is fairly easy to construct a threshold function that requires larger weights. Define the *Fibonacci numbers* as follows: $F_1 = 1$, $F_2 = 1$, and for all $n \geq 3$, $F_n = F_{n-2} + F_{n-1}$.

LEMMA 4.2.5 For all $n \geq 3$,

$$F_n = \sum_{i=1}^{n-2} F_i + 1.$$

PROOF: The proof is by induction on n. The claim is certainly true for $n = 3$. Suppose $F_{n-1} = \sum_{i=1}^{n-3} F_i + 1$. Then,

$$F_n = F_{n-2} + F_{n-1} = F_{n-2} + \sum_{i=1}^{n-3} F_i + 1 = \sum_{i=1}^{n-2} F_i + 1.$$

$\square$

THEOREM 4.2.6 The Boolean linear threshold function $\theta_n(F_1, \ldots, F_n, F_{n+1})$ has weight F_n.

PROOF: Suppose $f = \theta_n(F_1, \ldots, F_n, F_{n+1})$. Suppose $(w_1, \ldots, w_n, h)$ is an arbitrary presentation of f. The proof uses the same technique as Theorem 4.2.4. We will quickly sketch the proof and leave the details to the reader (Problems 4 and 5).

Suppose n is even. The proof is similar for odd n. For $1 \leq i \leq n/2$, let

$$t_i \;=\; (\underbrace{0, \ldots, 0}_{2(i-2)}, 0, 0, 1, 1, \underbrace{0, 1, 0, 1 \ldots, 0, 1}_{n-2i})$$

$$u_i \;=\; (\underbrace{1, \ldots, 1}_{2(i-2)}, 0, 0, 1, 0, \underbrace{0, 1, 0, 1 \ldots, 0, 1}_{n-2i}),$$

$$v_i \;=\; (\underbrace{1, \ldots, 1}_{2(i-2)}, 1, 0, 0, 1, \underbrace{0, 1, 0, 1 \ldots, 0, 1}_{n-2i}).$$

Therefore, for $1 \leq i \leq n/2$,

1. $\sigma_n(w_1, \ldots, w_n)(t_i) \geq h$,
2. $\sigma_n(w_1, \ldots, w_n)(u_i) < h$, and
3. $\sigma_n(w_1, \ldots, w_n)(v_i) < h$.

Therefore, for all $3 \leq k \leq n$, $w_k \geq \sum_{i=1}^{k-2} w_i + 1$ (inequalities (1) and (2) must be used for odd k and inequalities (1) and (3) must be used for even k).

Thus, the smallest weights are $w_1 = w_2 = 1$, and for $3 \leq k \leq n$, $w_k = \sum_{i=1}^{k-2} w_i + 1$. That is, by Lemma 4.2.5, $w_k = F_k$ for all $1 \leq k \leq n$. $\square$

LEMMA 4.2.7 For all $n \in \mathbb{N}$, $F_n \geq \lfloor \phi^n / \sqrt{5} \rfloor$, where $\phi = (1 + \sqrt{5})/2$.

PROOF: See, for example, Graham, Knuth, and Patashnik [54, Section 6.6]. $\square$

COROLLARY 4.2.8 The Boolean linear threshold function $\theta_n(F_1, \ldots, F_n, F_{n+1})$ has weight at least $\lfloor \phi^n / \sqrt{5} \rfloor$, where $\phi = (1 + \sqrt{5})/2$.

PROOF: The claim is an immediate consequence of Theorem 4.2.6 and Lemma 4.2.7. $\square$

It is clear that Corollary 4.2.8 is stronger than Theorem 4.2.4, since the former gives a lower bound slightly better than 1.618^n, and the latter a lower bound slightly better than 1.414^n.

4.3 A Threshold Function with Large Weights

In this section we will depart from the convention used up to this point and use bipolar states. For convenience, let $\mathbb{U}$ denote the set $\{-1, 1\}$. Define $\hat{\theta}_n$ to be ϑ_n with range restricted to linear threshold functions over $\mathbb{U}$. That is, $\hat{\theta}_n(w_1, \ldots, w_n, h): \mathbb{U}^n \to \mathbb{U}$, where for all $x_1, \ldots, x_n \in \mathbb{U}$,

$$\hat{\theta}_n(w_1, \ldots, w_n, h)(x_1, \ldots, x_n) = \vartheta_n(w_1, \ldots, w_n, h)(x_1, \ldots, x_n).$$

Suppose n is a power of 2, and $n = 2^m$. If A and B are sets, define the *symmetric difference* of A and B as follows:

$$A \Delta B = (A \cup B) \backslash (A \cap B).$$

Let $\mathcal{M} = \{1, 2, \ldots, m\}$. Consider the n different sets $\alpha_1, \ldots, \alpha_n \subseteq \mathcal{M}$. The list $\alpha_1, \ldots, \alpha_n$ is said to be in *minimal change* order if the following two properties hold:

1. For all $1 \leq i < n$, $\|\alpha_i\| \leq \|\alpha_{i+1}\|$.
2. For all $1 \leq i < n$, $\|\alpha_i \Delta \alpha_{i+1}\| \leq 2$.

Name	Bit	Set	Name	Bit	Set
α_1	0000	$\emptyset$	α_9	0101	$\{2,4\}$
α_2	0001	$\{4\}$	α_{10}	0110	$\{2,3\}$
α_3	0010	$\{3\}$	α_{11}	0011	$\{3,4\}$
α_4	0100	$\{2\}$	α_{12}	0111	$\{2,3,4\}$
α_5	1000	$\{1\}$	α_{13}	1011	$\{1,3,4\}$
α_6	1100	$\{1,2\}$	α_{14}	1101	$\{1,2,4\}$
α_7	1010	$\{1,3\}$	α_{15}	1110	$\{1,2,3\}$
α_8	1001	$\{1,4\}$	α_{16}	1111	$\{1,2,3,4\}$

Table 4.1
The sets $\alpha_1, \ldots, \alpha_n$ for $n = 16$ ($m = 4$).

$(x_1,$	$x_2,$	$x_3,$	$x_4)$	$\text{int}(x_1, x_2, x_3, x_4)$	$(x_1,$	$x_2,$	$x_3,$	$x_4)$	$\text{int}(x_1, x_2, x_3, x_4)$
$-$	$-$	$-$	$-$	1	$+$	$-$	$-$	$-$	9
$-$	$-$	$-$	$+$	2	$+$	$-$	$-$	$+$	10
$-$	$-$	$+$	$-$	3	$+$	$-$	$+$	$-$	11
$-$	$-$	$+$	$+$	4	$+$	$-$	$+$	$+$	12
$-$	$+$	$-$	$-$	5	$+$	$+$	$-$	$-$	13
$-$	$+$	$-$	$+$	6	$+$	$+$	$-$	$+$	14
$-$	$+$	$+$	$-$	7	$+$	$+$	$+$	$-$	15
$-$	$+$	$+$	$+$	8	$+$	$+$	$+$	$+$	16

Table 4.2
Output of the int function with $m = 4$.

This implies that the list $\alpha_1, \ldots, \alpha_n$ starts with $\alpha_1 = \emptyset$, followed by the singleton sets, followed by the sets of size two, followed by the sets of size three, etc., ending in $\alpha_n = \mathcal{M}$. The proof of the following result is delayed until Problem 7.

LEMMA 4.3.1 For all $n \in \mathbb{N}$, there is a minimal-change ordering of the sets $\alpha_1, \ldots, \alpha_n \subseteq \mathcal{M}$.

For example, Table 4.1 shows a minimal-change ordering with $n = 16$.

Define $\text{int}: \mathbb{U}^m \to \{1, 2, \ldots, n\}$ to be the function that maps an m-tuple of elements from $\mathbb{U}$ to a natural number in the natural fashion (that is, replace all -1s with zeros and treat the resulting string as the binary encoding of a natural number, then add one).

$\varphi_{\alpha_1}(x_1, x_2, x_3, x_4)$	$=$	1	$\varphi_{\alpha_9}(x_1, x_2, x_3, x_4)$	$=$	$x_2 x_4$
$\varphi_{\alpha_2}(x_1, x_2, x_3, x_4)$	$=$	x_4	$\varphi_{\alpha_{10}}(x_1, x_2, x_3, x_4)$	$=$	$x_2 x_3$
$\varphi_{\alpha_3}(x_1, x_2, x_3, x_4)$	$=$	x_3	$\varphi_{\alpha_{11}}(x_1, x_2, x_3, x_4)$	$=$	$x_3 x_4$
$\varphi_{\alpha_4}(x_1, x_2, x_3, x_4)$	$=$	x_2	$\varphi_{\alpha_{12}}(x_1, x_2, x_3, x_4)$	$=$	$x_2 x_3 x_4$
$\varphi_{\alpha_5}(x_1, x_2, x_3, x_4)$	$=$	x_1	$\varphi_{\alpha_{13}}(x_1, x_2, x_3, x_4)$	$=$	$x_1 x_3 x_4$
$\varphi_{\alpha_6}(x_1, x_2, x_3, x_4)$	$=$	$x_1 x_2$	$\varphi_{\alpha_{14}}(x_1, x_2, x_3, x_4)$	$=$	$x_1 x_2 x_4$
$\varphi_{\alpha_7}(x_1, x_2, x_3, x_4)$	$=$	$x_1 x_3$	$\varphi_{\alpha_{15}}(x_1, x_2, x_3, x_4)$	$=$	$x_1 x_2 x_3$
$\varphi_{\alpha_8}(x_1, x_2, x_3, x_4)$	$=$	$x_1 x_4$	$\varphi_{\alpha_{16}}(x_1, x_2, x_3, x_4)$	$=$	$x_1 x_2 x_3 x_4$

Table 4.3
The φ-functions for $n = 16$ ($m = 4$).

More formally (see Problem 6), if $x = (x_1, \ldots, x_m) \in \mathsf{U}^m$, then

$$\mathrm{int}(x) = 2^{m-1} + 0.5 + \sum_{i=1}^{m} 2^{m-i-1} x_i.$$

For example, Table 4.2 shows the int function with $m = 4$. (In this table and subsequent tables in this section, we will, to enhance readability, denote -1 by "$-$" and $+1$ by "$+$".) Define $\mathrm{str}: \mathsf{Z} \to \mathsf{U}^m$ to be the inverse of int, that is, if $1 \leq x \leq n$, $\mathrm{str}(x) = (x_1, \ldots, x_m)$ iff $\mathrm{int}(x_1, \ldots, x_m) = x$.

If $\alpha \subseteq \mathcal{M}$, define $\varphi_\alpha : \mathsf{U}^m \to \mathsf{U}$ as follows:

$$\varphi_\alpha(x_1, \ldots, x_m) = \prod_{a \in \alpha} x_a.$$

For example, φ_α for all of the choices of α when $n = 16$ are shown in Table 4.3, and truth tables are shown in Table 4.4. Further define $\phi(\alpha) \in \mathsf{U}^n$ to be a string encoding the truth table of φ_α, that is, $\phi(\alpha) = (\phi(\alpha)_1, \ldots, \phi(\alpha)_n)$, where for $1 \leq i \leq n$, $\phi(\alpha)_i = \varphi_\alpha(\mathrm{str}(i))$. Thus, for example, column i of Table 4.4 is $\phi(\alpha_i)$, for $1 \leq i \leq 16$.

If $u, v \in \mathsf{U}^m$, define $[u, v] \in \mathsf{U}^m$ to be the pointwise product of u and v, that is, $[u, v] = (x_1, \ldots, x_m)$ where for all $1 \leq i \leq m$, $x_i = u_i \cdot v_i$ ("$\cdot$" denotes integer multiplication). We will find the following result useful.

LEMMA 4.3.2 For all $u, v \in \mathsf{U}^m$ and all $\alpha \subseteq \mathcal{M}$, $\phi(\alpha)_{\mathrm{int}([u, v])} = \phi(\alpha)_{\mathrm{int}(u)} \cdot \phi(\alpha)_{\mathrm{int}(v)}$.

PROOF: $\phi(\alpha)_{\mathrm{int}([u, v])} = \varphi_\alpha([u, v]) = \prod_{i \in \alpha} [u, v]_i = \prod_{i \in \alpha} u_i \cdot v_i = \prod_{i \in \alpha} u_i \cdot \prod_{i \in \alpha} v_i = \varphi_\alpha(u) \cdot \varphi_\alpha(v) = \phi(\alpha)_{\mathrm{int}(u)} \cdot \phi(\alpha)_{\mathrm{int}(v)}$. $\square$

$x_1x_2x_3x_4$	φ_{α_1}	φ_{α_2}	φ_{α_3}	φ_{α_4}	φ_{α_5}	φ_{α_6}	φ_{α_7}	φ_{α_8}	φ_{α_9}	$\varphi_{\alpha_{10}}$	$\varphi_{\alpha_{11}}$	$\varphi_{\alpha_{12}}$	$\varphi_{\alpha_{13}}$	$\varphi_{\alpha_{14}}$	$\varphi_{\alpha_{15}}$	$\varphi_{\alpha_{16}}$
− − − −	+	−	−	−	−	+	+	+	+	+	+	−	−	−	−	+
− − − +	+	+	−	−	−	−	+	+	−	−	+	−	+	+	+	−
− − + −	+	−	+	−	−	+	−	+	+	−	−	+	+	−	+	−
− − + +	+	+	+	−	−	+	−	−	−	−	+	−	−	+	+	+
− + − −	+	−	−	+	−	−	+	+	−	−	+	+	−	+	+	−
− + − +	+	+	−	+	−	−	+	−	+	−	−	−	+	−	+	+
− + + −	+	−	+	+	−	−	−	+	−	+	−	−	+	+	−	+
− + + +	+	+	+	+	−	−	−	−	+	+	+	+	−	−	−	−
+ − − −	+	−	−	−	+	−	−	−	+	+	+	−	+	+	+	−
+ − − +	+	+	−	−	+	−	−	+	−	+	−	+	−	−	+	+
+ − + −	+	−	+	−	+	−	+	−	+	−	−	+	−	+	−	+
+ − + +	+	+	+	−	+	−	+	+	−	−	+	−	+	−	−	−
+ + − −	+	−	−	+	+	+	−	−	−	−	+	+	+	−	−	+
+ + − +	+	+	−	+	+	+	−	+	+	−	−	−	−	+	−	−
+ + + −	+	−	+	+	+	+	+	−	−	+	−	−	−	−	+	−
+ + + +	+	+	+	+	+	+	+	+	+	+	+	+	+	+	+	+

Table 4.4
Truth tables for the φ-functions with $n = 16$ $(m = 4)$.

If $u, v \in \mathrm{U}^n$, define $\langle u, v \rangle \in \mathbf{Z}$ to be the integer inner product of u and v, that is,

$$\langle u, v \rangle = \sum_{i=1}^{n} u_i \cdot v_i,$$

where "." denotes integer multiplication. It is easy to see that the $\phi(\alpha)$ strings are mutually orthogonal under this definition of inner product:

LEMMA 4.3.3 For all $1 \leq i, j \leq n$,

$$\langle \phi(\alpha_i), \phi(\alpha_j) \rangle = \begin{cases} n & \text{if } i = j \\ 0 & \text{otherwise.} \end{cases}$$

PROOF: For all $1 \leq i \leq n$,

$$\langle \phi(\alpha_i), \phi(\alpha_i) \rangle = \sum_{k=1}^{n} \phi(\alpha_i)_k^2 = \sum_{k=1}^{n} 1 = n.$$

For all $1 \le i \ne j \le n$,

$$
\begin{aligned}
\langle \phi(\alpha_i), \phi(\alpha_j) \rangle &= \sum_{k=1}^{n} \phi(\alpha_i)_k \cdot \phi(\alpha_j)_k \\
&= \sum_{x \in \mathsf{U}^m} \varphi_{\alpha_i}(x) \cdot \varphi_{\alpha_j}(x) \\
&= \sum_{x \in \mathsf{U}^m} \prod_{k \in \alpha_i} x_k \cdot \prod_{k \in \alpha_j} x_k \\
&= \sum_{x \in \mathsf{U}^m} \prod_{k \in \alpha_i \Delta \alpha_j} x_k \\
&= \sum_{x \in \mathsf{U}^m} \varphi_{\alpha_i \Delta \alpha_j}(x) \\
&= 0.
\end{aligned}
$$

The latter equality holds because for all $\alpha \subset \mathcal{M}$, φ_α is a parity function (or the complement of a parity function) of a subset of its inputs, and hence (provided $\alpha \ne \emptyset$) is positive as often as it is negative. $\square$

Define $F: \mathsf{U}^n \to \mathsf{U}$ as follows. For all $x = (x_1, \ldots, x_n) \in \mathsf{U}^n$, $F(x_1, \ldots, x_n) = \mathrm{sign}\,(\langle x, \phi(\alpha_k) \rangle)$, where k is the largest index such that $\langle x, \phi(\alpha_k) \rangle \ne 0$. Note that F is well-defined (see Problem 8).

LEMMA 4.3.4 F is a linear threshold function.

PROOF: Suppose $x = (x_1, \ldots, x_n) \in \mathsf{U}^n$, and $F(x) = \mathrm{sign}\,(\langle x, \phi(\alpha_k) \rangle)$, where $\langle x, \phi(\alpha_k) \rangle \ne 0$ and for all $i > k$, $\langle x, \phi(\alpha_i) \rangle = 0$. Then,

$$
\begin{aligned}
&\mathrm{sign}\left(\sum_{i=1}^{n} (n+1)^{i-1} \langle x, \phi(\alpha_i) \rangle \right) \\
= \ &\mathrm{sign}\left(\sum_{i=1}^{k} (n+1)^{i-1} \langle x, \phi(\alpha_i) \rangle \right) \\
= \ &\mathrm{sign}\left((n+1)^{k-1} \langle x, \phi(\alpha_k) \rangle + \sum_{i=1}^{k-1} (n+1)^{i-1} \langle x, \phi(\alpha_i) \rangle \right),
\end{aligned}
$$

which is equal to the sign of whichever of the two terms has the largest magnitude. Furthermore, this is always the first term since for all $y, z \in \mathsf{U}^n$, $|\langle y, z \rangle| \le n$, and hence

$$
\left| \sum_{i=1}^{k-1} (n+1)^{i-1} \langle x, \phi(\alpha_i) \rangle \right| \le n \cdot \left| \sum_{i=1}^{k-1} (n+1)^{i-1} \right|
$$

$$= (n+1)^{k-1} - 1,$$

and $\left|(n+1)^{k-1}\langle x, \phi(\alpha_k)\rangle\right| \geq (n+1)^{k-1}$. Thus, since the sign of the first term is

$$\text{sign}\left((n+1)^{k-1}\langle x, \phi(\alpha_k)\rangle\right) = \text{sign}\left(\langle x, \phi(\alpha_k)\rangle\right) = F(x),$$

we deduce that

$$
\begin{aligned}
F(x) &= \text{sign}\left(\sum_{i=1}^{n}(n+1)^{i-1}\langle x, \phi(\alpha_i)\rangle\right) \\
&= \text{sign}\left(\sum_{i=1}^{n}(n+1)^{i-1}\sum_{j=1}^{n}x_j \cdot \phi(\alpha_i)_j\right) \\
&= \text{sign}\left(\sum_{j=1}^{n}\sum_{i=1}^{n}(n+1)^{i-1}\cdot \phi(\alpha_i)_j \cdot x_j\right) \\
&= \hat{\theta}_n(w_1, \ldots, w_n, 0),
\end{aligned}
$$

where for $1 \leq j \leq n$, $w_j = \sum_{i=1}^{n}(n+1)^{i-1}\cdot \phi(\alpha_i)_j$. $\square$

The proof of Lemma 4.3.4 showed that F has a presentation with zero threshold. The next result shows that the threshold in any presentation can be set equal to zero. Once we have proven this fact, we will henceforth work only with presentations of F that have zero threshold.

LEMMA 4.3.5 If $(w_1, \ldots, w_n, h)$ is a presentation of F, then so is $(w_1, \ldots, w_n, 0)$.

PROOF: Since $F(x_1, \ldots, x_n) = \text{sign}\left(\langle x, \phi(\alpha_i)\rangle\right)$ for some $1 \leq i \leq n$,

$$F(-x_1, \ldots, -x_n) = -F(x_1, \ldots, x_n).$$

Suppose $(w_1, \ldots, w_n, h)$ is a presentation of F. For all $(x_1, \ldots, x_n) \in \mathsf{U}^n$, if $F(x_1, \ldots, x_n) = 1$, then

$$\sum_{i=1}^{n}w_i x_i - h \geq 0 \tag{4.3.11}$$

and since $F(-x_1, \ldots, -x_n) = -F(x_1, \ldots, x_n)$,

$$-\sum_{i=1}^{n}w_i x_i - h \leq 0,$$

which implies that

$$\sum_{i=1}^{n} w_i x_i + h \geq 0. \tag{4.3.12}$$

Therefore, adding Inequalities (4.3.11, 4.3.12),

$$\sum_{i=1}^{n} w_i x_i \geq 0.$$

Similarly, if $F(x_1, \ldots, x_n) = -1$, one can prove (see Problem 9) that

$$\sum_{i=1}^{n} w_i x_i < 0.$$

Therefore, $F = \hat{\theta}_n(w_1, \ldots, w_n, 0)$. $\square$

LEMMA 4.3.6 For all $1 \leq j, k \leq n$,

$$\sum_{i=1}^{n} \phi(\alpha_i)_j \cdot \phi(\alpha_i)_k = \begin{cases} n & \text{if } j = k \\ 0 & \text{otherwise.} \end{cases}$$

PROOF: See Problem 10. $\square$

LEMMA 4.3.7 If $F = \hat{\theta}_n(w_1, \ldots, w_n, 0)$, then for all $x = (x_1, \ldots, x_n) \in \mathsf{U}^n$,

$$F(x) = \text{sign}\left(\sum_{i=1}^{n} w_i' \langle x, \phi(\alpha_i) \rangle\right),$$

where

$$w_i' = \frac{1}{n} \sum_{j=1}^{n} w_j \phi(\alpha_i)_j, \tag{4.3.13}$$

and

$$w_i = \sum_{j=1}^{n} w_j' \phi(\alpha_i)_j. \tag{4.3.14}$$

Rather than deal with F in the standard form, we will find it more convenient to express F in a new form.

PROOF: Suppose $F = \hat{\theta}_n(w_1, \ldots, w_n, 0)$. Therefore, for all $x = (x_1, \ldots, x_n) \in \mathsf{U}^n$,

$$F(x) = \text{sign}\left(\sum_{j=1}^{n} w_j x_j\right).$$

In order to prove Equation (4.3.13), we must show that

$$F(x) = \text{sign}\left(\sum_{j=1}^{n} w_j \cdot \frac{1}{n}\sum_{i=1}^{n}\phi(\alpha_i)_j \cdot \langle x, \phi(\alpha_i)\rangle\right).$$

Therefore, it is sufficient to prove that

$$x_j = \frac{1}{n}\sum_{i=1}^{n}\phi(\alpha_i)_j \cdot \langle x, \phi(\alpha_i)\rangle.$$

Now,

$$
\begin{aligned}
\sum_{i=1}^{n}\phi(\alpha_i)_j \cdot \langle x, \phi(\alpha_i)\rangle &= \sum_{i=1}^{n}\phi(\alpha_i)_j \sum_{k=1}^{n} x_k \cdot \phi(\alpha_i)_k \\
&= \sum_{k=1}^{n} x_k \sum_{i=1}^{n}\phi(\alpha_i)_j \cdot \phi(\alpha_i)_k \\
&= n x_j.
\end{aligned}
$$

(The last step follows by Lemma 4.3.6.) Therefore, Equation (4.3.13) holds. Equation (4.3.14) follows similarly (Problem 11). □

It will be easier to deal with F in this new form. We will prove a lower bound on the weights in this form, and later use Lemma 4.3.7 to derive a lower bound on the weights of any presentation of F. If $w_1, \ldots, w_n \in \mathbf{Z}$, and

$$\hat{\theta}_n(w_1, \ldots, w_n, 0)(x_1, \ldots, x_n) = \text{sign}\left(\sum_{i=1}^{n} w_i' \langle x, \phi(\alpha_i)\rangle\right),$$

where $w'_1, \ldots, w'_n$ are defined in the statement of Lemma 4.3.7, we will write

$$\hat{\theta}_n(w_1, \ldots, w_n, 0) = \mathcal{F}_n(w'_1, \ldots, w'_n).$$

LEMMA 4.3.8 If $F = \mathcal{F}_n(w_1, \ldots, w_n)$, then $w_i > 0$ for all $1 \leq i \leq n$.

PROOF: By the definition of F and Lemma 4.3.3, $F(\phi(\alpha_i)) = 1$ for all $1 \leq i \leq n$. But by the hypothesis and Lemma 4.3.3, $F(\phi(\alpha_i)) = \text{sign}(w_i)$. Therefore, $w_i \geq 0$ for all $1 \leq i \leq n$. Similarly, for all $1 \leq i \leq n$, $F(-\phi(\alpha_i)) = -1$, and $F(-\phi(\alpha_i)) = \text{sign}(-w_i)$. Hence, $\text{sign}(-w_i) = -1$, and so $w_i \neq 0$. $\square$

LEMMA 4.3.9 If $F = \mathcal{F}_n(w_1, \ldots, w_n)$, then $w_i \geq 1/n$ for $1 \leq i \leq n$.

PROOF: Suppose $F = \mathcal{F}_n(w'_1, \ldots, w'_n)$. That is, by Lemma 4.3.7, there exists $w_1, \ldots, w_n \in \mathbf{Z}$ such that

$$w'_i = \frac{1}{n} \sum_{j=1}^{n} w_j \phi(\alpha_i)_j.$$

Therefore, for $1 \leq i \leq n$, w'_i is a rational number with denominator n. Hence, by Lemma 4.3.8, $w'_i \geq 1/n$. $\square$

4.4 A Proof of the Weight Lower Bound

The following pair of rather technical lemmas contain the key to the weight lower bound. They demonstrate a lower bound for w_{i+1} of almost $2^{\|\alpha_i\|} w_i$. The first of these, Lemma 4.4.1, deals with the case in which $\|\alpha_{i+1}\| = \|\alpha_i\|$, and the second, Lemma 4.4.2, deals with the case in which $\|\alpha_{i+1}\| = \|\alpha_i\| + 1$.

LEMMA 4.4.1 Suppose $F = \mathcal{F}_n(w_1, \ldots, w_n)$. Suppose $\|\alpha_{i+1}\| = \|\alpha_i\| = k$ and $\alpha_i \Delta \alpha_{i+1} = \{a, b\}$. Let $v = (v_1, \ldots, v_m) \in \mathsf{U}^m$, where $v_a = v_b$, and

$$A = \{j \mid 1 \leq j \leq n, \ \alpha_j \subset \alpha_i \cup \alpha_{i+1}, \ \|\alpha_j \cap \{a, b\}\| = 1, \ \alpha_j \neq \alpha_i, \alpha_{i+1}\}.$$

Then,

$$w_{i+1} \geq (2^{k-1} - 1)w_i - \sum_{j \in A} w_j \phi(\alpha_i)_{\text{int}(v)} \phi(\alpha_j)_{\text{int}(v)}.$$

PROOF: The proof of this result is quite complicated, and is broken up into 6 properties which follow easily from the definitions, and 5 claims which require more work. The overall structure of the argument is sketched in Figure 4.2.

We will without loss of generality assume that $\alpha_i = \{1, 2, \ldots, k\}$ and $\alpha_{i+1} = \{1, 2, \ldots, k-1, k+1\}$, for some $1 \leq k < m$, and take $a = k$ and $b = k+1$ (the general case is proved similarly). Let $v = (v_1, \ldots, v_m) \in \mathsf{U}^m$, where $v_k = v_{k+1}$. Define $\text{syn}(v), \text{ant}(v), \text{sim}(v) \subset \mathsf{U}^m$

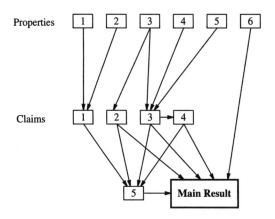

Figure 4.2
The structure of the proof of Lemma 4.4.1.

by

$$\text{syn}(v) \;=\; \{u = (u_1, \ldots, u_m) \mid u_i = v_i \text{ for } 1 \le i \le k+1\}$$
$$\text{ant}(v) \;=\; \{u = (u_1, \ldots, u_m) \mid u_i = v_i \text{ for } 1 \le i \le k-1, \; u_k = -v_k, \; u_{k+1} = -v_{k+1}\}$$
$$\text{sim}(v) \;=\; \text{syn}(v) \cup \text{ant}(v).$$

Note that the following properties hold.

1. For all $\alpha \subseteq \mathcal{M}$ where α contains an element larger than $k+1$,

$$\sum_{\text{str}(j) \in \text{sim}(v)} \phi(\alpha)_j \cdot \phi(\alpha_i)_j = 0.$$

2. For all $\alpha \subseteq \mathcal{M}$ where α contains an element larger than $k+1$,

$$\sum_{\text{str}(j) \notin \text{sim}(v)} \phi(\alpha)_j \cdot \phi(\alpha_i)_j = 0.$$

3. $\|\text{syn}(v)\| = \|\text{ant}(v)\| = 2^{m-k-1}$.
4. For all $y, z \in \text{syn}(v)$ and all $\alpha \subseteq \{1, 2, \ldots, k+1\}$, $\phi(\alpha)_{\text{int}(y)} = \phi(\alpha)_{\text{int}(z)}$.
5. For all $y, z \in \text{ant}(v)$ and all $\alpha \subseteq \{1, 2, \ldots, k+1\}$, $\phi(\alpha)_{\text{int}(y)} = \phi(\alpha)_{\text{int}(z)}$.
6. For all $y \in \text{syn}(v)$ and all $\alpha \subseteq \{1, 2, \ldots, k+1\}$, $\phi(\alpha)_{\text{int}(y)} = \phi(\alpha)_{\text{int}(v)}$.

Define $x = (x_1, \ldots, x_n) \in \mathsf{U}^n$ as follows. For $1 \le j \le n$,

$$x_j = \begin{cases} \phi(\alpha_i)_j & \text{if } \mathrm{str}(j) \in \mathrm{sim}(v) \\ -\phi(\alpha_i)_j & \text{otherwise.} \end{cases}$$

The proof will begin with the demonstration of five useful claims about $\langle x, \phi(\alpha) \rangle$ for all $\alpha = \alpha_1, \ldots, \alpha_n$.

Claim 1. If α contains an element larger than $k + 1$, then $\langle x, \phi(\alpha) \rangle = 0$.

Suppose α contains an element larger than $k + 1$. Then,

$$
\begin{aligned}
\langle x, \phi(\alpha) \rangle &= \sum_{j=1}^{n} x_j \cdot \phi(\alpha)_j \\
&= \sum_{\mathrm{str}(j) \in \mathrm{sim}(v)} \phi(\alpha)_j \cdot x_j + \sum_{\mathrm{str}(j) \notin \mathrm{sim}(v)} \phi(\alpha)_j \cdot x_j \\
&= \sum_{\mathrm{str}(j) \in \mathrm{sim}(v)} \phi(\alpha)_j \cdot \phi(\alpha_i)_j - \sum_{\mathrm{str}(j) \notin \mathrm{sim}(v)} \phi(\alpha)_j \cdot \phi(\alpha_i)_j \\
&= 0.
\end{aligned}
$$

(The last equality follows since by Properties (1,2) above, both terms of the sum are zero.)

Claim 2. $\langle x, \phi(\alpha_i) \rangle = 2^{m-k+1} - 2^m$.

By Property (3), if $\alpha = \alpha_i$,

$$
\begin{aligned}
\langle x, \phi(\alpha) \rangle &= \sum_{\mathrm{str}(j) \in \mathrm{sim}(v)} \phi(\alpha_i)_j^2 - \sum_{\mathrm{str}(j) \notin \mathrm{sim}(v)} \phi(\alpha_i)_j^2 \\
&= \|\mathrm{sim}(v)\| - \|\mathcal{M} \backslash \mathrm{sim}(v)\| \\
&= 2^{m-k} - (2^m - 2^{m-k}) \\
&= 2^{m-k+1} - 2^m.
\end{aligned}
$$

Claim 3. Let $s \in \mathrm{syn}(v)$ and $a \in \mathrm{ant}(v)$, where for all $k + 1 < i \le m$, $s_i = a_i$. For all $\alpha \subseteq \{1, 2, \ldots, k+1\}$, $\alpha \ne \alpha_i$, $\langle x, \phi(\alpha) \rangle = 2^{m-k} \phi(\alpha)_{\mathrm{int}(s)} \cdot \phi(\alpha_i)_{\mathrm{int}(s)} \cdot (1 - \phi(\alpha)_{\mathrm{int}([s, a])})$.

Suppose $\alpha \subseteq \{1, 2, \ldots, k+1\}$, $\alpha \ne \alpha_i$.

$$
\begin{aligned}
\langle x, \phi(\alpha) \rangle &= \sum_{j=1}^{n} x_j \cdot \phi(\alpha)_j \\
&= \sum_{\mathrm{str}(j) \in \mathrm{sim}(v)} \phi(\alpha)_j \cdot x_j + \sum_{\mathrm{str}(j) \notin \mathrm{sim}(v)} \phi(\alpha)_j \cdot x_j
\end{aligned}
$$

$$
\begin{aligned}
&= \sum_{\mathrm{str}(j)\in\mathrm{sim}(v)} \phi(\alpha)_j \cdot \phi(\alpha_i)_j - \sum_{\mathrm{str}(j)\notin\mathrm{sim}(v)} \phi(\alpha)_j \cdot \phi(\alpha_i)_j \\
&= 2 \sum_{\mathrm{str}(j)\in\mathrm{sim}(v)} \phi(\alpha)_j \cdot \phi(\alpha_i)_j - \sum_{j=1}^{n} \phi(\alpha)_j \cdot \phi(\alpha_i)_j \\
&= 2 \sum_{\mathrm{str}(j)\in\mathrm{sim}(v)} \phi(\alpha)_j \cdot \phi(\alpha_i)_j - \langle \phi(\alpha), \phi(\alpha_i) \rangle \\
&= 2 \sum_{\mathrm{str}(j)\in\mathrm{sim}(v)} \phi(\alpha)_j \cdot \phi(\alpha_i)_j \qquad \text{(by Lemma 4.3.3)} \\
&= 2 \sum_{\mathrm{str}(j)\in\mathrm{syn}(v)} \phi(\alpha)_j \cdot \phi(\alpha_i)_j + 2 \sum_{\mathrm{str}(j)\in\mathrm{ant}(v)} \phi(\alpha)_j \cdot \phi(\alpha_i)_j.
\end{aligned}
$$

Let $s \in \mathrm{syn}(v)$ and $a \in \mathrm{ant}(v)$, where for all $k+1 < i \le m$, $s_i = a_i$. By the above argument and Properties (3–5),

$$
\langle x, \phi(\alpha) \rangle = 2^{m-k} \phi(\alpha)_{\mathrm{int}(s)} \cdot \phi(\alpha_i)_{\mathrm{int}(s)} + 2^{m-k} \phi(\alpha)_{\mathrm{int}(a)} \cdot \phi(\alpha_i)_{\mathrm{int}(a)}.
$$

Hence, by Lemma 4.3.2 (remembering that multiplication and division over U are identical),

$$
\begin{aligned}
&\langle x, \phi(\alpha) \rangle \\
&= 2^{m-k}(\phi(\alpha)_{\mathrm{int}(s)} \cdot \phi(\alpha_i)_{\mathrm{int}(s)} + \phi(\alpha)_{\mathrm{int}(s)} \cdot \phi(\alpha_i)_{\mathrm{int}(s)} \cdot \phi(\alpha)_{\mathrm{int}([s,a])} \cdot \phi(\alpha_i)_{\mathrm{int}([s,a])}) \\
&= 2^{m-k} \phi(\alpha)_{\mathrm{int}(s)} \cdot \phi(\alpha_i)_{\mathrm{int}(s)} (1 + \phi(\alpha)_{\mathrm{int}([s,a])} \cdot \phi(\alpha_i)_{\mathrm{int}([s,a])}).
\end{aligned}
$$

Since $s \in \mathrm{syn}(v)$ and $a \in \mathrm{ant}(v)$, and $s_i = a_i$ for all $k+1 < i \le m$, we conclude that for all $1 \le j \le m$,

$$
[s,a]_j = \begin{cases} -1 & \text{if } j = k, k+1 \\ 1 & \text{otherwise.} \end{cases}
$$

Since

$$
\varphi_{\alpha_i}([s,a]) = \prod_{j=1}^{k} [s,a]_j,
$$

and $[s,a]_j = 1$ for all $1 \le i < k$, $[s,a]_k = -1$, we conclude that $\phi(\alpha_i)_{\mathrm{int}([s,a])} = -1$. Therefore,

$$
\langle x, \phi(\alpha) \rangle = 2^{m-k} \phi(\alpha)_{\mathrm{int}(s)} \cdot \phi(\alpha_i)_{\mathrm{int}(s)} \cdot (1 - \phi(\alpha)_{\mathrm{int}([s,a])}).
$$

Claim 4. $\langle x, \phi(\alpha_{i+1}) \rangle = 2^{m-k+1}$.

Since

$$\varphi_{\alpha_{i+1}}([s,a]) = (\prod_{j=1}^{k-1} [s,a]_j) \cdot [s,a]_{k+1},$$

and $[s,a]_j = 1$ for all $1 \le i < k$, $[s,a]_{k+1} = -1$, we conclude that $\phi(\alpha_{i+1})_{\text{int}([s,a])} = -1$. Hence, by Claim 3,

$$
\begin{aligned}
\langle x, \phi(\alpha_{i+1}) \rangle &= 2^{m-k} \phi(\alpha_{i+1})_{\text{int}(s)} \cdot \phi(\alpha_i)_{\text{int}(s)} \cdot (1 - \phi(\alpha_{i+1})_{\text{int}([s,a])})) \\
&= 2^{m-k}(1 - (-1)) \\
&= 2^{m-k+1}.
\end{aligned}
$$

Claim 5. $\langle x, \phi(\alpha) \rangle \ne 0$ iff either $\alpha = \alpha_i, \alpha_{i+1}$, or $\alpha = \alpha_j$ where $j \in A$, where

$$A = \{j \mid 1 \le j \le n, \ \alpha_j \subset \alpha_i \cup \alpha_{i+1}, \ \|\alpha_j \cap \{k, k+1\}\| = 1, \ \alpha_j \ne \alpha_i, \alpha_{i+1}\}.$$

By Claim 1, $\langle x, \phi(\alpha) \rangle$ can only be nonzero if $\alpha \subseteq \{1, 2, \ldots, k+1\} = \alpha_i \cup \alpha_{i+1}$. By Claims 2 and 4, $\langle x, \phi(\alpha) \rangle \ne 0$ if $\alpha = \alpha_i, \alpha_{i+1}$. Suppose $\alpha \subseteq \{1, 2, \ldots, k+1\}$, and $\alpha \ne \alpha_i$. By Claim 3, if $s \in \text{syn}(v)$ and $a \in \text{ant}(v)$, and for all $k+1 < i \le n$, $s_i = a_i$, then $\langle x, \phi(\alpha) \rangle$ is nonzero iff $\phi(\alpha)_{\text{int}([s,a])} = -1$. This is only possible if exactly one of $k, k+1 \in \alpha$, that is, $\alpha = \alpha_j$ for some $j \in A$.

This ends the proof of the claims. By the definition of F, Claim 5 implies that $F(x) = \text{sign}(\langle x, \phi(\alpha_{i+1}) \rangle)$, since $\phi(\alpha_{i+1})$ is the last of the ϕ-tuples that has nonzero inner product with x. Hence, by Claim 4, $F(x) = 1$. Therefore,

$$\sum_{i=1}^{n} w_i \langle x, \phi(\alpha_i) \rangle \ge 0.$$

Hence, by Claim 5,

$$\langle x, \phi(\alpha_i) \rangle w_i + \langle x, \phi(\alpha_{i+1}) \rangle w_{i+1} + \sum_{j \in A} \langle x, \phi(\alpha_j) \rangle w_j \ge 0.$$

Therefore, by Claims 2 and 4,

$$w_{i+1} \ge (2^{k-1} - 1)w_i - \sum_{j \in A} w_j \langle x, \phi(\alpha_j) \rangle / 2^{m-k+1}.$$

By Claim 5, for all $j \in A$, $\langle x, \phi(\alpha_j) \rangle \ne 0$, and hence by Claim 3,

$$\langle x, \phi(\alpha_j) \rangle = 2^{m-k+1} \phi(\alpha_j)_{\text{int}(s)} \cdot \phi(\alpha_i)_{\text{int}(s)}.$$

Therefore,

$$w_{i+1} \geq (2^{k-1} - 1)w_i - \sum_{j \in A} \phi(\alpha_j)_{\text{int}(s)} \cdot \phi(\alpha_i)_{\text{int}(s)} w_j.$$

Finally, since $s \in \text{syn}(v)$, by Property 6,

$$w_{i+1} \geq (2^{k-1} - 1)w_i - \sum_{j \in A} w_j \phi(\alpha_i)_{\text{int}(v)} \phi(\alpha_j)_{\text{int}(v)}.$$

$\square$

LEMMA 4.4.2 Suppose $F = \mathcal{F}_n(w_1, \ldots, w_n)$. Suppose $\|\alpha_i\| = k$ and $\|\alpha_{i+1}\| = k+1$ and $\alpha_i \Delta \alpha_{i+1} = \{a\}$. Let $v = (v_1, \ldots, v_m) \in \mathsf{U}^m$, where $v_a = 1$, and

$$A = \{j \mid 1 \leq j \leq n, \ \alpha_j \subset \alpha_{i+1}, \ \alpha_j \neq \alpha_i\}.$$

Then,

$$w_{i+1} \geq (2^k - 1)w_i - \sum_{j \in A} w_j \phi(\alpha_i)_{\text{int}(v)} \phi(\alpha_j)_{\text{int}(v)}.$$

PROOF: We will without loss of generality assume that $\alpha_i = \{1, 2, \ldots, k\}$ and $\alpha_{i+1} = \{1, 2, \ldots, k+1\}$, for some $1 \leq k < m$ (the general case is proved similarly). Thus, $a = k+1$. Let $v = (v_1, \ldots, v_m) \in \mathsf{U}^m$, where $v_{k+1} = 1$. As in the proof of Lemma 4.4.1, define $\text{syn}(v) \subset \mathsf{U}^m$ by

$$\text{syn}(v) = \{u = (u_1, \ldots, u_m) \mid u_i = v_i \text{ for } 1 \leq i \leq k+1\}$$
$$\text{sim}(v) = \text{syn}(v)$$

and define $x = (x_1, \ldots, x_n) \in \mathsf{U}^n$ as follows. For $1 \leq j \leq n$,

$$x_j = \begin{cases} \phi(\alpha_i)_j & \text{if } \text{str}(j) \in \text{sim}(v) \\ -\phi(\alpha_i)_j & \text{otherwise.} \end{cases}$$

Claim 1 of Lemma 4.4.1 still holds, that is, $\langle x, \phi(\alpha) \rangle = 0$ if α contains an element larger than $k+1$. Claim 2 must be modified slightly, since $\text{sim}(v)$ in this Lemma is half the size of the one in Lemma 4.4.1. Hence, $\langle x, \phi(\alpha_i) \rangle = 2^{m-k} - 2^m$. Following the first sequence of equalities of Claim 3 to the second-from-last line, we learn that for all other α,

$$\langle x, \phi(\alpha) \rangle = 2 \sum_{\text{str}(j) \in \text{sim}(v)} \phi(\alpha)_j \cdot \phi(\alpha_i)_j$$
$$= 2^{m-k} \phi(\alpha)_{\text{int}(v)} \cdot \phi(\alpha_i)_{\text{int}(v)}.$$

Since $v_{k+1} = 1$,

$$\varphi_{\alpha_{i+1}}(v) = \prod_{j=1}^{k+1} v_j = \prod_{j=1}^{k} v_j = \varphi_{\alpha_i}(v),$$

that is, $\phi(\alpha_{i+1})_{\text{int}(v)} = \phi(\alpha_i)_{\text{int}(v)}$. Therefore, by the above, $\langle x, \phi(\alpha_{i+1}) \rangle = 2^{m-k}$. Once again, this fact and Claim 2 imply that $F(x) = \text{sign}\,(\langle x, \phi(\alpha_{i+1}) \rangle) = 1$. Therefore,

$$\sum_{i=1}^{n} w_i \langle x, \phi(\alpha_i) \rangle \geq 0.$$

That is,

$$(2^{m-k} - 2^m) w_i + 2^{m-k} w_{i+1} + 2^{m-k} \sum_{j \in A} w_j \phi(\alpha_j)_{\text{int}(v)} \cdot \phi(\alpha_i)_{\text{int}(v)} \geq 0.$$

Hence,

$$w_{i+1} \geq (2^k - 1) w_i - \sum_{j \in A} w_j \phi(\alpha_i)_{\text{int}(v)} \phi(\alpha_j)_{\text{int}(v)}.$$

$\square$

Now that we have established Lemmas 4.4.1 and 4.4.2, we will now proceed to derive a series of concrete lower bounds for each of the weights in terms of earlier weights.

LEMMA 4.4.3 If $F = \mathcal{F}_n(w_1, \ldots, w_n)$, then

1. $w_1 \geq 1/n$.
2. For all i such that $\|\alpha_i\| = 1$, $w_i \geq 1/n$.
3. For all $i+1$ such that $\|\alpha_{i+1}\| = 2$, $w_{i+1} \geq w_i + 2/n$.

PROOF: Parts (1,2) of the hypothesis follow immediately from Lemma 4.3.9. Part (3) of the hypothesis is proved as follows. Suppose $\|\alpha_{i+1}\| = 2$. First, suppose that $\|\alpha_i\| = 1$. Without loss of generality, suppose $\alpha_i = \{1\}$ and $\alpha_{i+1} = \{1, 2\}$ (the general case is proved similarly). Let

$$v = (-1, \underbrace{1, 1, \ldots, 1}_{n-1}).$$

By Lemma 4.4.2,

$$w_{i+1} \geq w_i - \sum_{j \in A} w_j \phi(\alpha_i)_{\text{int}(v)} \phi(\alpha_j)_{\text{int}(v)},$$

where

$$A = \{j \mid 1 \leq j \leq n, \; \alpha_j \subset \alpha_{i+1}, \; \alpha_j \neq \alpha_i\}$$
$$= \{j \mid \alpha_j = \emptyset, \{2\}\}.$$

Therefore, since $\phi(\alpha_i)_{\text{int}(v)} = -1$ and for all $j \in A$, $\phi(\alpha_j)_{\text{int}(v)} = 1$,

$$w_{i+1} \geq w_i + \sum_{j \in A} w_j.$$

Hence, by Parts (1,2) above, since $\|A\| = 2$, $w_{i+1} \geq w_i + 2/n$, as claimed.

Now suppose $\|\alpha_i\| = 2$. Without loss of generality, assume that $\alpha_i = \{1,2\}$ and $\alpha_{i+1} = \{1,3\}$ (the general case is proved similarly). Once again, let

$$v = (-1, \underbrace{1, 1, \ldots, 1}_{n-1}).$$

Then, by Lemma 4.4.1,

$$w_{i+1} \geq w_i - \sum_{j \in A} w_j \phi(\alpha_i)_{\text{int}(v)} \phi(\alpha_j)_{\text{int}(v)},$$

where

$$A = \{j \mid 1 \leq j \leq n, \; \alpha_j \subset \alpha_i \cup \alpha_{i+1}, \; \|\alpha_j \cap \{2,3\}\| = 1, \; \alpha_j \neq \alpha_i, \alpha_{i+1}\}$$
$$= \{j \mid \alpha_j = \{2\}, \{3\}\}.$$

Hence, since $\phi(\alpha_i)_{\text{int}(v)} = -1$ and for $\alpha_j = \{2\}, \{3\}$, $\phi(\alpha_j)_{\text{int}(v)} = 1$, and by Part (2), $w_{i+1} \geq w_i + 2/n$. $\square$

LEMMA 4.4.4 For all i such that $\|\alpha_i\| \geq 2$ and all j such that $\|\alpha_j\| \leq 1$, $w_i > w_j$.

PROOF: We claim that for all i such that $\|\alpha_i\| \geq 2$ (that is, for all $i \geq m+2$), and all j such that $\|\alpha_j\| \leq 1$ (that is, $j \leq m+1$), $w_i > w_j$.

First, suppose $j = 1$. The proof is by induction on i. The claim is true for $i = m+2$, in which case $\|\alpha_{i-1}\| = 1$ and $\|\alpha_i\| = 2$, by the argument used in the first paragraph of the proof of Lemma 4.4.3 (neglecting to use Part (1) in the last line). If $w_i > w_1$, then by Lemma 4.4.3 (3), $w_{i+1} \geq w_i + 2/n > w_1$. This completes the proof for $j = 1$.

Now suppose that $j > 1$, in which case $\|\alpha_j\| = 1$. We can without loss of generality assume that the weights corresponding to the sets of size one are monotonically increasing, that is, for $1 < j \leq m$, $w_j \leq w_{j+1}$ (if this is not true, simply relabel the elements of $\mathcal{M}$). Because of this monotonicity, and since by Lemma 4.4.3 (3) $w_i > w_{i-1} \geq w_{m+1}$, the result follows. $\square$

LEMMA 4.4.5 For all $i+1$ such that $\|\alpha_{i+1}\| = 3$, $w_{i+1} \geq 3w_i$.

PROOF: Suppose $\|\alpha_{i+1}\| = 3$. First, suppose that $\|\alpha_i\| = 2$. Without loss of generality, suppose $\alpha_i = \{1, 2\}$ and $\alpha_{i+1} = \{1, 2, 3\}$ (the general case is proved similarly). Let

$$v = (-1, -1, \underbrace{1, 1, \ldots, 1}_{n-2}).$$

By Lemma 4.4.2,

$$w_{i+1} \geq 3w_i - \sum_{j \in A} w_j \phi(\alpha_i)_{\text{int}(v)} \phi(\alpha_j)_{\text{int}(v)},$$

where

$$
\begin{aligned}
A &= \{j \mid 1 \leq j \leq n,\ \alpha_j \subset \alpha_{i+1},\ \alpha_j \neq \alpha_i\} \\
&= \{j \mid \alpha_j = \emptyset, \{1\}, \{2\}, \{3\}, \{1, 3\}, \{2, 3\}\}.
\end{aligned}
$$

Define

$$
\begin{aligned}
A^+ &= \{j \mid \alpha_j = \{1\}, \{2\}, \{1, 3\}, \{2, 3\}\} \\
A^- &= \{j \mid \alpha_j = \emptyset, \{3\}\}.
\end{aligned}
$$

Therefore, since $\phi(\alpha_i)_{\text{int}(v)} = 1$, and for all $j \in A^+$, $\phi(\alpha_j)_{\text{int}(v)} = -1$, and for all $j \in A^-$, $\phi(\alpha_j)_{\text{int}(v)} = 1$,

$$w_{i+1} \geq 3w_i + \sum_{j \in A^+} w_j - \sum_{j \in A^-} w_j.$$

By Lemma 4.4.4, the positive terms of weights corresponding to the two sets of size two in A^+ have larger magnitude than the negative terms of weights corresponding to the two sets of size at most one in A^-. Hence, $w_{i+1} \geq 3w_i$, as claimed.

Now suppose $\|\alpha_i\| = 3$. Without loss of generality, assume that $\alpha_i = \{1, 2, 3\}$ and $\alpha_{i+1} = \{1, 2, 4\}$ (the general case is proved similarly). Once again, let

$$v = (-1, -1, \underbrace{1, 1, \ldots, 1}_{n-2}).$$

Then, by Lemma 4.4.1,

$$w_{i+1} \geq 3w_i - \sum_{j \in A} w_j \phi(\alpha_i)_{\text{int}(v)} \phi(\alpha_j)_{\text{int}(v)},$$

where

$$A = \{j \mid 1 \leq j \leq n, \ \alpha_j \subset \alpha_i \cup \alpha_{i+1}, \ \|\alpha_j \cap \{3,4\}\| = 1, \ \alpha_j \neq \alpha_i, \alpha_{i+1}\}$$
$$= \{j \mid \alpha_j = \{3\}, \{4\}, \{1,3\}, \{1,4\}, \{2,3\}, \{2,4\}\}.$$

Define

$$A^+ = \{j \mid \alpha_j = \{1,3\}, \{1,4\}, \{2,3\}, \{2,4\}\}$$
$$A^- = \{j \mid \alpha_j = \{3\}, \{4\}\}.$$

Hence, since $\phi(\alpha_i)_{\text{int}(v)} = 1$, and for $j \in A^+$, $\phi(\alpha_j)_{\text{int}(v)} = -1$, and for $j \in A^-$, $\phi(\alpha_j)_{\text{int}(v)} = 1$,

$$w_{i+1} \geq 3w_i + \sum_{j \in A^+} w_j - \sum_{j \in A^-} w_j.$$

By Lemma 4.4.4, the positive terms of weights corresponding to the four sets of size two in A^+ have larger magnitude than the negative terms of weights corresponding to the two sets of size one in A^-. Hence, $w_{i+1} \geq 3w_i$, as claimed. $\square$

LEMMA 4.4.6 Suppose $\|\alpha_t\| = 3$ and $\|\alpha_{t+1}\| = 4$. Then, for $i = t-1, t$,

$$w_i > \sum_{j=1}^{i-1} w_j.$$

PROOF: Suppose $s = m(m+1)/2 + 1$, $t = m(m^2+5)/6 + 1$. That is, $\|\alpha_s\| = 2$ and $\|\alpha_{s+1}\| = 3$, and $\|\alpha_t\| = 3$ and $\|\alpha_{t+1}\| = 4$.

As in the proof of Lemma 4.4.4, we can without loss of generality assume that the weights corresponding to the sets of size one are monotonically increasing, that is, for $1 < j \leq m$, $w_j \leq w_{j+1}$ (if this is not true, simply relabel the elements of $\mathcal{M}$). Because of this monotonicity, and the monotonicity of the weights corresponding to sets of size two (Lemma 4.4.3 (3)),

$$\sum_{j=1}^{s} w_j \leq w_1 + w_s m(m+1)/2.$$

By Lemma 4.4.4, $w_1 < w_s$, and hence

$$\sum_{j=1}^{s} w_j < w_s(m^2 + m + 2)/2. \tag{4.4.15}$$

Furthermore, by Lemma 4.4.5, it can be proved by induction (Problem 12) that

$$w_{t-1} > \sum_{j=s+1}^{t-2} w_j + (3^{t-s-1} + 1)w_s/2$$

$$= \sum_{j=s+1}^{t-1} w_j + (3^{m(m-1)(m-2)/6-1} + 1)w_s/2.$$

Since for all $m \geq 4$, $(3^{m(m-1)(m-2)/6-1} + 1)/2 > (m^2 + m + 2)/2$, we conclude from Equation (4.4.15) that

$$w_{t-1} > \sum_{j=1}^{t-2} w_j.$$

By Lemma 4.4.5, $w_t \geq 3w_{t-1}$. Hence, by the above, $w_t \geq w_{t-1} + 2w_{t-1} > \sum_{j=1}^{t-1} w_j$.
□

LEMMA 4.4.7 If $F = \mathcal{F}_n(w_1, \ldots, w_n)$, then

1. For each i such that $\|\alpha_{i+1}\| \geq 3$, $w_{i+1} \geq (2^{\|\alpha_{i+1}\|-1} - 1)w_i$.
2. For each i such that $\|\alpha_i\| \geq 3$ and $\|\alpha_{i+2}\| \geq 4$, $w_i > \sum_{j=1}^{i-1} w_j$.

PROOF: The proof is by induction on i such that $\|\alpha_{i+1}\| \geq 3$. The base case occurs when $\|\alpha_{i+1}\| = 3$. Part (1) of the base case was proved in Lemma 4.4.5, and Part (2) was proved in Lemma 4.4.6.

Now, suppose that $\|\alpha_{i+1}\| = k$ for some $k \geq 4$, and that the induction hypothesis holds for all α_j such that $3 \leq \|\alpha_j\| < k$. We will first prove Part (1). There are two cases to consider. In the first case, $\|\alpha_i\| = k - 1$. Without loss of generality, suppose $\alpha_i = \{1, 2, \ldots, k-1\}$ and $\alpha_{i+1} = \{1, 2, \ldots, k\}$ (the general case is proved similarly). Choose a such that $a \in \alpha_i$ and $a \notin \alpha_{i-1}$ (this is possible since $\|\alpha_i\| = \|\alpha_{i-1}\|$). Define $v \in \mathbb{U}^n$ as follows: $v_a = -1$, and for all other j with $1 \leq j \leq n$, $v_j = 1$. By Lemma 4.4.2, since $v_k = 1$,

$$w_{i+1} \geq (2^{\|\alpha_{i+1}\|-1} - 1)w_i - \sum_{j \in A} w_j \phi(\alpha_i)_{\text{int}(v)} \phi(\alpha_j)_{\text{int}(v)},$$

where

$$A = \{j \mid 1 \leq j \leq n, \ \alpha_j \subset \alpha_{i+1}, \ \alpha_j \neq \alpha_i\}.$$

Define

$$A^+ = \{j \mid \phi(\alpha_j)_{\text{int}(v)} = -1\}$$
$$A^- = \{j \mid \phi(\alpha_j)_{\text{int}(v)} = 1\}.$$

Therefore, since $\phi(\alpha_i)_{\text{int}(v)} = -1$,

$$w_{i+1} \geq (2^{\|\alpha_{i+1}\|-1} - 1)w_i + \sum_{j \in A^+} w_j - \sum_{j \in A^-} w_j.$$

Note that, because of the choice of v, A^+ contains α_{i-1}. Since $j \leq i-1$ for all $j \in A$, we know that $j < i-1$ for all $j \in A^-$. Therefore, by the induction hypothesis (2), the magnitude of the positive term is larger than that of the negative term, and hence we conclude that $w_{i+1} \geq (2^{\|\alpha_{i+1}\|-1} - 1)w_i$, as claimed.

In the second case, $\|\alpha_i\| = k$. Without loss of generality, assume that $\alpha_i = \{1, 2, \ldots, k\}$ and $\alpha_{i+1} = \{1, 2, \ldots, k-1, k+1\}$ (the general case is proved similarly). Let α be the set in A that has the highest index. Note that α must have index less than i, but unlike the previous case it may not necessarily be α_{i-1}, since α_{i-1} may contain both k and $k+1$ and thus may not be a member of A. Choose a such that $a \in \alpha_i$ and $a \notin \alpha$, $a \neq k, k+1$ (this is possible since $\alpha_i \Delta \alpha_{i-1} \neq \{k, k+1\}$). Define $v \in \mathbf{U}^n$ as follows: $v_a = -1$, and for all other j with $1 \leq j \leq n$, $v_j = 1$. Then, by Lemma 4.4.1,

$$w_{i+1} \geq (2^{\|\alpha_{i+1}\|-1} - 1)w_i - \sum_{j \in A} w_j \phi(\alpha_i)_{\text{int}(v)} \phi(\alpha_j)_{\text{int}(v)},$$

where

$$A = \{j \mid 1 \leq j \leq n, \ \alpha_j \subset \alpha_i \cup \alpha_{i+1}, \ \|\alpha_j \cap \{k, k+1\}\| = 1, \ \alpha_j \neq \alpha_i, \alpha_{i+1}\}.$$

Define

$$A^+ = \{j \mid \phi(\alpha_j)_{\text{int}(v)} = -1\}$$
$$A^- = \{j \mid \phi(\alpha_j)_{\text{int}(v)} = 1\}.$$

Hence, since $\phi(\alpha_i)_{\text{int}(v)} = -1$,

$$w_{i+1} \geq (2^{\|\alpha_{i+1}\|-1} - 1)w_i + \sum_{j \in A^+} w_j - \sum_{j \in A^-} w_j.$$

Note that, because of the choice of v, A^+ contains α. Since α is the highest indexed set in A, and it has index less than i, then by the induction hypothesis (2), the magnitude of the positive term is larger than that of the negative term, and hence we conclude that $w_{i+1} \geq (2^{\|\alpha_{i+1}\|-1} - 1)w_i$, as claimed. This completes the inductive proof of Part (1).

Since $w_{i+1} \geq (2^{\|\alpha_{i+1}\|-1} - 1)w_i > 2w_i$ and by the induction hypothesis (2), $w_i > \sum_{j=1}^{i-1} w_j$, clearly $w_{i+1} > \sum_{j=1}^{i} w_j$. This completes the inductive proof of Part (2). $\square$

We are now almost ready for the main theorem, which gives a lower bound on the weights used in the nonstandard form of F. But before we begin, we need two elementary counting results:

LEMMA 4.4.8 For all $n \in \mathbf{N}$, the following two identities hold:

$$\sum_{i=0}^{n} i \cdot \binom{n}{i} = n2^{n-1} \tag{4.4.16}$$

$$\sum_{i=0}^{n} 2^{-i} \cdot \binom{n}{i} = (3/2)^n \tag{4.4.17}$$

PROOF: Identity (4.4.16) can be proved by induction on n, but the following argument is more intuitive. Write down every string of n bits. Since there are $\binom{n}{i}$ strings with exactly i ones, we must have written exactly

$$\sum_{i=0}^{n} i \cdot \binom{n}{i}$$

ones. But since we have written exactly as many ones as zeros, and we have written $n2^n$ bits, there must be $n2^{n-1}$ ones. This established Identity (4.4.16).

Identity (4.4.17) follows by induction on $n \in \mathbf{N}$. The identity holds for $n = 0$, in which case both sides are equal to one. Suppose that

$$\sum_{i=0}^{n-1} 2^{-i} \cdot \binom{n-1}{i} = (3/2)^{n-1}. \tag{4.4.18}$$

To choose i items out of n, we must either choose the first, in which case we must choose $i-1$ more items out of the remaining $n-1$, or not choose the first item, in which case we must choose the i items out of the remaining $n-1$. Hence, for all $1 \leq i \leq n$,

$$\binom{n}{i} = \binom{n-1}{i-1} + \binom{n-1}{i}.$$

Therefore,

$$
\begin{aligned}
\sum_{i=0}^{n} 2^{-i} \cdot \binom{n}{i} &= \sum_{i=1}^{n-1} 2^{-i} \cdot \binom{n}{i} + 2^{-n} + 1 \\
&= \sum_{i=1}^{n-1} 2^{-i} \cdot \binom{n-1}{i-1} + \sum_{i=1}^{n-1} 2^{-i} \cdot \binom{n-1}{i} + 2^{-n} + 1 \\
&= \sum_{i=0}^{n-2} 2^{-i-1} \cdot \binom{n-1}{i} + \sum_{i=1}^{n-1} 2^{-i} \cdot \binom{n-1}{i} + 2^{-n} + 1 \\
&= \sum_{i=0}^{n-1} 2^{-i-1} \cdot \binom{n-1}{i} + \sum_{i=0}^{n-1} 2^{-i} \cdot \binom{n-1}{i} \\
&= (3/2)^{n-1}/2 + (3/2)^{n-1} \qquad \text{(by Equation (4.4.18), twice)} \\
&= (3/2)^{n}.
\end{aligned}
$$

Thus, Identity (4.4.17) holds. $\Box$

Now, we are ready for the main theorem:

THEOREM 4.4.9 If $F = \mathcal{F}_n(w_1, \ldots, w_n)$, then

$$
w_n \geq \frac{n^{(n-\log n-1)/2} e^{\gamma(\log^2 n + 3\log n + 8)} (\log^2 n - \log n + 1)}{e^{8\gamma n^\beta} 2^{n-1}}
$$

where $\beta = \log(3/2) \approx 0.585$, $\gamma = \ln(4/3) \approx 0.288$.

PROOF: Suppose $F = \mathcal{F}_n(w_1, \ldots, w_n)$. Let $k = m(m+1)/2 + 1$. That is, $\|\alpha_k\| = 2$, and $\|\alpha_{k+1}\| = 3$. Let $H = \{i \mid \|\alpha_i\| \geq 3\}$. Then, by Lemma 4.4.7 (1),

$$
w_n \geq w_k \cdot \prod_{i \in H} (2^{\|\alpha_i\|-1} - 1) = w_k \cdot \prod_{i \in H} (2^{\|\alpha_i\|-1}) \cdot \prod_{i \in H} (1 - 2^{1-\|\alpha_i\|}).
$$

We will derive separate lower bounds for each of the three factors of the right-hand side of this inequality. Firstly, by Lemma 4.4.3,

$$
w_k \geq \frac{1}{n} + \frac{2}{n}(m(m-1)/2) = (m^2 - m + 1)/n = (\log^2 n - \log n + 1)/n.
$$

We can evaluate the second factor by noting that

$$
\log \left(\prod_{i \in H} 2^{\|\alpha_i\|-1} \right) = \sum_{i=k+1}^{n} (\|\alpha_i\| - 1)
$$

$$= \sum_{i=3}^{m} i \cdot \binom{m}{i} - (n-k)$$

$$= \sum_{i=1}^{m} i \cdot \binom{m}{i} - \sum_{i=1}^{2} i \cdot \binom{m}{i} - (n-k)$$

$$= nm/2 - m - 2m(m-1)/2 - (n - (m(m+1)/2 + 1))$$

$$\text{(by Lemma 4.4.8 (4.4.16))}$$

$$= (n\log n - \log^2 n + \log n)/2 - (n-1).$$

Hence the second factor is at least $2^{(n\log n - \log^2 n + \log n)/2 - (n-1)} = n^{(n-\log n+1)/2}/2^{n-1}$. We can also bound the third factor, since for $0 < x \le 1/4$, $\ln(1-x) \ge -4\gamma x$, where γ is minimized by $\ln(1 - (1/4)) = -4\gamma(1/4)$, so

$$\gamma = -\ln(3/4) = \ln(4/3) \approx 0.288.$$

Then,

$$\ln\left(\prod_{i \in H}(1 - 2^{1-\|\alpha_i\|})\right) \ge -\sum_{i=3}^{m} 4\gamma 2^{1-i} \cdot \binom{m}{i}$$

$$= 8\gamma \sum_{i=0}^{2} 2^{-i} \cdot \binom{m}{i} - 8\gamma \sum_{i=0}^{m} 2^{-i} \cdot \binom{m}{i}$$

$$= 8\gamma(1 + m/2 + m(m-1)/8) - 8\gamma(3/2)^m$$

$$\text{(by Lemma 4.4.8 (4.4.17))}$$

$$= \gamma(m^2 + 3m + 8) - 8\gamma n^\beta$$

where $\beta = \log(3/2)$. Hence the third factor is at least $e^{\gamma(\log^2 n + 3\log n + 8) - 8\gamma n^\beta}$, and the claimed result follows. $\square$

Finally, we can derive our lower bound on the weight of F.

COROLLARY 4.4.10 F has weight at least

$$\frac{n^{(n-\log n - 1)/2} e^{\gamma(\log^2 n + 3\log n + 8)}(\log^2 n - \log n + 1)}{e^{8\gamma n^\beta} 2^{n-1}}$$

where $\beta = \log(3/2) \approx 0.585$, $\gamma = \ln(4/3) \approx 0.288$.

PROOF: For convenience, define

$$\ell(n) = \frac{n^{(n-\log n - 1)/2} e^{\gamma(\log^2 n + 3\log n + 8)}(\log^2 n - \log n + 1)}{e^{8\gamma n^\beta} 2^{n-1}}.$$

Suppose $F = \hat{\theta}_n(w_1, \ldots, w_n, 0)$. Suppose, for a contradiction, that $|w_i| < \ell(n)$ for all $1 \leq i \leq n$. By Lemma 4.3.7, $F = \mathcal{F}_n(w_1, \ldots, w_n)$, where

$$w_i' = \frac{1}{n} \sum_{j=1}^{n} w_j \phi(\alpha_i)_j \leq \frac{1}{n} \sum_{j=1}^{n} |w_j| < \frac{1}{n} \sum_{j=1}^{n} \ell(n) = \ell(n).$$

Hence, in particular, $w_n' < \ell(n)$. But this contradicts Theorem 4.4.9. Therefore, $|w_i| \geq \ell(n)$ for all $1 \leq i \leq n$. $\square$

Note that the lower bound of Corollary 4.4.10 is smaller than the upper bound of Theorem 4.2.1 by a factor of only $2^{O(n^\beta)}$.

4.5   Problems

1. If a Boolean linear threshold function has presentation $(w_1, \ldots, w_n, h)$ under normal logic, find a presentation for the same function under bipolar logic. If a Boolean linear threshold function has presentation $(w_1, \ldots, w_n, h)$ under bipolar logic, find a presentation for the same function under normal logic.

2. Prove Theorem 4.1.8.

3. Prove that for all Boolean linear threshold functions $f : \mathbf{B}^n \to \mathbf{B}$, there exists a presentation $(w_1, \ldots, w_n, h)$ such that $f = \theta_n(w_1, \ldots, w_n, h)$ and for all $x, y \in \mathbf{B}^n$, if $x \neq y$, then $\sigma_w(n_1, \ldots, n_w)(x) \neq \sigma_w(n_1, \ldots, n_w)(y)$.

4. Complete the proof of Theorem 4.2.6 when n is even.

5. Complete the proof of Theorem 4.2.6 when n is odd.

6. Show that the function $\text{int} : \mathbf{U}^m \to \mathbf{Z}$ defined in Section 4.3 has the desired properties. That is, if we define

$$\text{int}(x) = 2^{m-1} + 0.5 + \sum_{i=1}^{m} 2^{m-i-1} x_i,$$

then $\text{int}(x)$ is the value obtained by replacing all -1s in x with zeros and treating the resulting string as the binary encoding of a natural number, then adding one to it.

7. Generalize the construction in Table 4.1 to give an algorithm for generating sets in minimal change order, and hence (or otherwise) prove Lemma 4.3.1 by providing a proof that your construction is correct.

8. Show that the function F defined on p. 80 is well-defined. That is, show that for all $x = (x_1, \ldots, x_n) \in \mathbf{U}^n$, there exists $1 \leq k \leq n$ such that $\langle x, \phi(\alpha_k) \rangle \neq 0$.

9. Complete the proof of Lemma 4.3.5 by showing that if $F(x_1, \ldots, x_n) = 0$, then

$$\sum_{i=1}^{n} w_i x_i < 0.$$

10. Prove Lemma 4.3.6 by demonstrating that the matrix as constructed in Table 4.4 is symmetric if the columns are permuted into the right order.

11. Complete the proof of Lemma 4.3.7 by proving that Equation (4.3.14) holds.

12. Complete the proof of Lemma 4.4.6 by showing that

$$w_{t-1} \geq \sum_{j=s+1}^{t-2} w_j + (3^{t-s-1} + 1)w_s/2$$

4.6   Bibliographic Notes

Theorem 4.2.1 is due to Muroga, Toda, and Takasu [89], and appears in more detail in Muroga [88]. Weaker versions of this result was more recently rediscovered by Hong [64], Raghavan [111], and Natarajan [91] using a modernized version of essentially the same technique.

Theorem 4.2.2 is due to Yajima and Ibaraki [150], and Smith [130], and is attributed to Dahlin by Muroga [88]. The bound can be improved to $C(n) > 2^{n(n-1)/2 + 16}$ by observing that $C(8) > 2^{44}$ (Muroga, Tsuboi, and Baugh [90]). Theorem 4.2.3 is not the best possible; an easy improvement can be made by using Stirling's approximation to give a lower bound of $2^{n^2 - O(n \log n)}$. Variations on this argument can be found in Winder [149] and Hu [66].

The lower bound of $\Omega(2^{n/2})$ on the weights of a Boolean linear threshold function obtained by using the counting argument in the comment following Theorem 4.2.3 appears to be a "folk theorem". It appears in Parberry [95]. Hampson and Volper [56] obtained the same result. Theorem 4.2.6 is another "folk theorem", known to the author, Piotr Berman and Nainan Kovoor, and Ron Rivest, but previously unpublished. Muroga [87] demonstrates a Boolean linear threshold function that has weight $\Omega(2^n)$. The larger lower bound described in Sections 4.3 and 4.4 is from Håstad [134].

5 Alternating Circuits

In Chapter 2 we were introduced to the *classical circuit* model, which is a circuit model of computing based on gates that compute two-input conjunction and disjunction, and unary complement. Classical circuits can be viewed as very limited neural networks, since, as we saw in in Section 4.1, conjunction, disjunction, and complement are linear threshold functions. However, this model is lacking in at least one regard. The typical neuron has tremendously large fan-in, often estimated at around 10^6 to 10^8 synapses per neuron, as opposed to a fan-in of 2 in classical circuits. In this chapter we add large fan-in to our circuit model by allowing gates that compute conjunction and disjunction of an arbitrary number of Boolean values. The resulting circuit model is called an *AND-OR circuit*.

This chapter is divided into four major sections. Section 5.1 contains the formal definition of the AND-OR circuit model, and introduces the *alternating circuit*, a conveniently structured form of AND-OR circuit that consists of alternating layers of conjunction and disjunction gates. Section 5.2 explains some important techniques for constructing alternating circuits. Section 5.3 is devoted to alternating circuits with exponential size. Although the size of these circuits scales so poorly as to make them appear almost useless, we will find some reasonable applications for them later. Section 5.4 considers alternating circuits of polynomial size, and gives a circuit-based account of the theory of $\mathcal{NP}$-completeness.

5.1 AND-OR Circuits and Alternating Circuits

An AND-OR circuit is a classical circuit (see Section 2.3) with the restriction on fan-in removed. Thus, the AND-gates can compute the conjunction of any number of values, and the OR-gates can compute the disjunction of any number of values. More formally, an *AND-OR circuit* is a 5-tuple $C = (V, X, Y, E, \ell)$, where

$$V \text{ is a finite ordered set}$$
$$X \cap V = \emptyset$$
$$Y \subseteq V$$
$$(V \cup X, E) \text{ is a directed, acyclic graph}$$
$$\ell : V \to \{\text{AND}, \text{OR}, \text{NOT}, 0, 1\}.$$

It is not strictly necessary to have the NOT-gates scattered arbitrarily throughout the circuit:

THEOREM 5.1.1 For every n-input AND-OR circuit of depth d and size s there exists an equivalent n-input AND-OR circuit of depth at most d and size at most $2s + n$ in which all of the NOT-gates are at level 1.

PROOF: Let $C = (V, X, Y, E, \ell)$ be an n-input AND-OR circuit. We assume without loss of generality that the fan-in of any gate $v \in V$ with $\ell(v) = \text{NOT}$ is 1, and that C does not contain two consecutive NOT-gates, that is, there does not exist $u, v \in V$ such that $\ell(u) = \ell(v) = \text{NOT}$, and $(u, v) \in E$.

First, define $N \subseteq V \times V$ to be the set of pairs of gates which are connected via a NOT-gate. That is,

$$N = \{(g_1, g_2) \mid \text{there exists } g_3 \in V \text{ such that } \ell(g_3) = \text{NOT and } (g_1, g_3), (g_3, g_2) \in E\}.$$

Now define a new circuit $C' = (V', X, Y', E', \ell')$, where

$$V' = \{g, \overline{g} \mid g \in V, g \neq \text{NOT}\} \cup \{\overline{x} \mid x \in X\}$$
$$Y' = \{y'_1, \ldots, y'_m\},$$

where $Y = \{y_1, \ldots, y_m\}$, and for $1 \leq i \leq m$, y'_i is defined by

$$y'_i = \begin{cases} \overline{g} & \text{if } \ell(y_i) = \text{NOT, where } (g, y_i) \in E \\ y_i & \text{if } \ell(y_i) \neq \text{NOT}. \end{cases}$$

E' is defined as follows. $(x, \overline{x}) \in E'$ for all $x \in X$, and for every pair of vertices $g_1, g_2 \in V' \cup X\}$:

Case 1: $(g_1, g_2) \in E$. Then, $(g_1, g_2), (\overline{g}_1, \overline{g}_2) \in E'$.

Case 2: $(g_1, g_2) \in N$. Then, $(g_1, \overline{g}_2), (\overline{g}_1, g_2) \in E'$.

ℓ' is defined as follows. $\ell'(\overline{x}) = \text{NOT}$ for all $x \in X$. The other gates fall into one of four categories:

Case 1: $\ell(g) = \text{AND}$. Then, $\ell'(g) = \text{AND}$, and $\ell'(\overline{g}) = \text{OR}$.

Case 2: $\ell(g) = \text{OR}$. Then, $\ell'(g) = \text{OR}$, and $\ell'(\overline{g}) = \text{AND}$.

Case 3: $\ell(g) = 0$. Then, $\ell'(g) = 0$, and $\ell'(\overline{g}) = 1$.

Case 4: $\ell(g) = 1$. Then, $\ell'(g) = 1$, and $\ell'(\overline{g}) = 0$.

Clearly C' has depth d and size at most $2s + n$, and all of its NOT-gates are at level 1. It remains to show that C' computes the same function as C. Let $v'(g)$ denote the value of g in C', for all $g \in V' \cup X\}$. We claim that for all $g, \overline{g} \in V' \cup X$, $v'(g) = v(g)$, and $v'(\overline{g}) = \neg v(g)$. The proof of the claim is by induction on level. The hypothesis is certainly true if g is at level 0 (that is, g is an input), or level 1 (that is, g is a NOT-gate). Now suppose that g is at level $i > 1$. The hypothesis is certainly true if $\ell'(g) = 0$, or $\ell'(g) = 1$, for some $1 \le i \le n$. Suppose $\ell'(g) = \text{AND}$. Suppose g has k inputs, with $g_1, \ldots, g_j$ the vertices such that $(g_i, g) \in E$ and $\ell(g_i) \ne \text{NOT}$, for $1 \le i \le j$, and $g_{j+1}, \ldots, g_k$ the vertices such that $(g_i, g) \in N$ for $j + 1 \le i \le k$. Then, $g_1, \ldots, g_j$ are the vertices such that $(g_i, g) \in E'$ for $1 \le i \le j$, and $\overline{g}_{j+1}, \ldots, \overline{g}_k$ are the vertices such that $(\overline{g}_i, g) \in E'$ for $j + 1 \le i \le k$. Therefore,

$$
\begin{aligned}
v'(g) &= (v'(g_1) \wedge \cdots \wedge v'(g_j)) \wedge (v'(\overline{g}_{j+1}) \wedge \cdots \wedge v'(\overline{g}_k)) \\
&= (v(g_1) \wedge \cdots \wedge v(g_j)) \wedge (\neg v(g_{j+1}) \wedge \cdots \wedge \neg v(g_k)) \\
&\quad \text{(by the induction hypothesis)} \\
&= v(g).
\end{aligned}
$$

and

$$
\begin{aligned}
v'(\overline{g}) &= (v'(\overline{g}_1) \vee \cdots \vee v'(\overline{g}_j)) \vee (v'(g_{j+1}) \vee \cdots \vee v'(g_k)) \\
&= (\neg v(g_1) \vee \cdots \vee v\neg(g_j)) \vee (v(g_{j+1}) \vee \cdots \vee v(g_k)) \\
&\quad \text{(by the induction hypothesis)} \\
&= \neg v(g) \quad \text{(by Corollary 4.1.6)}.
\end{aligned}
$$

The case $\ell'(g) = \text{OR}$ is similar.

Therefore, $v'(y') = v(y)$ for all $y \in Y$ and inputs $b_1, \ldots, b_n \in \mathbf{B}$. That is, C' is equivalent to C. $\square$

Figure 5.2 shows the AND-OR circuit obtained from the one in Figure 5.1 by applying Theorem 5.1.1. Note that some of the gates in the new circuit are redundant (the size and depth bounds given in the statement of the Theorem are worst-case only). Figure 5.3 shows the new circuit with the redundant gates removed.

Theorem 5.1.1 allows us to put all AND-OR circuits into a useful kind of normal form. An *alternating circuit* is an AND-OR circuit in which all of the gates in any given layer (apart from the first) compute the same function, and the layers alternate between gates computing AND and gates computing OR.

COROLLARY 5.1.2 For every n-input AND-OR circuit of size s and depth d there is an equivalent alternating circuit of size at most $2s + n$ and depth at most d.

PROOF: Let $C = (V, X, Y, E, \ell)$ be an n-input AND-OR circuit. We assume, by Theorem 5.1.1, that there are NOT-gates only in the first level. For each $v, w \in V$ such that $(v, w) \in E$ and $\ell(v) = \ell(w)$, delete v from V, and for all $u \in V \cup X$ such that $(u, v) \in E$, delete (u, v) from E and add (u, w) to E. Repeat this process until no such v, w can be found. The new circuit is equivalent to the old since AND and OR are associative. $\square$

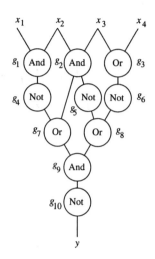

Figure 5.1
An AND-OR circuit.

Figure 5.4 shows that alternating circuit obtained from the AND-OR circuit in Figure 5.3 using Corollary 5.1.2.

We will use alternating circuits in preference to AND-OR circuits from this point onwards. Let us redefine the depth and size of an alternating circuit to exclude layer 1 (which consists of NOT-gates). It is convenient to think of an alternating circuit as being a function of a set of *literals*, where a literal is either an input or its complement. Our motivation is based primarily on the desire for a cleaner model, but we are not totally divorced from reality, since NOT-gates are relatively cheap compared to AND and OR-gates (particularly since we have placed no bound on the fan-in of the latter), and in some applications the complements of the inputs are routinely available, for example, if the inputs are stored in digital memory. Omitting the NOT-gates can only have a relatively small effect on the size of alternating circuits, since they can have most n NOT-gates. We must also modify our model so that the vertex set includes both input vertices $x_i \in X$ and nodes representing their complements $\overline{x}_i$.

The results of this section extend in a fairly straightforward way to circuits with multiple outputs (except for the fact that the depth in Corollary 5.1.2 may increase by 1).

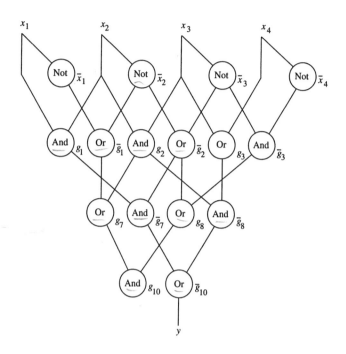

Figure 5.2
An AND-OR circuit equivalent to the one in Figure 5.1 with all of the NOT-gates at level 1
constructed using Theorem 5.1.1.

5.2   Computing with Alternating Circuits

Alternating circuits can be used to solve a variety of problems. Any finite mathematical
object can easily be encoded as a sequence of bits. For example, an integer can be
encoded in binary. A sequence of integers can be encoded by repeating each bit in the
numbers (replacing 0 with 00, and 1 with 11 wherever it occurs), and separating each
pair of integers by 01. A set can be represented as a sequence of members. A function
over a finite domain can be represented as a sequence of input-output pairs.

The finite alternating circuits defined in the previous section have a finite number of
inputs. These circuits can be used to compute arbitrary functions by constructing a
circuit for each input size. This is reasonable, since we will in practice only need circuits
with a small fixed number of inputs, which is just as well, since our technology at any
given moment will only allow us to build circuits with a small fixed number of inputs.
The definition of "small" will undoubtedly increase slowly with time as our needs increase

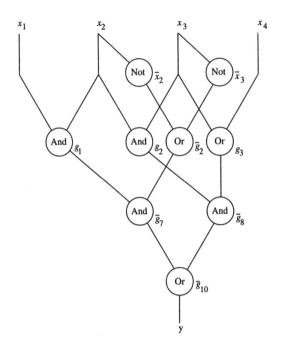

Figure 5.3
The circuit in Figure 5.2 with the redundant gates removed.

and our technology advances. It is interesting to consider how the resources of size and depth increase with input size.

We will concentrate for a good part of the time on functions that have a single Boolean output. As in Chapter 2, we will think of the Boolean value 1 as representing the logical truth value **true** and the Boolean value 0 as representing the logical truth value **false**. We can then express the parity function as a decision problem: given n bits, is there an odd number of them which are 1? A circuit is said to *solve* such a decision problem if for all instances of the decision problem, it outputs 1 iff the answer to the question on that instance is affirmative. For example, a circuit solves the parity problem iff on input $x_1, \ldots, x_n$, it outputs 1 iff $\|\{i \mid x_i = 1\}\|$ is odd. In order to be precise, we will express decision problems, such as parity, in the following format:

PARITY
INSTANCE: $x_1, \ldots, x_n \in \mathbf{B}$.
QUESTION: Is $\|\{i \mid x_i = 1\}\|$ odd?

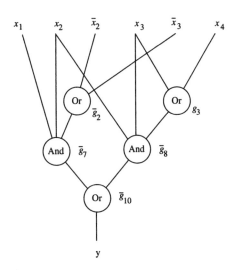

Figure 5.4
An alternating circuit equivalent to the one in Figure 5.3.

For added convenience, we will use set notation to express decision problems. A *language* is a set of binary strings. The *language corresponding to a problem* is the set of instances for which the answer to the question is "yes". We will use the name of the problem as a synonym for the language corresponding to that problem, writing for example, $(x_1, \ldots, x_n) \in$ PARITY to denote that the answer to instance $x_1, \ldots, x_n$ of the parity problem is "yes", that is, $\|\{i \mid x_i = 1\}\|$ is odd. A finite circuit with n inputs is said to *accept* an input $x \in \mathbf{B}^n$ if it outputs 1 on input x, and to *reject* x otherwise. We say that a circuit family $C = (C_1, C_2, \ldots)$ *recognizes* language L if it solves the problem corresponding to L, that is, for all inputs x, the circuit accepts x iff $x \in L$.

The main technique that we will use for constructing circuits is called *divide-and-conquer*, a standard approach in Computer Science. This technique is applied to circuit design as follows. In order to design a circuit to solve a given problem P, we will decompose P into smaller subproblems and construct individual circuits for each of them (the "divide" part), and then assemble these subcircuits into the circuit we need for P (the "conquer" part). The easiest divide-and-conquer method is called *concatenation* of circuits. This is performed by taking the outputs from one circuit and feeding them into the inputs of a second circuit:

THEOREM 5.2.1 Suppose $n_1, n_2, n_3 \in \mathbf{N}$. If $f_1 : \mathbf{B}^{n_1} \to \mathbf{B}^{n_2}$ can be computed by an alternating circuit of size z_1 and depth d_1, and $f_2 : \mathbf{B}^{n_2} \to \mathbf{B}^{n_3}$, can be computed by an alternating circuit of size z_2 and depth d_2, then the function $f_2 f_1 : \mathbf{B}^{n_1} \to \mathbf{B}^{n_3}$ defined by

$$f_2 f_1(x_1, \ldots, x_{n_1}) = f_2(f_1(x_1, \ldots, x_{n_1}))$$

for all $x_1, \ldots, x_{n_1} \in \mathbf{B}$ can be computed by an alternating circuit of size $z_1 + z_2$ and depth $d_1 + d_2$.

PROOF: Suppose $n_1, n_2, n_3 \in \mathbf{N}$, and $f_1 : \mathbf{B}^{n_1} \to \mathbf{B}^{n_2}$ can be computed by an alternating circuit C_1 of size z_1 and depth d_1, $f_2 : \mathbf{B}^{n_2} \to \mathbf{B}^{n_3}$ can be computed by an alternating circuit C_2 of size z_2 and depth d_2, then the function $f_2 f_1 : \mathbf{B}^{n_1} \to \mathbf{B}^{n_3}$. Then, concatenating the circuits C_1 followed by C_2 gives rise to a circuit that computes $f_2 f_1$ in size $z_1 + z_2$ and depth $d_1 + d_2$. □

A savings in depth of one layer can be made if the subcircuits have the right property:

THEOREM 5.2.2 Suppose $n_1, n_2, n_3 \in \mathbf{N}$. Suppose $f_1 : \mathbf{B}^{n_1} \to \mathbf{B}^{n_2}$ can be computed by an alternating circuit C_1 of size z_1 and depth d_1, and $f_2 : \mathbf{B}^{n_2} \to \mathbf{B}^{n_3}$ can be computed by an alternating circuit C_2 of size z_2 and depth d_2, where the last layer of C_1 and the first layer of C_2 consist of gates with the same node function (either both AND or both OR). The function $f_2 f_1 : \mathbf{B}^{n_1} \to \mathbf{B}^{n_3}$ defined by

$$f_2 f_1(x_1, \ldots, x_{n_1}) = f_2(f_1(x_1, \ldots, x_{n_1}))$$

for all $x_1, \ldots, x_{n_1} \in \mathbf{B}$ can be computed by an alternating circuit of size $z_1 + z_2$ and depth $d_1 + d_2 - 1$.

PROOF: The proof is identical to that of Theorem 5.2.1, noting that this construction gives a circuit with two adjacent layers of gates that compute the same function, which can be combined using the technique of Corollary 5.1.2 to save a single layer without additional expense in size. □

We will call the depth-reduction technique in Theorem 5.2.2 *compression* of alternating circuits. The following trick, called *inversion*, will enable us to use compression to save another layer of gates at the expense of an increase in size.

THEOREM 5.2.3 Any function $f : \mathbf{B}^n \to \mathbf{B}$ that can be computed by a depth 2 alternating circuit with ANDgates of fan-in p on level 1, and r ORgates of fan-in q on level 2, can be computed by a depth 2 alternating circuit of size $p^q r$ with ORgates on level 1. The same proposition holds if AND and OR are interchanged.

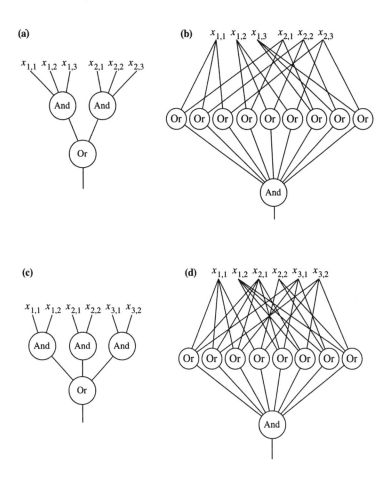

Figure 5.5
Two alternating circuits (a), (c), and equivalent inverted circuits (b), (d), respectively.

PROOF: The result follows because AND and OR each distribute over the other, that is, for all $x_{i,j} \in \mathbf{B}$, $1 \leq i \leq q$, $1 \leq j \leq p$,

$$(x_{1,1} \wedge x_{1,2} \wedge \cdots \wedge x_{1,p}) \vee (x_{2,1} \wedge x_{2,2} \wedge \cdots \wedge x_{2,p}) \vee \cdots \vee (x_{q,1} \wedge x_{q,2} \wedge \cdots \wedge x_{q,p})$$
$$= (x_{1,1} \vee x_{2,1} \vee x_{q,1}) \wedge (x_{1,1} \vee x_{2,1} \vee x_{q,2}) \wedge \cdots \wedge (x_{1,p} \vee x_{2,p} \vee x_{q,p}).$$

The same identity holds if AND and OR are interchanged. These identities can be proved by induction on n, and the proposition can then be proved by induction on the number of gates in the first layer. □

For example, Figure 5.5 shows two alternating circuits, and the equivalent inverted alternating circuits obtained by applying Theorem 5.2.3. Note that the size increase in Theorem 5.2.3 will be quite large if the output gates have large fan-in q, but it can be reasonable if $q = O(1)$. Inversion swaps the order of two layers of gates in return for an increase in size. Swapping two layers of gates enables us to save depth using compression.

5.3   Exponential Size

If size is no barrier, then alternating circuits can be used to compute any Boolean function in very small depth.

THEOREM 5.3.1 For all $f : \mathbf{B}^n \to \mathbf{B}$, there is an alternating circuit of size $2^{n-1} + 1$ and depth 2 that computes f.

PROOF: A finite alternating circuit for f is constructed as follows. Let

$$T = \{(b_1, \ldots, b_n) \in \mathbf{B}^n \mid f(b_1, \ldots, b_n) = 1\}.$$

Suppose $T = \{(b_{1,1}, \ldots, b_{1,n}), \ldots (b_{m,1}, \ldots, b_{m,n})\}$ for some $1 \leq m \leq 2^n$. Let

$$F = \{(c_1, \ldots, c_n) \in \mathbf{B}^n \mid f(c_1, \ldots, c_n) = 0\}.$$

Suppose $F = \{(c_{1,1}, \ldots, c_{1,n}), \ldots (c_{m',1}, \ldots, c_{m',n})\}$ for some $1 \leq m' \leq 2^n$. Let $x_i[0]$ denote $\overline{x}_i$, $x_i[1]$ denote x_i, $\overline{x}_i[0]$ denote x_i, and $\overline{x}_i[1]$ denote $\overline{x}_i$.
    Suppose $m \leq 2^{n-1}$. Then, since $x_1[b_{i,1}] \wedge \cdots \wedge x_n[b_{i,n}] = 1$ iff $(x_1, \ldots, x_n) = (b_{i,1}, \ldots, b_{i,n})$ for $1 \leq i \leq m$,

$$f(x_1, \ldots, x_n) = (x_1[b_{1,1}] \wedge \cdots \wedge x_n[b_{1,n}]) \vee \cdots \vee (x_1[b_{m,1}] \wedge \cdots \wedge x_n[b_{m,n}]),$$

and hence f_n can be computed by a depth 2 alternating circuit, where the first layer consists of m AND-gates, and the second layer consists of a single OR-gate with inputs from all of the gates in the first layer. This circuit has size $m + 1 \leq 2^{n-1} + 1$.

Suppose $m \geq 2^{n-1}$. Then, since

$$
\begin{aligned}
f(x_1, \ldots, x_n) &= \neg(x_1[c_{1,1}] \wedge \cdots \wedge x_n[c_{1,n}]) \vee \cdots \vee (x_1[c_{m',1}] \wedge \cdots \wedge x_n[c_{m',n}]) \\
&= (\overline{x}_1[c_{1,1}] \vee \cdots \vee \overline{x}_n[c_{1,n}]) \wedge \cdots \wedge (\overline{x}_1[c_{m',1}] \vee \cdots \vee \overline{x}_n[c_{m',n}]),
\end{aligned}
$$

f_n can be computed by a depth 2 alternating circuit, where the first layer consists of m' OR-gates, and the second layer consists of a single AND-gate with inputs from all of the gates in the first layer. This circuit has size $m' + 1 = 2^n - m + 1 \leq 2^{n-1} + 1$. $\square$

For example, consider the 4-input parity function, $f(x_1, \ldots, x_4) = x_1 \oplus x_2 \oplus x_3 \oplus x_4$. $T = \{0001, 0010, 0100, 1000, 0111, 1011, 1101, 1110\}$, and hence

$$
\begin{aligned}
f(x_1, \ldots, x_4) &= (\overline{x}_1 \wedge \overline{x}_2 \wedge \overline{x}_3 \wedge x_4) \vee (\overline{x}_1 \wedge \overline{x}_2 \wedge x_3 \wedge \overline{x}_4) \vee \\
&\quad (\overline{x}_1 \wedge x_2 \wedge \overline{x}_3 \wedge \overline{x}_4) \vee (x_1 \wedge \overline{x}_2 \wedge \overline{x}_3 \wedge \overline{x}_4) \vee \\
&\quad (\overline{x}_1 \wedge x_2 \wedge x_3 \wedge x_4) \vee (x_1 \wedge \overline{x}_2 \wedge x_3 \wedge x_4) \vee \\
&\quad (x_1 \wedge x_2 \wedge \overline{x}_3 \wedge x_4) \vee (x_1 \wedge x_2 \wedge x_3 \wedge \overline{x}_4).
\end{aligned}
$$

This gives rise to the circuit shown in Figure 5.6.

We will also find the following variant of Theorem 5.3.1 for multi-output circuits quite useful for designing modules for use in the construction of larger circuits.

THEOREM 5.3.2 For all $f : \mathbf{B}^n \to \mathbf{B}^m$, there is an alternating circuit of size $2^n + m$ and depth 2 that computes f. There is a circuit of this size and depth with AND-gates in the first layer, and a circuit of this size and depth with OR-gates in the first layer.

PROOF: We use the construction of Theorem 5.3.1 using the set T if AND-gates are required in the first layer, and F if OR-gates are required in the first layer. If we use a copy of the circuit from Theorem 5.3.1 for each of the m outputs, we get a circuit of size $m(2^{n-1} + 1)$, with $m2^{n-1}$ gates in the first layer and m in the second layer. However, by construction of the sets T and F, the first layer can contain at most 2^n different gates, one for each member of $\mathbf{B}^n$. Therefore, the size is at most $2^n + m$ and the depth is 2. $\square$

Theorem 5.3.1 compares favourably with Theorem 2.3.1, which gives classical circuits of size $O(2^n)$ and depth $O(n)$. Unfortunately, the circuits constructed in both Theorems have exponential size (that is, size that grows exponentially with n), and hence cannot be considered a practical method for constructing circuits for all but the smallest values of n. It is interesting to ask whether exponential size is necessary. It is certainly necessary if we wish to maintain depth 2. In fact, Theorem 5.3.1 has optimal size for circuits of depth 2.

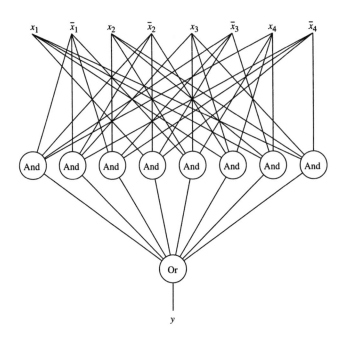

Figure 5.6
An alternating circuit of depth 2 computing $y = x_1 \oplus x_2 \oplus x_3 \oplus x_4$.

THEOREM 5.3.3 Any depth 2 alternating circuit for computing PARITY must have size at least $2^{n-1} + 1$.

PROOF: Suppose there exists a depth 2 circuit C for PARITY. Further suppose that the first level consists of AND-gates, and the second level is an OR-gate (we will return to the other case later).

Each $b = (b_1, \ldots, b_n) \in$ PARITY must make at least one gate on the first level output 1. Therefore, there must exist an AND-gate A on the first level whose inputs are a subset of

$$X = \{x_1[b_1], \ldots, x_n[b_n]\}$$

(using the notation from the proof of Theorem 5.3.1). Suppose A has inputs that form a proper subset of X. Without loss of generality, suppose it computes

$$\text{AND}(x_1[b_1], \ldots, x_{n-1}[b_{n-1}]).$$

Then, A outputs 1 on input $(b_1, \ldots, b_{n-1}, \bar{b}_n)$, which implies (since the second level of C is an OR-gate) that C outputs 1. Therefore, C outputs 1 on inputs $(b_1, \ldots, b_n)$ and

$(b_1, \ldots, b_{n-1}, \overline{b}_n)$. But it is impossible to have both

$$(b_1, \ldots, b_n), (b_1, \ldots, b_{n-1}, \overline{b}_n) \in \text{PARITY}.$$

Therefore, A must have inputs exactly X.

We conclude that there must be a distinct AND-gate on the first level for each member of PARITY. Therefore, there are at least 2^{n-1} gates on the first level, and at least $2^{n-1}+1$ gates in all (it is obvious that no depth 1 circuit can compute parity).

We now return to the case in which C has OR-gates on the first level and an AND-gate on the second level. First, use Theorem 5.1.1 to convert C into a circuit for the complement of PARITY with AND-gates on the first level and an OR-gate on the second level, and then repeat the above argument using the complement of PARITY instead of PARITY. $\square$

An obvious question to ask is whether we can reduce the size of the circuit described in Theorem 5.3.1, and trade it for increased depth. The answer is that this is not possible beyond a certain size: some functions intrinsically require exponential size circuits.

THEOREM 5.3.4 There exists a function that requires an alternating circuit of size $\Omega(2^{n/2})$.

PROOF: Let $\mathcal{C}(z, n)$ be the number of circuits with z gates and n inputs. How large is $\mathcal{C}(z, n)$? There are less than $2^{z(z-1)}$ different ways of wiring together z gates (since this is the number of directed graphs on z vertices), and at most 3^{nz} different ways of wiring them to the inputs (each of z gates can be connected to x_i, $\overline{x}_i$, or neither of the above, for $1 \leq i \leq n$). There are at most z ways of choosing the output gate, and 2^z ways of choosing the functions that the gates compute. We have counted each circuit on z gates at least once, so therefore

$$\mathcal{C}(z, n) \leq z 2^{z^2} 3^{nz}. \tag{5.3.1}$$

Clearly there are 2^{2^n} Boolean functions with n inputs (on each of the 2^n inputs there are 2 possible outputs). If every Boolean function on n inputs can be computed by a circuit with z gates, then

$$\mathcal{C}(z, n) \geq 2^{2^n}. \tag{5.3.2}$$

It cannot be the case that $z \leq n$, for otherwise by Equation (5.3.1), $\mathcal{C}(z, n) \leq 2^{O(n^2)}$, which contradicts Equation (5.3.2). Therefore, it must be the case that $z \geq n$. Then, by Equation (5.3.1), $\mathcal{C}(z, n) \leq 2^{O(z^2)}$, which by Equation 5.3.2 implies that $2^{O(z^2)} \geq 2^{2^n}$, that is, $z = \Omega(2^{n/2})$. $\square$

Can this size lower bound, which is polynomially smaller than the upper bound of Theorem 5.3.1, be met? Surprisingly it can be met with a circuit of depth 3.

THEOREM 5.3.5 If $f: \mathbf{B}^n \to \mathbf{B}$, then there is an alternating circuit of size $O(2^{n/2})$ and depth 3 that computes f.

PROOF: Let $f: \mathbf{B}^n \to \mathbf{B}$. Without loss of generality, assume n is even (a similar approach will work when n is odd, see Problem 1). We will construct a circuit for f using a standard divide-and-conquer technique.

For each $x_1, \ldots, x_{n/2} \in \mathbf{B}$, define $g(x_1, \ldots, x_{n/2}): \mathbf{B}^{n/2} \to \mathbf{B}$ by

$$g(x_1, \ldots, x_{n/2})(x_{n/2+1}, \ldots, x_n) = f(x_1, \ldots, x_n).$$

By Theorem 5.3.2, the $2^{n/2}$ functions $g(x_1, \ldots, x_{n/2})$ for $x_1, \ldots, x_{n/2} \in \mathbf{B}$ can be computed by a single multi-output circuit of depth 2 and size $2^{n/2+1}$, with the first layer consisting of OR-gates and the second layer consisting of AND-gates.

For each $b_1, \ldots, b_{n/2} \in \mathbf{B}$, define $h(b_1, \ldots, b_{n/2}): \mathbf{B}^n \to \mathbf{B}$ by

$$h(b_1, \ldots, b_{n/2})(x_1, \ldots, x_n) = (x_i = b_i \text{ for } 1 \le i \le n/2) \wedge$$
$$g(x_1, \ldots, x_{n/2})(x_{n/2+1}, \ldots, x_n).$$

The circuit $\mathcal{C}$ constructed above can easily be modified to compute the $2^{n/2}$ functions $h(b_1, \ldots, b_{n/2})$ for $b_1, \ldots, b_{n/2} \in \mathbf{B}$ by simply taking the AND-gate that computes $g(b_1, \ldots, b_{n/2})(x_{n/2}, \ldots, x_n)$, and giving it extra inputs from $x_1[b_1], \ldots, x_{n/2}[b_{n/2}]$ (using the notation from the proof of Theorem 5.3.1). The resulting circuit still has depth 2 and size $2^{n/2+1}$.

Finally, we note that

$$f(x_1, \ldots, x_n) = h(\underbrace{0, \ldots, 0}_{n/2})(x_1, \ldots, x_n) \vee \cdots \vee h(\underbrace{1, \ldots, 1}_{n/2})(x_1, \ldots, x_n),$$

and f can therefore be computed by a circuit of depth 3 and size $2^{n/2+1} + 1$. $\square$

For example, Figures 5.7 and 5.8 show the construction of a depth 3 circuit for a function f with 4 inputs and the input-output behaviour shown in Table 5.1. Figure 5.7 shows the two steps in the construction of the circuit for computing the functions $g(0,0)$, $g(0,1)$, $g(1,0)$, $g(1,1)$. Figure 5.8 shows the resulting circuit for f.

x_1	x_2	x_3	x_4	$f(x_1, x_2, x_3, x_4)$	x_1	x_2	x_3	x_4	$f(x_1, x_2, x_3, x_4)$
0	0	0	0	0	1	0	0	0	0
0	0	0	1	1	1	0	0	1	0
0	0	1	0	0	1	0	1	0	0
0	0	1	1	0	1	0	1	1	1
0	1	0	0	0	1	1	0	0	1
0	1	0	1	1	1	1	0	1	1
0	1	1	0	0	1	1	1	0	0
0	1	1	1	1	1	1	1	1	0

Table 5.1
Truth table for a 4-input Boolean function f.

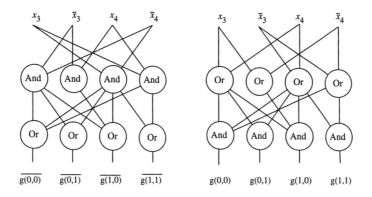

Figure 5.7
Construction of alternating circuit using Theorem 5.3.5 for the function f defined in Table 5.1. Left: Circuit for complement of $g(0,0)$, $g(0,1)$, $g(1,0)$, $g(1,1)$. Right: Circuit for $g(0,0)$, $g(0,1)$, $g(1,0)$, $g(1,1)$.

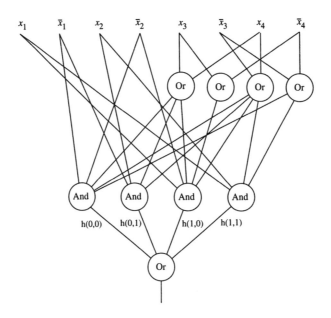

Figure 5.8
Construction of alternating circuit using Theorem 5.3.5 for the function f defined in Table 5.1. The
top two layers of the circuit compute $h(0,0)$, $h(0,1)$, $h(1,0)$, $h(1,1)$, and should be compared with
Figure 5.7.

5.4   Polynomial Size

The problem with the methods for circuit design presented in the previous section (Theorem 5.3.1, Theorem 5.3.2 and Theorem 5.3.5) is that they produce circuits whose size
grows exponentially with n. Such a method cannot be called scalable, since such circuits
will only be buildable for very small values of n, and great advances in technology will be
required for even a modest increase in the size of the problems tackled. It is reasonable
to expect that only circuits whose size grows subexponentially with n stand any chance
of being practical in the forseeable future. Unfortunately, as we saw in Theorem 5.3.4,
not all functions have polynomial size circuits. It is interesting to consider those that do.

We saw in Section 5.3 that a *problem* is a set of input and output requirements (Figure 5.9 (a)). If we have in mind a computational model, and what it means for a problem
to be computed in that model (Figure 5.9 (b)), we can define a class of problems that
can be computed by it (Figure 5.9 (c)). We will meet two such definitions in this section,
and more in subsequent sections.

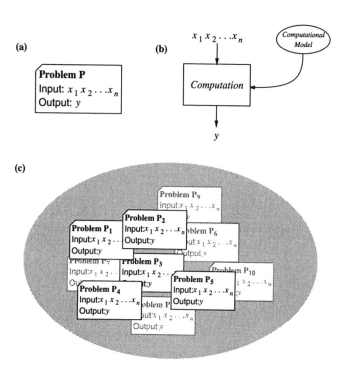

Figure 5.9
(a) A problem, (b) computation of a problem, and (c) a problem class.

The first such class of problems is $\mathcal{P}$, defined to be the set of decision problems which can be solved by an alternating circuit of polynomial size, that is, a circuit $C = (C_1, C_2, \ldots)$, where for some $c \in \mathbf{N}$ and all $n \geq 1$, the size of C_n is bounded above by n^c (see Figure 5.10). We will call the problems in $\mathcal{P}$ *tractable* and those not in $\mathcal{P}$ *intractable*, for the reasons outlined in the first paragraph of this section.

To enhance readability we will describe decision problems not as being functions of a sequence of bits, but as functions of mathematical objects wherever appropriate. This is reasonable since all finite mathematical objects can be encoded as a sequence of bits. This approach is useful in that it adds a level of abstraction that insulates the reader from messy details at the bit level. However, there is a pitfall to be avoided here. If the encoding scheme is suitably sparse, then every function that is computable by an alternating circuit can be made a member of $\mathcal{P}$. For example, if a function $f : \mathbf{N} \to \mathbf{B}$ is computable in size 2^n when the input is encoded in binary, then simply encode it

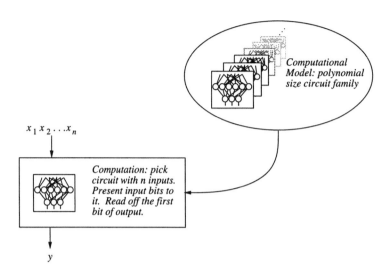

Figure 5.10
Computation for problem class $\mathcal{P}$.

in unary. The number of gates will then be linear in the number of inputs. However, such chicanery will not enable us to compute useful functions with a modest amount of hardware. It is reasonable to insist that inputs encode a sufficiently large amount of information about the mathematical objects in question. We will insist that the input encoding is sufficiently dense, that is, it is not more than polynomially larger than the tersest description of the input.

Let $\mathcal{NP}$ denote the set of existential decision problems of the form:

> Given a mathematical object x, does there exist a mathematical object y no more than polynomially larger than x such that $f(x, y) = 1$, where $f \in \mathcal{P}$.

If such a y exists, and an adversary claimed to have found one, then that claim could be verified with a polynomial size circuit for f. Restating the problems in terms of binary encodings rather than mathematical objects:

> For a fixed $c \in \mathbb{N}$ and $f \in \mathcal{P}$, on input $x_1, \ldots, x_n$, does there exist $x_{n+1}, \ldots, x_{n^c}$ such that $f(x_1, \ldots, x_{n^c}) = 1$.

(See Figure 5.11.)

One of the most important and interesting open problems in computational complexity

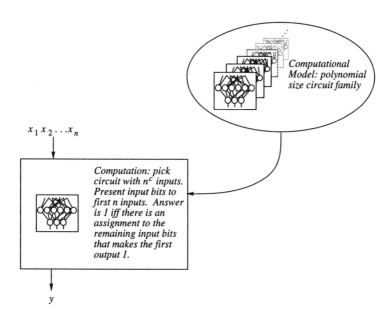

$x_1 x_2 \ldots x_n$

Computation: pick circuit with n^c inputs. Present input bits to first n inputs. Answer is 1 iff there is an assignment to the remaining input bits that makes the first output 1.

Computational Model: polynomial size circuit family

y

Figure 5.11
Computation for problem class $\mathcal{NP}$.

theory is whether $\mathcal{P} = \mathcal{NP}$, that is, whether existential questions that can be verified in polynomial size can be solved in polynomial size. It is clear that $\mathcal{P} \subseteq \mathcal{NP}$, since every problem in $\mathcal{P}$ can be rephrased in the appropriate form with y being the empty string in the "mathematical objects" version of the definition of $\mathcal{NP}$, and $c = 1$ in the "binary encoding" version of the definition. Furthermore, every problem in $\mathcal{NP}$ can be solved in exponential[1] size by Theorem 5.3.1. The relationship between $\mathcal{P}$ and $\mathcal{NP}$ is summarized in Figure 5.12.

It is possible to encode any finite alternating circuit $C_n = (V, X, Y, E, \ell)$ as a finite sequence of bits using the encoding scheme described earlier in this section. However, the following encoding scheme is slightly easier to manipulate. Suppose, for simplicity, that $Y = \{y\}$. Let $C = (V, X, Y, E, \ell)$ be a finite alternating circuit, where $V = g_1, \ldots, g_m$, and for $1 \leq i, j \leq m$, if $(g_i, g_j) \in E$, then $i < j$. Gate g_i is represented as a string of $2n + i + 2$ bits

$$\alpha_1 \alpha_2 \alpha_3 \beta_1 \gamma_1 \ldots \beta_n \gamma_n \delta_1 \ldots \delta_{i-1}.$$

---

[1] We take exponential to mean 2^{n^c} for some $c \in \mathbb{N}$.

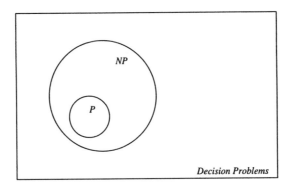

Figure 5.12
The classes $\mathcal{P}$ and $\mathcal{NP}$.

The first three bits $\alpha_1\alpha_2\alpha_3$ represent $\ell(g_i)$, with

$$\ell(g_i) = \text{AND} \quad \text{iff} \quad \alpha_1\alpha_2\alpha_3 = 001$$
$$\ell(g_i) = \text{OR} \quad \text{iff} \quad \alpha_1\alpha_2\alpha_3 = 010$$
$$\ell(g_i) = 0 \quad \text{iff} \quad \alpha_1\alpha_2\alpha_3 = 011$$
$$\ell(g_i) = 1 \quad \text{iff} \quad \alpha_1\alpha_2\alpha_3 = 100.$$

The next $2n$ bits $\beta_1\gamma_1\ldots\beta_n\gamma_n$ represent connections between g_i and the inputs, with

$$(x_j, g_i) \in E \quad \text{iff} \quad \beta_j = 1$$
$$(\overline{x}_j, g_i) \in E \quad \text{iff} \quad \gamma_j = 1.$$

The next $i - 1$ bits $\delta_1\ldots\delta_{i-1}$ represent connections between $g_1, \ldots, g_{i-1}$ and g_i, with $(g_j, g_i) \in E$ iff $\delta_j = 1$.

Each input x_i is represented by a string of $2i + 1$ zeros, and $\overline{x}_i$ is represented by a string of $2i + 2$ zeros. The output y is represented by a string

$$\alpha_1\alpha_2\alpha_3\beta_1\gamma_1\ldots\beta_n\gamma_n\delta_1\ldots\delta_{i-1},$$

where $\alpha_1\alpha_2\alpha_3 = 101$, $\beta_i = \gamma_i = 0$ for $1 \leq i \leq n$, and $(g_j, y) \in E$ iff $\delta_j = 1$. The circuit C is represented by concatenating together, in order, the representations of $x_1, \overline{x}_1, \ldots, x_n, \overline{x}_n,\ g_1, \ldots, g_m, y$. Thus, for example, the circuit in Figure 5.13 (a) is represented by the string 00000000000000000000011001001011000011010000010101000-01000001100010000001101010000000010, which can be decomposed as follows:

$$\underbrace{000}_{x_1}\ \underbrace{0000}_{\overline{x}_1}\ \underbrace{00000}_{x_2}\ \underbrace{000000}_{\overline{x}_2}$$

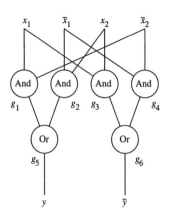

Figure 5.13
A small alternating circuit.

Circuits can be used to solve problems involving circuits. For example, it is easy to construct an alternating circuit $C = (C_1, C_2, \ldots)$ which checks that its input is the valid encoding of an alternating circuit. Note that many of the C_i will output 0 no matter what the input, since valid encodings only come in certain sizes. This is no problem, but it leads us naturally to our next question.

In general, finite alternating circuits that output 0 in response to all inputs are usually not of much use, and can be replaced by a single gate that always outputs 0. It would be nice to be able to distinguish these unnecessarily complicated circuits from any other. We will say that a finite circuit is *satisfiable* if there is an input which makes it output 1. The *satisfiability problem* for alternating circuits (abbreviated SAT) is the problem of determining whether a given alternating circuit is satisfiable. We will consider the problem of constructing a circuit which solves the satisfiability problem, that is, a circuit which on input a binary string encoding a finite alternating circuit C, outputs 1 iff there is an input to C that makes C output 1. We will assume that the circuit outputs 0 if the input does not encode a valid alternating circuit.

SAT is interesting for a number of reasons. Suppose we have two finite alternating circuits C_1 and C_2, each with n inputs, and wish to know whether they are equivalent in

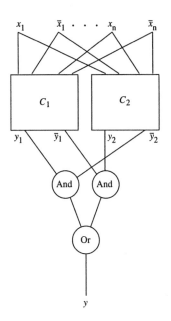

Figure 5.14
An alternating circuit that is satisfiable iff C_1 is not equivalent to C_2.

the sense that they both compute the same function, or conversely, whether or not there is some input on which they give different outputs. Suppose C_1 has output y_1 and C_2 has output y_2, and that (as in the proof of Theorem 5.1.1), their complements $\bar{y}_1$ and $\bar{y}_2$ are also available. We can solve the problem of whether C_1 and C_2 are equivalent if we can determine whether the circuit shown in Figure 5.14 is satisfiable. This is an example of using a solution to one problem (satisfiability) to solve another (equivalence). More formally, we will say that the equivalence problem is *reducible to* the satisfiability problem.

Let us examine this concept of reducibility more closely. First, let us formally define the satisfiability and equivalence problems as decision problems.

SATISFIABILITY (SAT)
INSTANCE: An alternating circuit C.
QUESTION: Is C satisfiable?

NONEQUIVALENCE (NONEQ)

INSTANCE: Alternating circuits C_1, C_2.

QUESTION: Is there an input for which the outputs of C_1 and C_2 differ?

In general, we will say that problem A is *reducible* to problem B if for every input x there is an input $f(x)$ such that $x \in A$ iff $f(x) \in B$. For example, an instance of NONEQ consists of two alternating circuits C_1 and C_2. The corresponding instance of SAT is the alternating circuit C shown in Figure 5.14. If $(C_1, C_2) \in$ NONEQ then there is an input that makes $y_1 = \bar{y}_2$ and $y_2 = \bar{y}_1$, and hence at least one of the extra AND-gates will output 1, which makes the output $y = 1$. Conversely, if $(C_1, C_2) \notin$ NONEQ then for all inputs, $y_1 = y_2$ and $\bar{y}_1 = \bar{y}_2$, and hence neither of the extra AND-gates will output 1, which makes the output $y = 0$. Therefore, $(C_1, C_2) \in$ NONEQ iff $C \in$ SAT.

In general, we will say that problem A is *$\mathcal{P}$-reducible* to problem B if A is reducible to B, and there is a polynomial size circuit which computes the reduction f (that is, a polynomial size circuit that given an instance of A as input, outputs the corresponding instance of B). We will write $A \leq_p B$ to denote "A is $\mathcal{P}$-reducible to B". Clearly NONEQ $\leq_p$ SAT, since it is easy to construct a polynomial size circuit which, when given an input encoding C_1 and C_2, outputs an encoding of the circuit shown in Figure 5.14 (all it needs to do is insert a few zeros into the descriptions of gates in C_2, and add a few extra gates connecting C_1 and C_2). $\mathcal{P}$-reducibility is an important technique for constructing polynomial size circuits for new problems from polynomial size circuits for old problems.

LEMMA 5.4.1 If $A \leq_p B$, and $B \in \mathcal{P}$, then $A \in \mathcal{P}$.

PROOF: Suppose $B \in \mathcal{P}$, that is, there is a circuit for B of size n^b, for some $b \in \mathbf{N}$. Further suppose there is a circuit C of size n^c, for some $c \in \mathbf{N}$, that reduces A to B. A circuit for A can be obtained by combining the polynomial size circuit for B and the polynomial size circuit C which reduces A to B, as shown in Figure 5.15. Since C has size n^c, C has at most n^c outputs. Therefore, the circuit for B has size n^{bc}, and so the entire circuit has polynomial size, $n^{bc} + n^c$. $\square$

Consider the following problem, called the *circuit value problem*:

CIRCUIT VALUE (CVP)

INSTANCE: An n-input alternating circuit C, and $x_1, \ldots, x_n \in \mathbf{B}$.

QUESTION: What is the output of C on input $x_1, \ldots, x_n$?

It is clear that CVP $\in \mathcal{P}$, and it can be deduced that SAT $\in \mathcal{NP}$.

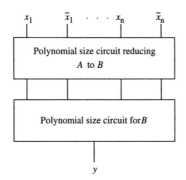

Figure 5.15
The polynomial size circuit for A, given $A \leq_p B$ and $B \in \mathcal{P}$.

LEMMA 5.4.2 The following two inclusions hold:

1. CVP $\in \mathcal{P}$.
2. SAT $\in \mathcal{NP}$.

PROOF: Suppose $C = (V, X, Y, E, \ell)$ is an alternating circuit of size z and depth d, where $X = \{x_1, \ldots, x_n\}$. Suppose $v_1, \ldots, v_n \in \mathbf{B}$. The following algorithm computes a value $v[g]$ for all $g \in V \cup X$.

1.   **for** $i := 1$ **to** n **do** $v[x_i] := v_i$
2.   **for** $i := 1$ **to** d **do**
3.   **for** each gate g at level i **do**
4.   Let $g_1 \in X \cup V$ be such that $(g_1, g) \in E$
5.   Let $g_2 \in X \cup V$ be such that $(g_2, g) \in E$ and $g_1 \neq g_2$, if one exists
6.   **if** $\ell(g) = $ AND **then** $v[g] := v[g_1] \wedge v[g_2]$
7.   **else if** $\ell(g) = $ OR **then** $v[g] := v[g_1] \vee v[g_2]$
8.   **else if** $\ell(g) = $ NOT **then** $v[g] := \neg v[g_1]$

It can be proved by induction on the level of g that on termination, for all $g \in V \cup X$, $v[g]$ contains the value of g on input $v_1, \ldots, v_n \in \mathbf{B}$. Lines 4–8 each take $O(1)$ time. Therefore, the for-loop on lines 2–8 takes $O(z)$ time. Line 1 takes $O(n)$ time. Therefore, the algorithm takes time $O(n + z)$, which is polynomial in the size of C. Therefore, by Theorem 2.3.3, there is a polynomial size circuit for CVP, and hence CVP $\in \mathcal{P}$, as required in part 1 of this lemma..

Hence, SAT $\in \mathcal{NP}$ (simply take f in the definition of $\mathcal{NP}$ to be the CVP-function). This proves part 2 of the lemma. $\square$

It is hardly surprising that NONEQ $\leq_p$ SAT, since all members of $\mathcal{NP}$ are $\mathcal{P}$-reducible to SAT. We will say that a problem is $\mathcal{NP}$-*hard* if every problem in $\mathcal{NP}$ is $\mathcal{P}$-reducible to it, and that it is $\mathcal{NP}$-*complete* if it is $\mathcal{NP}$-hard and a member of $\mathcal{NP}$.

THEOREM 5.4.3 SAT is $\mathcal{NP}$-complete.

PROOF: We have already established that SAT $\in \mathcal{NP}$ (Lemma 5.4.2 (2)). It remains to show that SAT is $\mathcal{NP}$-hard, that is, for all $A \in \mathcal{NP}$, $A \leq_p$ SAT. Suppose $A \in \mathcal{NP}$ (see Figure 5.16 (a)). Then, there exists a constant $c \in \mathbf{N}$ and a circuit family $C_A = (C_1, C_2, \ldots)$ such that for every $n \in \mathbf{N}$ there is a circuit C_{n^c} such that for all $(a_1, \ldots, a_n) \in \mathbf{B}$, $(a_1, \ldots, a_n) \in A$ iff there exists $a_{n+1}, \ldots, a_{n^c}$ such that the output of C_{n^c} on input $a_1, \ldots, a_{n^c}$ is 1 (see Figure 5.16 (b)).

Suppose $a_1, \ldots, a_n \in \mathbf{B}$. We construct a Boolean circuit as follows. Let $C = C_{n^c}$, $C = (V, X, Y, E, \ell)$ where $X = \{x_1, \ldots, x_{n^c}\}$ and $V = \{g_1, \ldots, g_s\}$. Construct a new circuit $C' = (V', X', Y', E', \ell')$ from C by replacing the first n inputs with fixed Boolean values representing $a_1, \ldots, a_n$, and leaving the remaining inputs as inputs to the new circuit (see Figure 5.16 (c)). That is,

$$
\begin{aligned}
V' &= V \cup \{g_i', \overline{g}_i' \mid 1 \leq i \leq n\} \\
X' &= \{x_{n+1}, \ldots, x_{n^c}\} \\
(g_i, g_j) &\in E' \text{ iff } (g_i, g_j) \in E & 1 \leq i, j \leq s \\
(x_i, g_j) &\in E' \text{ iff } (x_i, g_j) \in E & n+1 \leq i \leq n^c,\ 1 \leq j \leq s \\
(\overline{x}_i, g_j) &\in E' \text{ iff } (\overline{x}_i, g_j) \in E & n+1 \leq i \leq n^c,\ 1 \leq j \leq s \\
(g_i', g_j) &\in E' \text{ iff } (x_i, g_j) \in E & 1 \leq i \leq n,\ 1 \leq j \leq s \\
(\overline{g}_i', g_j) &\in E' \text{ iff } (\overline{x}_i, g_j) \in E & 1 \leq i \leq n,\ 1 \leq j \leq s \\
\ell'(g_i) &= \ell(g_i) & 1 \leq i \leq s \\
\ell'(g_i') &= a_i & 1 \leq i \leq n \\
\ell'(\overline{g}_i') &= \neg a_i & 1 \leq i \leq n.
\end{aligned}
$$

Clearly the output of C on input $a_1, \ldots, a_{n^c}$ is equal to the output of C' on input $a_{n+1}, \ldots, a_{n^c}$. Therefore, $(a_1, \ldots, a_n) \in A$ iff there exists $a_{n+1}, \ldots, a_{n^c}$ such that the output of C_{n^c} on input $a_1, \ldots, a_{n^c}$ is 1, iff there exists $a_1, \ldots, a_{n^c}$ such that the output of C' on input $a_{n+1}, \ldots, a_{n^c}$ is 1, iff C' is satisfiable. Furthermore, there is a polynomial size circuit which, on input $a_1, \ldots, a_n$ will output a description of C' (see Figure 5.16 (d)). That is, $A \leq_p$ SAT. $\square$

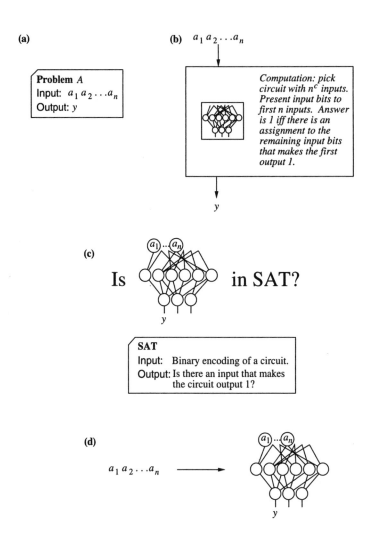

Figure 5.16
(a) The problem A, (b) computation of $A \in \mathcal{NP}$, (c) an instance of SAT equivalent to A, and (d) the reduction from A to SAT.

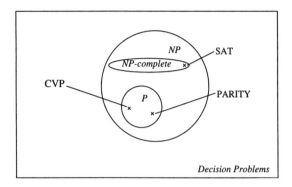

Figure 5.17
$\mathcal{NP}$-complete problems.

$\mathcal{NP}$-complete problems are interesting since, by Lemma 5.4.1, if one of them is in $\mathcal{P}$, then $\mathcal{P} = \mathcal{NP}$. It is widely conjectured that $\mathcal{P} \neq \mathcal{NP}$. If this conjecture is true, then by Theorem 5.4.3, SAT requires exponential size circuits, and Figure 5.17 depicts the true state of affairs.

There is a particularly easy way to prove new $\mathcal{NP}$-completeness theorems from old ones:

LEMMA 5.4.4 If $A \leq_p B$ and $B \leq_p C$, then $A \leq_p C$.

PROOF: The proof of this result is almost identical to that of Lemma 5.4.1. The details are left to the reader (Problem 2). □

THEOREM 5.4.5 If B is $\mathcal{NP}$-hard and $B \leq_p C$, then C is also $\mathcal{NP}$-hard.

PROOF: Since B is $\mathcal{NP}$-hard, for all problems $A \in \mathcal{NP}$, $A \leq_p B$. Since $B \leq_p C$, by Lemma 5.4.4, $A \leq_p C$. Therefore, C is $\mathcal{NP}$-hard. □

Therefore, to prove that a new problem C is $\mathcal{NP}$-complete, it is sufficient to show that $C \in \mathcal{NP}$ and that $B \leq_p C$ for some known $\mathcal{NP}$-hard problem B.

5.5 Problems

1. Complete the proof of Theorem 5.3.5 when n is odd. Show that the size is $3 \cdot 2^{(n-1)/2} + 1$.

2. Prove that "$\leq_p$" is transitive (Lemma 5.4.4), that is, if $A \leq_p B$ and $B \leq_p C$, then $A \leq_p C$.

3. Prove that NONEQ $\in \mathcal{NP}$.

4. Show that nonuniformity in $\mathcal{P}$ can the pushed back to the inputs. That is, show that any language that can be recognized by a polynomial-size circuit can be recognize by a polynomial-size circuit which is $\mathcal{P}$-uniform except for a single layer of gates that ignore their inputs and output either 0 or 1 continuously.

5.6   Bibliographic Notes

The reader who has already been exposed to computational complexity theory will notice that the standard definitions of the complexity classes found in these texts differ from those used in this chapter in one important way: our complexity classes are *nonuniform*. The complexity class that we have called $\mathcal{P}$ is more commonly called $\mathcal{P}/\text{poly}$ (see, for example, Karp and Lipton [73]).

Nonuniform alternating circuits are a natural machine model upon which to base a nonuniform complexity theory. For instance, the proof of Cook's Theorem (Theorem 5.4.3) is particularly painless. Turing machines and the concept of nondeterministic computation always seem to strike the uninitiated reader as arbitrary, puzzling, and confusing, and certainly contribute to the fact that the standard proof of Cook's Theorem is, as far as the novice is concerned, intricate and tedious. The uniform versions of Theorems 5.4.3 and 6.2.4 are due to Cook [33]. For more information on the standard theory of $\mathcal{NP}$-completeness, see Garey and Johnson [46].

Theorem 5.3.3 is due to Lupanov [80, 81]. Theorem 5.3.5 appears without proof in Redkin [112]. Problem 1 is from Spielman [132].

6 Small, Shallow Alternating Circuits

Chapter 5 was primarily concerned with the size of alternating circuits. Now we turn our attention to the depth. More specifically, motivated by the empirical observation that important circuits in the brain appear to have very few layers of gates, we are interested in alternating circuits of polynomial size with depth very much smaller than size. Section 6.1 considers alternating circuits with of polynomial size and polylog depth, and contains an introduction to the theory of $\mathcal{P}$-completeness. Here, we meet the circuit complexity classes $\mathcal{AC}$ and $\mathcal{NC}$. It appears that some important circuits in the brain have very small depth, perhaps only 3 or 4. Therefore, although it is reasonable to have size scale in our circuit model, it is perhaps unnecessary to have depth scale. Section 6.2 is devoted to alternating circuits of polynomial size and constant depth, in which we meet the circuit complexity class $\mathcal{AC}^0$. Section 6.3 is devoted to the $\mathcal{AC}^0$ hierarchy, in which these alternating circuits are grouped in increasing order of depth.

6.1 Polynomial Size and Polylog Depth

Some of the polynomial size circuits for problems in $\mathcal{P}$ have small depth, for example, the circuit for the parity problem demonstrated in Section 5.4 has size $O(n)$, but depth exponentially smaller at $O(\log n)$. While all problems in $\mathcal{P}$ have polynomial depth circuits (if the depth were greater than a polynomial, then so would the size be), it is interesting to consider which of them have depth exponentially smaller than size, that is, growing polynomially with $\log n$. We will use the notation $\log^c n$ to denote the function $(\log n)^c$, and use the term *polylog* to denote a function of the form $\log^c n$ for some $c \in \mathbf{R}$.

Let $\mathcal{AC}$ denote the set of decision problems which can be solved by an alternating circuit of polynomial size and polylog depth. For example, we will see that the parity function can be computed in linear size and logarithmic depth.

LEMMA 6.1.1 If "$\circ$" is an associative binary operation over $\mathbf{B}$ that can be computed by a classical circuit of depth d and size z, then for all $n \in naturals$, $x_1 \circ x_2 \circ \cdots \circ x_n$ can be computed by a classical circuit of depth $d\lceil \log n \rceil$, and size $(n-1)z$.

PROOF: We will construct a circuit C_n for computing $x_1 \circ x_2 \circ \cdots \circ x_n$ from copies of the circuit C for computing two-input "$\circ$". If $n = 2$, a single copy of C suffices, giving depth and size 1. If $n > 2$, C_n is constructed from a copy of $C(\lceil n/2 \rceil)$ and a copy of $C(\lfloor n/2 \rfloor)$, with their outputs connected to a single copy of C (see Figure 6.1). For example, Figure 6.2 shows the construction for $n = 11$.

If $D(n)$ is the depth of C_n, then $D(2) = d$ and for all $n > 2$, $D(n) = D(\lceil n/2 \rceil) + d$. It can be verified by induction on n that $D(n) = d\lceil \log n \rceil$. If $S(n)$ is the size of C_n,

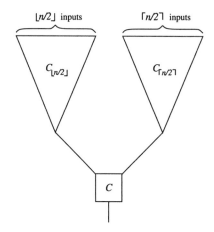

Figure 6.1
Recursive construction of C_n from Lemma 6.1.1.

then $S(2) = z$ and for all $n > 2$, $S(n) = S(\lceil n/2 \rceil) + S(\lfloor n/2 \rfloor) + z$. It can be verified by induction on n that $S(n) = (n-1)z$. $\square$

THEOREM 6.1.2 The n-input parity function $x_1 \oplus \cdots \oplus x_n$ can be computed in size $4n - 5$ and depth $\lceil \log n \rceil + 1$.

PROOF: Two depth 2, size 6 alternating circuits for computing the parity of two inputs are shown in Figure 6.3. Either can be used as the building block in a classical circuit to compute the n-input parity function $x_1 \oplus \cdots \oplus x_n$ in depth $2\lceil \log n \rceil$ and size $6n - 6$, by Lemma 6.1.1. By alternating between the sub-circuits in Figure 6.3, can use compression (Theorem 5.2.2) to save almost half of the layers. This results in a circuit of depth $\lceil \log n \rceil + 1$ and size $4n - 2$. The constructed circuit computes both parity and its complement. Since only parity is required, 3 redundant gates can be removed to give the required size. $\square$

For example, Figure 6.4 shows the classical parity circuit on 4 inputs. and Figure 6.5 the alternating circuit constructed using Theorem 6.1.2. Note that one more layer can be saved using inversion (Theorem 5.2.3) in return for an increase in size to $O(n^2)$.

The polynomial size condition on $\mathcal{AC}$ circuits implies that $\mathcal{AC} \subseteq \mathcal{P}$, but it is unknown whether this containment is proper. It is widely conjectured that $\mathcal{P} \neq \mathcal{AC}$. Figure 6.6

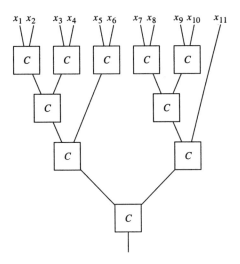

Figure 6.2
The circuit C_n from Lemma 6.1.1 with $n = 11$.

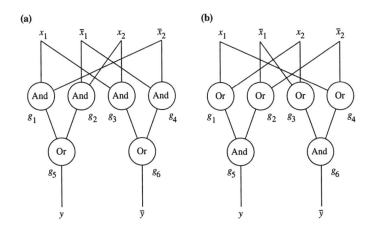

Figure 6.3
Two alternating circuits computing $y = x_1 \oplus x_2$ and its complement.

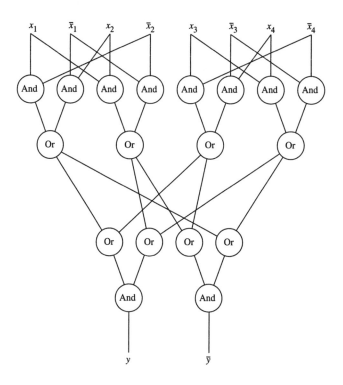

Figure 6.4
A classical circuit computing $y = x_1 \oplus x_2 \oplus x_3 \oplus x_4$ and its complement.

shows the conjectured relationship between $\mathcal{AC}$ and $\mathcal{P}$.

Although it is not known for sure whether there is a problem in $\mathcal{P}$ that is not in $\mathcal{AC}$, there is a good candidate: the circuit value problem introduced in Section 5.4. We say that a problem A is $\mathcal{AC}$-*reducible* to problem B, written $A \leq_c B$, if there exists a function f computable by an alternating circuit of polynomial size and polylog depth such that for every x, $x \in A$ iff $f(x) \in B$.

LEMMA 6.1.3 If $A \leq_c B$, and $B \in \mathcal{AC}$, then $A \in \mathcal{AC}$.

PROOF: The proof is similar to that of Lemma 5.4.1. Suppose $B \in \mathcal{AC}$, that is, there is a circuit for B of size n^b and depth $\log^{b'} n$, for some $b, b' \in \mathbf{N}$. Further suppose there is a circuit C of size n^c and depth $\log^{c'} n$, for some $c, c' \in \mathbf{N}$, which reduces A to B. A circuit for A can be obtained by combining the polynomial size, polylog depth circuit for B and the polynomial size, polylog depth circuit C which reduces A to B, as was shown

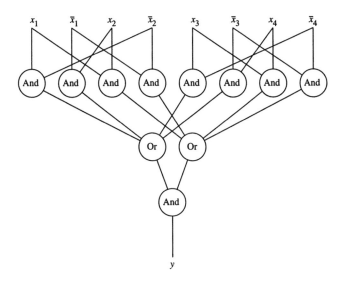

Figure 6.5
An alternating circuit computing $y = x_1 \oplus x_2 \oplus x_3 \oplus x_4$.

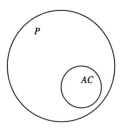

Figure 6.6
The classes $\mathcal{AC}$ and $\mathcal{P}$.

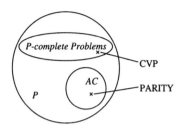

Figure 6.7
$\mathcal{P}$-complete problems.

previously in Figure 5.15. Since C has size n^c, C has at most n^c outputs. Therefore, the circuit for B has size n^{bc} and depth $c \log^{b'} n$, and so the entire circuit has polynomial size and polylog depth. $\Box$

We will say that a problem is $\mathcal{P}$-*hard* if every problem in $\mathcal{P}$ is $\mathcal{AC}$-reducible to it, and that it is $\mathcal{P}$-*complete* if it is $\mathcal{P}$-hard and a member of $\mathcal{P}$.

THEOREM 6.1.4 CVP is $\mathcal{P}$-complete.

PROOF: The proof is similar to that of Theorem 5.4.3. We have already established (see Lemma 5.4.2 (1)) that CVP $\in \mathcal{P}$. It remains to show that CVP is $\mathcal{P}$-hard, that is, for all $A \in \mathcal{P}$, $A \leq_c$ CVP. Suppose $A \in \mathcal{P}$. Then, there is a polynomial size circuit which recognizes A. It is easy to construct a circuit of polynomial size and constant depth (it consists purely of constant-gates which output either 0 or 1 regardless of their input) which inputs $x_1, \ldots, x_n$ and outputs a description of A with a copy of the input $x_1, \ldots, x_n$. The output is an instance of CVP which is a member of CVP iff $x \in A$. Therefore, $A \leq_c$ CVP. $\Box$

$\mathcal{P}$-complete problems are interesting since, by Lemma 6.1.3, if one of them is in $\mathcal{AC}$, then $\mathcal{AC} = \mathcal{P}$. If the conjecture that $\mathcal{AC} \neq \mathcal{P}$ is correct, then by Theorem 6.1.4, the circuit value problem requires polynomial depth if it is to be solved by polynomial size circuits, and Figure 6.7 reflects the true state of affairs.

Define $\mathcal{AC}^k$ to be the set of problems that can be solved by alternating circuits of polynomial size, and depth $O(\log^k n)$, for $k \geq 0$. Clearly $\mathcal{AC}^k \subseteq \mathcal{AC}^{k+1}$ for $k \geq 0$, and

$$\mathcal{AC} = \cup_{k \geq 0} \mathcal{AC}^k.$$

The relationship between classical and alternating circuits is obvious: a classical circuit is a special case of an AND-OR circuit, and furthermore:

THEOREM 6.1.5 For every finite AND-OR circuit of size s and depth d there is a finite classical circuit of size $s^2 + sn$ and depth $d\lceil\log(s+n)\rceil$.

PROOF: Let C be a finite AND-OR circuit of size s, depth d, and fan-in f. The new circuit C' is constructed by replacing every AND-gate in C with a subcircuit of fan-in 2 AND-gates of size $f-1$ and depth $\lceil\log f\rceil$ from Lemma 6.1.1. and similarly for OR-gates. Since $f \le s + n$, the result follows. □

There are classical (bounded fan-in) analogs of the complexity classes studied so far in this section. Define $\mathcal{NC}^k$ to be the set of problems that can be solved with fan-in 2, in polynomial size and depth $O(\log^k n)$, for $k \ge 1$. Clearly $\mathcal{NC}^k \subseteq \mathcal{NC}^{k+1}$ for $k \ge 1$. Define

$$\mathcal{NC} = \cup_{k \ge 0}\mathcal{NC}^k.$$

COROLLARY 6.1.6 1. For $k \ge 0$, $\mathcal{NC}^k \subseteq \mathcal{AC}^k$.
2. For $k \ge 0$, $\mathcal{AC}^k \subseteq \mathcal{NC}^{k+1}$.
3. $\mathcal{NC} = \mathcal{AC}$.

PROOF: Part (1) is obvious, since fan-in 2 circuits are a special case of unbounded fan-in circuits. Part (2) is a corollary of Theorem 6.1.5. Part (3) follows immediately from part (2). □

Figure 6.8 shows the relationships between $\mathcal{NC}^k$ and $\mathcal{AC}^k$. $\mathcal{AC}^0$, the class of problems that can be solved in polynomial size and *constant* depth, is of particular interest, and is the subject of the next section.

We have already seen that the parity problem is in $\mathcal{AC}^1$ (Theorem 6.1.2). Actually, the logarithmic depth, linear size circuit for PARITY in that result has fan-in 2, so PARITY $\in \mathcal{NC}^1$. It is interesting to note that the unbounded fan-in of $\mathcal{AC}$-circuits allows a significant reduction in depth with only a small increase in size.

THEOREM 6.1.7 For every $k \in \mathbb{N}$, there is an alternating circuit for PARITY of depth $\lceil k\log n/\log\log n\rceil$ and size $O(2^{k\sqrt{\log n}} n/\sqrt[k]{\log n})$.

PROOF: Suppose $m \in \mathbb{N}$, $m > 4$ (we will return to the exact value of m later). For the moment, suppose that n is an integer power of m (we will return to the more general case later). Consider the following circuit $C(n, m)$ which recursively computes n-input

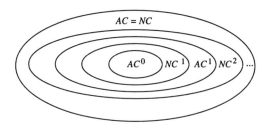

Figure 6.8
The classes $\mathcal{NC}^k$ and $\mathcal{AC}^k$.

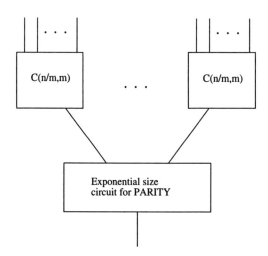

Figure 6.9
Recursive construction of $C(n, m)$, a shallow circuit for computing parity.

parity. $C(1, m)$ is the identity circuit. If $n \geq m$, $C(n, m)$ is constructed by dividing the inputs into m disjoint sets, and use m copies of $C(n/m, m)$ to find the parity within each set, and then taking the parity of the parities using Theorem 5.3.1 (see Figure 6.9).

That $C(n, m)$ computes PARITY is obvious, since "$\oplus$" is an associative operation. We can improve the depth of our construction by using the observation that Theorem 5.3.1 can be used to construct both circuits with AND on the first layer, and alternately with OR on the first layer. If we alternate between the two, then we can use compression (Theorem 5.2.2) to save depth. Then, if $D(n)$ is the depth of $C(n, m)$, $D(1) = 0$ and for $n > 1$ a power of m, $D(n) \leq D(n/m)+1$. Therefore, $D(n) \leq \log n/\log m$. Let $S(n)$ be the size of $C(n, m)$. Then, $S(1) = 0$ and for $n > m$ a power of m, $S(n) \leq mS(n/m)+2^m+1$. Therefore, $S(n) = O(2^m n/m)$.

Now suppose n is not an integer power of m. Since

$$x_1 \oplus \cdots \oplus x_n = x_1 \oplus \cdots \oplus x_n \oplus \underbrace{0 \oplus \cdots \oplus 0}_{k}$$

for all $k \geq 0$, we can compute the parity of n inputs by padding it out with the appropriate number of zeros to bring the input size up to $m\lceil n/m \rceil$, the next multiple of m. The above construction can then be repeated with m copies of $C(\lceil n/m \rceil, m)$, giving depth $D(n) \leq D(\lceil n/m \rceil)+1$ and size $S(n) \leq mS(\lceil n/m \rceil)+2^m+1$. The solution to these new recurrence relations is $D(n) = \lceil \log n/\log m \rceil$ and $S(n) = O(2^m n/m)$ (see Problem 1).

Choosing $m = \lceil \sqrt[k]{\log n} \rceil$ and $C_n = C(n, \lceil \log n \rceil)$ gives a AND-OR circuit of depth $\lceil k \log n/\log \log n \rceil$ and size $O(2^{\sqrt[k]{\log n}} n/\sqrt[k]{\log n})$. □

The size bound in Theorem 6.1.7 is quite close to linear, since even if we take $k = 2$, $2^{\sqrt{\log n}}$ grows more slowly than n^ϵ for any $\epsilon \in \mathbf{R}^+$ (it is easy to verify that $2^{\sqrt{\log n}} \leq n^\epsilon$ provided $n \geq 2^{1/\epsilon^2}$). The proof technique used in Theorem 6.1.7 was tailored to the fact that PARITY is associative, but the technique can be generalized to give a comparable depth reduction for any Boolean function, with a slightly larger overhead in size.

THEOREM 6.1.8 Any function computed by a classical circuit of depth d and size z can be computed by an alternating circuit of depth $\lceil d/\delta \rceil +1$ and size $z 2^{2^\delta} +1$, for any $\delta \in \mathbf{N}$.

PROOF: Divide the classical circuit horizontally into strips of depth δ. Each gate on the bottom of a strip can depend on at most 2^δ gates from the previous strip, and thus its role can be played by an alternating circuit of size $2^{2^\delta}+1$ and depth 2 by Theorem 5.3.1. Once again, we can alternate between subcircuits with AND on the first layer and subcircuits with OR on the first layer, and use compression (Theorem 5.2.2) to get depth $\lceil d/\delta \rceil +1$ and size $z 2^{2^\delta} +1$. □

COROLLARY 6.1.9 For every $k \in \mathbb{N}$, any function that can be computed by a classical circuit of depth $D(n)$ and size $S(n)$ can be computed by an alternating circuit of depth $\lceil kD(n)/\log\log S(n)\rceil + 1$ and size $2^{\sqrt[k]{\log S(n)}}S(n) + 1$.

PROOF: The claimed result follows immediately from Theorem 6.1.8 by taking $\delta = \lfloor(\log\log S(n))/k\rfloor$. □

Corollary 6.1.9 is particularly interesting when $S(n)$ is a polynomial in n, in which case it states that the depth of a classical circuit can be reduced by a factor of $\log\log n$ in return for a quite small increase in size (by a factor that is, as we have seen, smaller than n^ϵ for any $\epsilon > 0$). Therefore, an $\mathcal{AC}$ circuit is substantially shallower than any $\mathcal{NC}$ circuit for the same function. Thus, we can conclude that scaling fan-in has its benefits in depth savings.

6.2 Polynomial Size and Constant Depth

We saw in Theorem 5.3.1 that every Boolean function can be computed in constant depth with exponential size, but this cannot be considered practical for any but the very smallest values of n. Unfortunately, as we saw in Theorem 5.3.4, some Boolean functions intrinsically require exponential size (regardless of depth). However, some interesting functions can be computed in constant depth with only polynomial size. For example, we will see in this section that computing the sum of two integers is in $\mathcal{AC}^0$.

Consider the problem of adding two n-bit natural numbers represented in binary (the extension to negative integers is tedious but not difficult, see Problem 6). Suppose $x, y \in \mathbb{N}$, and we are to compute $z = x + y$. Suppose the binary representation of x is $x_1 x_2 \cdots x_n$, the binary representation of y is $y_1 y_2 \cdots y_n$, and the binary representation of z is $z_1 z_2 \cdots z_{n+1}$. Thus, for example,

$$x = \sum_{i=1}^{n} x_i 2^{n-i}.$$

The sum can be drawn as:

$$
\begin{array}{ccccc}
  & x_1 & x_2 & \cdots & x_n \\
+ & y_1 & y_2 & \cdots & y_n \\
\hline
z_1 & z_2 & z_3 & \cdots & z_{n+1}.
\end{array}
$$

Let c_i be 1 if there is a carry into the ith bit of the result z_i (that is, a carry out of the ith bit of the sum $x_i + y_i$) and define the *carry* of x and y to be $c_1 \cdots c_n$.

THEOREM 6.2.1 The carry of two n-bit natural numbers and its complement can be computed by an alternating circuit of size $O(n^2)$ and depth 3.

PROOF: Define g_i to be 1 if there is a carry generated in the ith bit of the operands, for $1 \leq i \leq n$, and define p_i to be 1 if there is a carry propagated in the ith bit of the operands, for $1 \leq i < n$. That is, $g_i = x_i \wedge y_i$, and $p_i = x_i \vee y_i$. Let $f_{i,j}$ be 1 if there is a carry generated in the jth bit of the operands and propagated all the way through the ith bit, for $1 \leq i \leq n$, $i \leq j \leq n$. That is,

$$f_{i,j} = p_i \wedge p_{i+1} \wedge \cdots \wedge p_{j-1} \wedge g_j. \qquad (6.2.1)$$

Then,

$$c_i = f_{i,i} \vee f_{i,i+1} \vee \cdots \vee f_{i,n}. \qquad (6.2.2)$$

for $1 \leq i \leq n$. The first layer of the circuit consists of $n - 1$ OR-gates computing p_i for $1 \leq i \leq n$. The second layer consists of $O(n^2)$ AND-gates computing $f_{i,j}$ for $1 \leq i \leq j \leq n$ using Equation (6.2.1). The third and final layer computes c_i for $1 \leq i \leq n$ using Equation (6.2.2). The correctness of the construction can easily be verified by induction on n.

It remains to show how to compute the complements of the carry bits in depth 3 and size $O(n^2)$. Theorem 5.1.1 can be used to produce a circuit of depth 3 and size $O(n^2)$ for the complement of the carry bits, but unfortunately this is of little use since the circuit produced has AND-gates in the first layer, and thus the combined circuit for the carry and its complement must have depth 4 as an alternating circuit (although as an AND-OR circuit it has depth 3.

Define a_i to be 1 if carry can be absorbed in the ith bit of the operands, for $1 \leq i \leq n$, and define n_i to be 1 if there is no carry generated in the ith bit of the operands, for $1 \leq i < n$. That is, $a_i = \overline{x}_i \wedge \overline{y}_i$, and $n_i = \overline{x}_i \vee \overline{y}_i$. Let $g_{i,j}$ be 1 if carry is absorbed in the jth bit of the operands and is not generated all the way through the ith bit, for $1 \leq i \leq n$, $i \leq j \leq n$. That is,

$$g_{i,j} = n_i \wedge n_{i+1} \wedge \cdots \wedge n_{j-1} \wedge a_j. \qquad (6.2.3)$$

Then,

$$\overline{c}_i = g_{i,i} \vee g_{i,i+1} \vee \cdots \vee g_{i,n}. \qquad (6.2.4)$$

for $1 \leq i \leq n$. The first layer of the circuit consists of $n - 1$ OR-gates computing n_i for $1 \leq i \leq n$. The second layer consists of $O(n^2)$ AND-gates computing $g_{i,j}$ for $1 \leq i \leq j \leq n$ using Equation (6.2.3). The third and final layer computes $\overline{c}_i$ for $1 \leq i \leq n$ using Equation (6.2.4). $\square$

THEOREM 6.2.2 The sum of two n-bit natural numbers can be computed by an alternating circuit of size $O(n^2)$ and depth 3.

PROOF: First, compute the carry of x and y in $O(n^2)$ size and depth 3 using the alternating circuit from Theorem 6.2.1. Then, $z_1 = c_1$, $z_{n+1} = x_n \oplus y_n$, and for $1 \le i < n$,

$$z_{i+1} = x_i \oplus y_i \oplus c_{i+1}.$$

Using Theorem 5.3.1 and Theorem 5.1.1, it is easily seen that

$$x_i \oplus y_i = (x_i \vee y_i) \wedge (\overline{x}_i \vee \overline{y}_i), \qquad (6.2.5)$$

and

$$\neg(x_i \oplus y_i) = (x_i \vee \overline{y}_i) \wedge (\overline{x}_i \vee y_i). \qquad (6.2.6)$$

Therefore, $x_i \oplus y_i$ and its complement for $1 \le i \le n$ can be computed in layers 1 and 2, and $(x_i \oplus y_i) \oplus c_{i+1}$ in layers 3 and 4. The obvious construction which concatenates the carry circuits from Theorem 6.2.1 with the parity circuits gives an AND-OR circuit of depth 5 with both layers 3 and 4 composed of OR-gates; these two layers can be combined into one using compression (Theorem 5.2.2).

For example, Figure 6.10 shows an alternating circuit for computing the second bit z_2 of the sum of two 4-bit numbers. Figures 6.11, 6.12, and 6.13 show the parts of that circuit that compute $(x_1 \oplus y_1) \oplus c_2$, c_2, and $\overline{c}_2$, respectively.

The circuit constructed thus far has $n + 1$ output gates, each of which are AND-gates with inputs from two OR-gates with at most n inputs. These last two layers can be inverted to give a layer of $O(n^2)$ AND-gates followed by a layer of $n + 1$ OR-gates (Theorem 5.2.3). Thus, layers 3 and 4 of this new circuit are both AND-gates, which can be combined using compression (Theorem 5.2.2). This reduces the depth to 3, and leaves the size at $O(n^2)$. $\square$

The following variant of Theorem 6.2.2 appears obscure, but we will actually find it to be quite useful.

THEOREM 6.2.3 The sum of two n-bit natural numbers, one of which has at most k ones in its binary representation, can be computed by an alternating circuit of size $O(kn)$ and depth 3.

PROOF: The construction is similar to that of Theorem 6.2.2, and is left to the reader (see Problem 4). $\square$

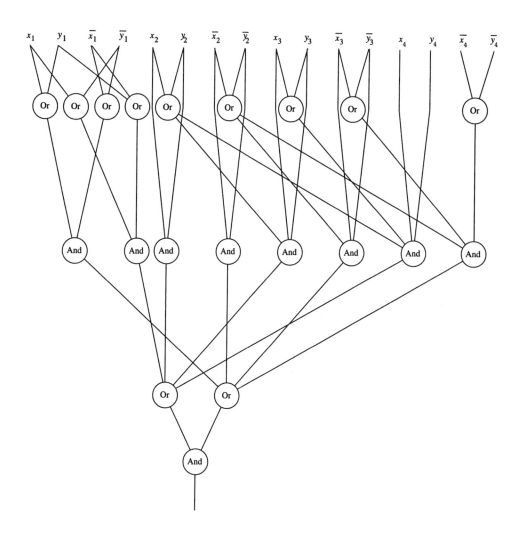

Figure 6.10
Alternating circuit for computing the second bit z_2 of the sum of two 4-bit numbers.

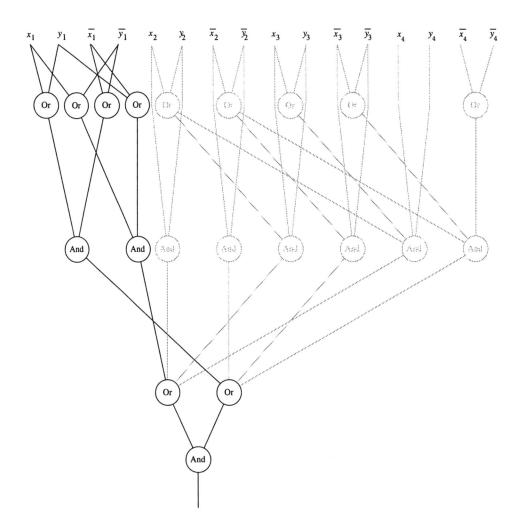

Figure 6.11
Part of the alternating circuit from Figure 6.10 that computes $(x_1 \oplus y_1) \oplus c_2$.

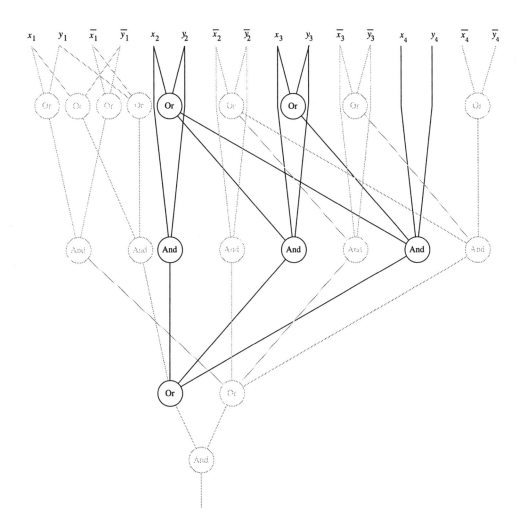

Figure 6.12
Part of the alternating circuit from Figure 6.10 that computes the carry bit c_2.

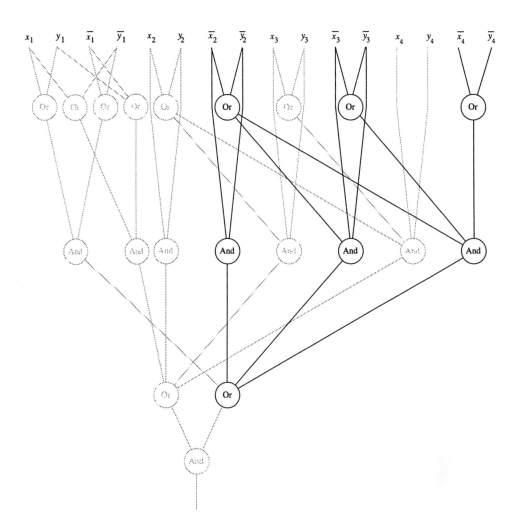

Figure 6.13
Part of the alternating circuit from Figure 6.10 that computes the complement of the carry bit c_2.

The circuit constructed in Theorem 6.2.2 has OR-gates in the first layer. It is possible to construct a circuit of the same size and depth that has AND-gates in the first layer (Problem 7).

It is interesting to ask whether SAT is any easier when restricted to constant depth circuits. It is intuitively clear that it is not since the difficulty seems to stem from the fact that there are exponentially many inputs, not from the fact that the circuit may have large depth. Consider the following problem.

3SAT

INSTANCE: An alternating circuit C of depth 2 with first layer gates of fan-in 3.

QUESTION: Is C satisfiable?

It is perhaps not surprising that 3SAT is $\mathcal{NP}$-complete.

THEOREM 6.2.4 3SAT is $\mathcal{NP}$-complete.

PROOF: It is clear that 3SAT $\in \mathcal{NP}$, since 3SAT is a subproblem of SAT. We claim that SAT $\leq_p$ 3SAT. By Theorem 5.4.5, this is enough to show that 3SAT is $\mathcal{NP}$-complete.

Let $C = (V, X, Y, E, \ell)$ be an alternating circuit, where $X = \{x_1, \ldots, x_n\}$, $V = \{g_1, \ldots, g_m\}$, and $Y = \{g_m\}$. Without loss of generality we may assume that C is a classical circuit, since the reduction described in Theorem 6.1.5 can be computed in polynomial size. We will construct a new circuit $C' = (V', X', Y', E', \ell')$ as follows.

$X' = X \cup \{g_1, \ldots, g_m\}$. The inputs $x_1, \ldots, x_n$ will play the role of the inputs to C, and the inputs $g_1, \ldots, g_m$ will play the role of the corresponding gates in C. For each gate $g_i \in V$ there are three gates $a_i, b_i, c_i \in V'$, with $\ell'(a_i) = \ell'(b_i) = \ell'(c_i) = $ OR for $1 \leq i \leq m$. These three gates form a unit called a *gate enforcer*. There is also an additional gate z with $\ell'(z) = $ AND, $(a_i, z), (b_i, z), (c_i, z) \in E'$ for $1 \leq i \leq m$, and $Y' = \{z\}$.

Consider $g_i \in V$. Since C is a classical circuit, g_i has fan-in 2. Suppose the inputs to g_i come from $v_1, v_2 \in V \cup \{x_1, \ldots, x_n\}$ (that is, $(v_1, g_i), (v_2, g_i) \in E$). For $1 \leq i < m$, if $\ell(g_i) = $ OR, then

$$(v_1, a_i), (v_2, a_i), (\overline{g}_i, a_i),$$
$$(\overline{v}_1, b_i), (g_i, b_i),$$
$$(\overline{v}_2, c_i), (g_i, c_i) \in E'$$

(see Figure 6.14(a)), and if $\ell(g_i) = $ AND, then

$$(\overline{v}_1, a_i), (\overline{v}_2, a_i), (g_i, a_i),$$

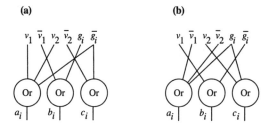

Figure 6.14
The gate enforcer for g_i, (a) when $\ell(g_i) = $ OR, and (b) when $\ell(g_i) = $ AND.

$$(v_1, b_i), (\overline{g}_i, b_i),$$
$$(v_2, c_i), (\overline{g}_i, c_i) \in E'$$

(see Figure 6.14(b)). If $\ell(g_m) = $ OR, then $(v_1, a_m), (v_2, a_m), (a_m, z) \in E'$, and otherwise $\ell(g_m) = $ AND and $(v_1, z), (v_2, z) \in E'$.

If C is satisfiable, then it can be verified by induction on n (Problem 12(12a)) that if the inputs $x_1, \ldots, x_n$ of C' are set to the assignment that satisfies C, and inputs g_i of C' are set to the value of gate g_i in C on that input, then all of the OR-gates on the first level of C' (a_i, b_i, c_i for $1 \leq i \leq m$) output 1, which makes the AND-gate z output 1, and thus C' is satisfiable.

Now suppose that C' is satisfiable. Suppose input $b_1, \ldots, b_{n+m-1}$ satisfies C', that is, $v_{C'}(y) = 1$. It can be proved by induction on n (Problem 12(12b)) that $v_C(g_i) = v_{C'}(g_i)$, for $1 \leq i < m$, and hence deduced that $v_C(y) = 1$, that is, C is satisfiable.

Therefore, C' is satisfiable iff C is satisfiable. C' clearly has depth 2, and all gates on the first level have fan-in at most 3. Furthermore, it can be shown that the transformation from C to C' is simple enough to be computed in polynomial size. Therefore, SAT $\leq_p$ 3SAT, completing the proof that 3SAT is $\mathcal{NP}$-complete. $\square$

Figure 6.15 shows an alternating circuit, and Figure 6.16 shows the corresponding depth 2 circuit that is satisfiable iff the original is.

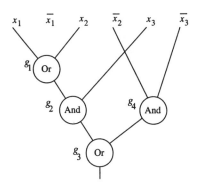

Figure 6.15
An alternating circuit.

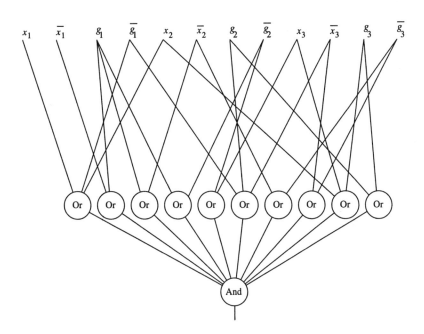

Figure 6.16
An alternating circuit that is satisfiable iff the circuit in Figure 6.15 is satisfiable.

6.3 The $\mathcal{AC}^0$ Hierarchy

Define $\mathcal{AC}_k^0$ to be the class of problems that have polynomial size alternating circuits of depth k. Then,

$$\mathcal{AC}^0 = \bigcup_{k \geq 0} \mathcal{AC}_k^0.$$

The sequence of language classes

$$\mathcal{AC}_1^0 \subseteq \mathcal{AC}_2^0 \subseteq \mathcal{AC}_3^0 \subseteq \cdots$$

is called the $\mathcal{AC}^0$ *hierarchy*.

It is interesting to ask whether the containments in this hierarchy are all proper (referred to as *separating the* $\mathcal{AC}^0$ *hierarchy*), or whether there exists a k such that $\mathcal{AC}_k^0 = \mathcal{AC}_{k+1}^0$. The latter is referred to as *collapsing the* $\mathcal{AC}^0$ *hierarchy*, since if $\mathcal{AC}_k^0 = \mathcal{AC}_{k+1}^0$, then for all $\ell \geq k$, $\mathcal{AC}_k^0 = \mathcal{AC}_\ell^0$ (see Problem 10). It is easy to prove that $\mathcal{AC}_1^0 \subset \mathcal{AC}_2^0$, since $\mathcal{AC}_1^0$ consists merely of conjunctions and disjunctions of a subset of the inputs and their complements. It is also easy to prove that $\mathcal{AC}_2^0 \subset \mathcal{AC}_3^0$:

THEOREM 6.3.1 The addition of two n-bit integers is in $\mathcal{AC}_3^0$ but not in $\mathcal{AC}_2^0$.

PROOF: Addition is in $\mathcal{AC}_3^0$ by Theorem 6.2.2. It can be shown that any depth 2 alternating circuit for computing the first bit of the carry of two n-bit natural numbers requires size at least 2^{n-1} Therefore, the first bit of the sum of two natural numbers requires exponential size to compute in depth 2. (See Problem 9). □

In fact, the entire $\mathcal{AC}^0$ hierarchy can be separated as a consequence of the following result, which we state without proof:

THEOREM 6.3.2 For all $k \in \mathbb{N}$, there is a function in $\mathcal{AC}_k^0$ that is not in $\mathcal{AC}_{k+1}^0$.

It is also possible to separate $\mathcal{AC}^0$ from $\mathcal{NC}^1$. We know that $\mathcal{AC}^0 \subseteq \mathcal{NC}^1$ (Corollary 6.1.6 (2)). We have learned that PARITY $\in \mathcal{NC}^1$ (Theorem 6.1.2). We also know that PARITY $\notin \mathcal{AC}_2^0$ (Theorem 5.3.3). This result can be extended to the following, which we also state without proof:

THEOREM 6.3.3 PARITY $\notin \mathcal{AC}^0$.

6.4   Problems

1. It can be shown that for all continuous and monotonically increasing functions $f : \mathbf{R} \to \mathbf{R}$ with the property that $f(x) \in \mathbf{Z} \Rightarrow x \in \mathbf{Z}$, $\lceil f(\lceil x \rceil) \rceil = \lceil f(x) \rceil$ (see Graham, Knuth, and Patashnik [54, p. 71]). Deduce that $\lceil \lceil n/m \rceil / m \rceil = \lceil n/m^2 \rceil$. Hence, show that the solution to the following recurrence relations: $D(1) = 0$, and for all $n > 1$, $D(n) \le D(\lceil n/m \rceil) + 1$; $S(1) = 0$ and for all $n > 1$, $S(n) \le mS(\lceil n/m \rceil) + 2^m + 1$ is $D(n) = \lceil \log n / \log m \rceil$ and $S(n) = O(2^m n/m)$.

2. Give an exact figure for the size of the carry circuit of Theorem 6.2.1 as a function of n.

3. Give an exact figure for the size of the addition circuit of Theorem 6.2.2 as a function of n.

4. Show that the sum of two n-bit natural numbers, one of which has at most k ones in its binary representation, can be computed by an alternating circuit of size $O(kn)$ and depth 3 (Theorem 6.2.3). (Hint: Observe that in the proof of Theorem 6.2.2, carry can only be generated in k places.)

5. Show that an n-bit natural number can be incremented by an alternating circuit of size $O(n^2)$ and depth 2.

6. Suppose we represent $x \in \mathbf{Z}$ in binary as follows, using n bits. If $x \ge 0$, and $0 \le x < 2^{n-1} - 1$, store x in the normal fashion (see Section 6.2). If $x < 0$, and $-2^{n-1} \le x \le -1$, store $2^n - x$ in the normal fashion. This is called *two's complement representation* in n bits. Show that the alternating circuit of Theorem 6.2.2 can be used to add integers stored in this manner.

7. The alternating circuit for addition in Theorem 6.2.2 starts with OR-gates on the first layer. Construct a circuit with the same size and depth that has AND-gates on the first layer.

8. Show that the sum of two n-bit natural numbers, can be computed by an alternating circuit of size $O(n^{4/3})$ and depth 5. (Hint: Start by dividing the inputs into n/b blocks of b bits, where b will be chosen later.)

9. Show, using the technique of Theorem 5.3.3, that any depth 2 alternating circuit for computing the first bit of the carry of two n-bit natural numbers requires size at least 2^{n-1}. Use this fact to complete the proof of Theorem 6.3.1.

10. Let C be a set of functions that have domain $\mathbf{B}^n$ for all $n \in \mathbf{N}$, and range $\mathbf{B}$. Define CC_k^0 to be the class of functions computable by polynomial size, depth k circuits with node function set C. Prove that if there exists $k \in \mathbf{N}$ such that $CC_k^0 = CC_{k+1}^0$, then for all $\ell \ge k$, $CC_k^0 = CC_\ell^0$.

11. Show that for all $c \in \mathbb{N}$, and every alternating circuit of depth d and polynomial size, there is an equivalent alternating circuit of depth d and polynomial size in which every gate on the first level is connected to at least $c \log n$ literals.

12. Complete the proof of Theorem 6.2.4 by showing that

    (a) If C is satisfiable, then C' is satisfiable.

    (b) If C' is satisfiable, then C is satisfiable.

13. Show that 2SAT, the analog of 3SAT with fan-in 2 on the first level, can be solved in polynomial size.

14. Theorem 6.2.4 showed that 3SAT is $\mathcal{NP}$-complete for alternating circuits with OR at the first level and AND at the second level. What can be said about SAT when the order of these layers is reversed?

6.5   Bibliographic Notes

$\mathcal{NC}$ is an abbreviation of "Nick's Class", named by Cook [34] after the seminal contribution of Pippenger [104], who discovered an important and pivotal relationship between $\mathcal{NC}$ and conventional Turing machine based computation. (See also Ruzzo [119].) The classes $\mathcal{AC}^k$ for $k \geq 1$ first appeared in Cook [32]. The class $\mathcal{AC}^0$ was first studied by Furst, Saxe, and Sipser [44], and was named by Barrington [13]. The uniform version of Theorem 6.1.4 is due to Ladner [75]. The proof in that reference is somewhat sketchy; a more detailed proof appears in Parberry [94]. For more information on the complexity theory of parallel computation, see Hong [63], and Parberry [94].

A weaker form of Corollary 6.1.9 is due to Chandra, Stockmeyer, and Vishkin [27]. Our result is the obvious generalization, and tightens the sloppy analysis of Theorem 5.2.8 of Parberry [95]. Theorems 6.2.1 and 6.2.2 are also due to Chandra, Stockmeyer, and Vishkin [27], although they were less concerned about the exact value of the constant in the depth bound. The depth 4, polynomial size alternating circuit for addition in Theorem 6.2.2 can also be found in be found in Wegener [146]. The reduction in depth to 3 is reported in Wegener [147].

Chandra, Fortune and Lipton have shown by a sophisticated argument that the number of edges (and hence the size) of the circuit for computing carry in constant depth described in Theorem 6.2.1 (and hence also the addition circuit in Theorem 6.2.2) can be reduced from $O(n^2)$ to an almost linear function. Define $f^{(1)}(x) = f(x)$, and for $i > 1$, $f^{(i)}(x) = f(f^{(i-1)}(x))$. Define $f_1(n) = 2^n$, and for $i > 1$, $f_i(n) = f_{i-1}^{(n)}(2)$. Chandra, Fortune and Lipton [26] have shown that there is an AND-OR circuit for carry of depth $6d + 3$ and size $n f_d^{-1}(n)^2$. Surprisingly, they also found a matching lower bound on the number of edges [25].

Theorem 6.3.2 is from Sipser [126]. Theorem 6.3.3 was originally proved by Furst, Saxe, and Sipser [44]. Successive improvements on the size bound were found by Yao [151], Håstad [133], and Dingzhu [38]. A more readable proof can be found in Wegener [146].

7 Threshold Circuits

Chapters 5 and 6 studied a circuit model in which the gates compute only very simple linear threshold functions. Now we extend the model by allowing the gates to compute any of the Boolean linear threshold functions from Chapter 4. The resulting circuit is called a *threshold circuit*. We start by considering various restrictions on the weights used in the circuit. In Section 7.1 the weights are allowed to be arbitrary integers. In Section 7.2 the weights are restricted to ± 1. In Section 7.3 the weights are restricted to scale polynomially. Section 7.4 compares and contrasts various threshold circuit complexity classes, with particular reference to $\mathcal{TC}^0$, the analog of $\mathcal{AC}^0$ using threshold circuits. Section 7.5 is devoted to the $\mathcal{TC}^0$ hierarchy, the threshold-based analog of the $\mathcal{AC}^0$ hierarchy.

7.1 Weighted Threshold Circuits

A threshold circuit is defined similarly to an AND-OR circuit (see Section 5.1), the only difference being that the functions computed by the nodes are now permitted to be Boolean linear threshold functions (see Chapter 4) instead of just AND, OR, and NOT. Formally, a *threshold circuit* is a 5-tuple $C = (V, X, Y, E, \ell)$, where

$$V \text{ is a finite ordered set}$$
$$X \cap V = \emptyset$$
$$Y \subseteq V$$
$$(V \cup X, E) \text{ is a directed, acyclic graph}$$
$$\ell : V \to \Theta.$$

We will depict a gate computing $\theta_n(w_1, \ldots, w_n, h)$ as in Figure 7.1, with the weights as labels on the edges, and the threshold as a label on the gate.

We will assume, without loss of generality, that all presentations of the Boolean linear threshold functions used in threshold circuits are integer presentations (by Corollary 3.3.6). In addition to the *size* and *depth* of these circuits, we will be interested in

Figure 7.1
A gate computing $\theta_n(w_1, \ldots, w_n, h)$.

two additional resources relating to the weights used in the circuit. The first, called *maximum weight*, is defined to be the magnitude of the largest weight used in the circuit. The second, called the *weight*, is defined to be the sum of the magnitude of all of the weights used in the circuit. Clearly, the weight, the maximum weight, and the size of a circuit are all related. In a circuit of size z, weight w, and maximum weight m, $1 \leq m \leq w$, and $z - 1 \leq w \leq mz$.

As with alternating circuits, we will allow threshold circuits to be functions of literals, that is, we permit them to have a layer of NOT-gates at the inputs. This layer will not be counted in either the size or the depth. The requirement that threshold circuits be allowed to have negative weights can be waived, given that we have defined them to be functions of literals:

THEOREM 7.1.1 For every n-input threshold circuit of depth d, size s and maximum weight w, there exists an equivalent n-input threshold circuit in which all weights are positive, of depth at most d, size at most $2s$, and maximum weight w.

PROOF: Negative weights can be replaced by NOT-gates using Lemma 4.1.3. These can be pushed back to the inputs using the proof technique of Theorem 5.1.1, substituting Theorem 4.1.5 for Corollary 4.1.6. None of these results increase the magnitude of the weights. □

In the remainder of this chapter we will investigate the computing power of small depth threshold circuits of polynomial size. It is useful to distinguish between three different types of threshold circuits. The first type, called *unit-weight* threshold circuits, have maximum weight 1. By Theorem 7.1.1, we can without loss of generality assume that all weights within this type of circuit are 1, and thus we will leave out the weights when we depict them graphically. (This is ignoring, of course, the "invisible" first layer of NOT-gates, which by Lemma 4.1.3 are threshold-gates that have weight -1.) The second type, called *small-weight* threshold circuits, have maximum weight bounded above by a polynomial in the number of inputs to the circuit (equivalently for polynomial size circuits, a polynomial in the size of the circuit). Each weight of a small-weight threshold circuit can be described using $O(\log n)$ bits. The third type, called *unrestricted-weight* threshold circuits, have no restrictions on their weights.

By Theorem 4.2.1, each weight of an unrestricted weight threshold circuit can be described using a polynomial number of bits. Therefore, a finite polynomial size threshold circuit with n inputs can always be described using a polynomial number of bits. This is intuitively pleasing, since the "size" of a mathematical object should be a polynomial of the number of bits needed to describe it. An examination of the proof of Theorem 7.1.1

will reveal that it holds for unit-weight, small-weight, and unrestricted-weight threshold circuits, since the techniques used do not change the magnitude of the weights. It should be clear from remarks made in Section 4.1 that AND-OR (and hence alternating) circuits are a special case of threshold circuits.

7.2   Unit Weight Threshold Circuits

In this section we examine the computing power of unit-weight threshold circuits with polynomial size and constant depth. A function $f : \mathbf{B}^n \to \mathbf{B}^m$ is called *symmetric* if its output remains the same regardless of the order of the input bits.

THEOREM 7.2.1 Any symmetric function $f : \mathbf{B}^n \to \mathbf{B}$ can be computed by a unit-weight threshold circuit with size $2n + 3$ and depth 2.

PROOF: A symmetric function $f : \mathbf{B}^n \to \mathbf{B}$ can be uniquely defined by the set

$$S_f = \{ m \in \mathbf{N} \mid f(x) = 1 \text{ for all } x \in \mathbf{B}^n \text{ with exactly } m \text{ ones} \}.$$

Suppose $S_f = \{ m_1, \ldots, m_k \}$.

The circuit uses k pairs of gates on the first level. The ith pair has one gate active when the number of ones in the input is at least m_i (this is a unit-weight threshold-gate with threshold m_i connected to the inputs $x_1, \ldots, x_n$), and the other gate active when the number of ones in the input is at most m_i (by Lemmas 4.1.2 and 4.1.3, this is a unit-weight threshold-gate with threshold $n - m_i$ connected to the complements of the inputs $\overline{x}_1, \ldots, \overline{x}_n$). When given an input x such that $f(x) = 0$, exactly one of each pair is active, therefore, exactly k gates are active. When given an input x such that $f(x) = 1$, one pair has both of its gates active, and all other pairs have exactly one of its gates active, therefore exactly $k + 1$ gates are active. The output gate therefore has threshold value $k + 1$ and inputs from all of the first level gates. This circuit has depth 2, and since $k \le n + 1$, size at most $2(n + 1) + 1$. □

For example, Figure 7.2 shows a threshold circuit for computing PARITY in depth 2 and size 5. Note that this circuit has a size smaller than the size bound in Theorem 7.2.1. The size bound in Theorem 7.2.1 can actually be reduced by a constant multiple without increase in depth (Problem 1). A similar result holds for symmetric functions with multiple outputs:

COROLLARY 7.2.2 Any symmetric function $f : \mathbf{B}^n \to \mathbf{B}^m$ can be computed by a unit-weight threshold circuit with size $2n + m + 2$ and depth 2.

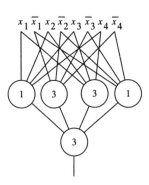

Figure 7.2
A threshold circuit computing the symmetric function $x_1 \oplus x_2 \oplus x_3 \oplus x_4$.

PROOF: Suppose $f: \mathbf{B}^n \to \mathbf{B}^m$ is a symmetric function. Computing each individual bit of the output of f is a symmetric function, and hence by Theorem 7.2.1 can be computed in depth 2 and size $2n+1$. Thus, the obvious circuit for computing f uses m such circuits and has depth 2 and size $2nm + m$. However, the first layer of this combined circuit can have at most $2(n+1)$ different gates, giving the required size bound. $\square$

Gates in the second layer of the threshold circuits constructed in Theorem 7.2.1 and Corollary 7.2.2 have an interesting property. They have unit weights, threshold k, and the number of ones in their input is guaranteed (by the rest of the circuit) to be either k or $k - 1$. Let us call this kind of Boolean linear threshold function a *balanced* one. The following result enables a savings in depth whenever balanced threshold-gates are used in any layer of a circuit but the last. This does not, of course, give a savings in depth for the circuits constructed in Theorem 7.2.1 or Corollary 7.2.2, but it will enable a reduction in depth whenever these circuits are used as building blocks in the interior of another circuit.

LEMMA 7.2.3 Let g_0 be a unit-weight threshold-gate that has inputs only from balanced threshold-gates $g_1, \ldots, g_m$ where for all $1 \le i < j \le m$, gates g_i and g_j have distinct inputs. The gates $g_0, g_1, \ldots, g_m$ can be replaced by a single threshold-gate.

PROOF: Let g_0 be a unit-weight threshold-gate that has inputs only from balanced threshold-gates $g_1, \ldots, g_m$. Suppose gates $g_1, \ldots, g_m$ collectively have inputs $x_1, \ldots, x_n$, and that for all $1 \le i < j \le m$, gates g_i and g_j have nonoverlapping inputs. Suppose g_i has weight k_i, for $0 \le i \le m$. We claim that the entire circuit can be replaced by a

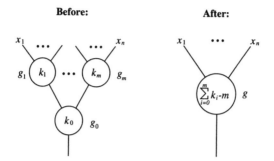

Figure 7.3
Before and after pictures for Lemma 7.2.3.

threshold-gate g with threshold $\sum_{i=0}^{m} k_i - m$ (see Figure 7.3).

Suppose g_0 outputs 0. Then, at most $k_0 - 1$ of the gates $g_1, \ldots, g_m$ output 1. Therefore, at most $k_0 - 1$ of the gates g_i for $1 \leq i \leq m$ see k_i ones, and the rest see $k_i - 1$ ones. Hence, $x_1, \ldots, x_n$ can have at most

$$\sum_{i=1}^{m}(k_i - 1) + (k_0 - 1) = \sum_{i=0}^{m} k_i - (m + 1)$$

ones. Therefore, g outputs 0.

Conversely, suppose g_0 outputs 1. Then, at least k_0 of the gates $g_1, \ldots, g_m$ output 1. Therefore, at least k_0 of the gates g_i for $1 \leq i \leq m$ see k_i ones, and the rest see $k_i - 1$ ones. Hence, $x_1, \ldots, x_n$ must have at least

$$\sum_{i=1}^{m}(k_i - 1) + k_0 = \sum_{i=0}^{m} k_i - m$$

ones. Therefore, g outputs 1.

We have shown that g outputs 1 iff g_0 outputs 1. Therefore, the circuit containing $g_0, g_1, \ldots, g_m$ can be replaced by the threshold-gate g, as claimed. $\square$

There is an analogous version of Lemma 7.2.3 that applies when the balanced threshold-gates have non-unit weights, and may have inputs from shared sources. However, the result as stated is sufficient for our needs, and we leave the details of the generalization to the interested reader (Problems 4 and 5). Theorem 7.2.1 has many interesting applications, including the problem of adding together a set of numbers, which we will call the *iterated addition* problem.

LEMMA 7.2.4 The sum of n natural numbers of m bits has at most $m + \lfloor \log n \rfloor + 1$ bits.

PROOF: It can be proved (see Problem 6) that any natural number z can be written using exactly $\lfloor \log z \rfloor + 1$ bits. A natural number with m bits can be at most $2^m - 1$ (see Problem 6). Therefore, the sum of n numbers of m bits is bounded above by $n(2^m - 1)$. Hence, the sum of n numbers of m bits can have at most

$$\lfloor \log(n(2^m - 1)) \rfloor + 1 \leq m + \lfloor \log n \rfloor + 1$$

bits. □

THEOREM 7.2.5 The addition of n m-bit natural numbers can be performed with a unit-weight threshold circuit of size $O(m^2 \log \log \log n / \log \log n + mn + n \log n)$ and depth 6.

PROOF: The circuit is constructed in six steps as follows. We will first describe the general algorithm, and then investigate its implementation as a circuit.

Step 1. Write the n numbers in binary in the rows of an $n \times m$ array of bits. For example, the leftmost part of Figure 7.4 shows the first step in computing the sum $255 + 255 + 255 + 255 + 255 + 255 + 255 + 224$, taking $n = 8$, $m = 8$.

Step 2. For $1 \leq i \leq m$, take the ith column of the array (counting from 1 at the least-significant, or rightmost end), add the number of ones in the column, multiply by 2^{i-1} and lay the result in binary as one of the rows of a new rectangular matrix. For example, in Figure 7.4 the rightmost 5 columns have 7 ones, resulting in the upper 5 rows of the lower matrix, and the leftmost 3 columns have 8 ones, resulting in the lower 3 rows. The old matrix has m columns, so the new matrix has m rows.

The number of ones in each column of the old matrix is between 0 and n (inclusive), which requires $\lfloor \log n \rfloor + 1$ bits. Thus, row i of the new matrix consists of $\lfloor \log n \rfloor + 1$ bits encoding the number of ones in the column i of the old matrix, shifted left by $i - 1$ bits. In particular, row m has $\lfloor \log n \rfloor + 1$ bits shifted left by $m - 1$ bits, for a total of $m + \lfloor \log n \rfloor$ bits. The new matrix therefore has dimension $m \times (m + \lfloor \log n \rfloor)$ and consists mostly of zero entries with $\lfloor \log n \rfloor + 1$ possibly non-zero bits in each row arranged in blocks down the back-diagonal. These bits are called *dirty* bits, and are shown at the end of Figure 7.4.

Step 3. Repeat step 2. The old matrix has $m + \lfloor \log n \rfloor$ columns, so the new matrix has $m + \lfloor \log n \rfloor$ rows. The back-diagonal structure of the old matrix guarantees that the new matrix has $m + \lfloor \log n \rfloor$ columns. The dirty region in each row now has only $\lfloor \log(\lfloor \log n \rfloor + 1) \rfloor + 1 \leq \lfloor \log \lfloor \log n \rfloor \rfloor + 2$ dirty bits. It can be proven that $\lfloor \log \lfloor \log n \rfloor \rfloor =$

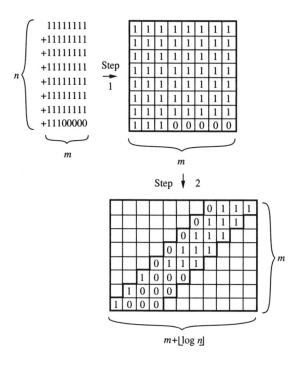

Figure 7.4
Steps 1 and 2 of the circuit in Theorem 7.2.5. Blank entries are all zero.

$\lfloor \log \log n \rfloor$ (the tools needed to prove this are used in Problem 1 of Section 6.4). Step 3 is shown in Figure 7.5.

Step 4. Let $\ell = \lfloor \log \log n \rfloor + 2$. Since each row of the current matrix has ℓ dirty bits in each row, and each subsequent row has the dirty bits shifted left by one bit, we conclude that each column has ℓ dirty bits. Take the dirty bits from each column and use them as the columns of a new $\ell \times (m + \lfloor \log n \rfloor)$ matrix. Step 4 is shown in Figure 7.6.

Step 5. Divide the matrix into $\ell \times \ell$ squares. Treat each square as ℓ number of ℓ bits. Add the ℓ numbers in each square, obtaining a result word of ℓ bits and a carry word of ℓ bits. Concatenate the result words into a single word. Shift the carry words ℓ bits right and concatenate them together into a single word. The result is two words of $m + \lfloor \log n \rfloor + 1$ bits. See, for example, Figure 7.7.

Step 6. Add the result word and the carry word. Step 6 is shown in Figure 7.8.

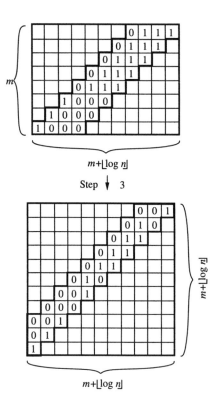

Figure 7.5
Step 3 of the circuit in Theorem 7.2.5. Blank entries are all zero.

It can be shown that in each of the matrices used in the above construction, if each row of the matrix is treated as the binary representation of a natural number, then the sum of the rows equals the sum of the input numbers. This is sufficient to demonstrate correctness of the algorithm.

Analysis of Step 1: Step 1 requires no gates.

Analysis of Step 2: The iterated addition of n zeros and ones is a symmetric function with $O(\log n)$ outputs, which can therefore be computed in depth 2 and size $O(n)$ (by Corollary 7.2.2). Duplicating this circuit for each of m columns gives a circuit of depth 2 and size $O(mn)$ for Step 2.

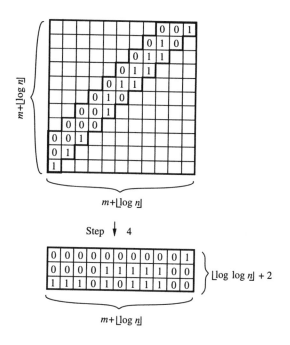

Step ↓ 4

Figure 7.6
Step 4 of the circuit in Theorem 7.2.5. Blank entries are all zero.

Analysis of Step 3: Step 3 is a repeat of Step 2, but it need only operate on the $O(\log n)$ dirty bits in each column, and hence has depth 2 and size only $O((m + \log n) \log n)$.

Analysis of Step 4: Step 4 requires no gates.

Analysis of Step 5: Since each square had $O(\log \log^2 n)$ bits, the sum of each square can be computed by an alternating circuit of depth 2 and size $2^{\log \log^2 n}$ by Theorem 5.3.2. Duplicating this circuit for each of $(m + \lfloor \log n \rfloor)/(\log \log n + 1)$ squares gives size $O(m + \log n)2^{\log \log^2 n} / \log \log n)$.

Analysis of Step 6: By Lemma 7.2.4, the numbers to be added together in Step 6 have $m + \lfloor \log n \rfloor + 1$ bits. The addition can be implemented with an alternating circuit of depth 3 and size $O((m + \log n)^2)$, by Theorem 6.2.2. The size can further be reduced by noting that the carry word consists of blocks of ℓ bits, each block being the carry from the sum of an ℓ block of bits, and hence by Lemma 7.2.4 has at most $\lfloor \log \ell \rfloor + 1 = O(\log \log \log n)$ ones per block. Therefore, by Theorem 6.2.3, the alternating circuit for Step 6 has size $O((m + \log n)^2 \log \log \log n / \log \log n)$.

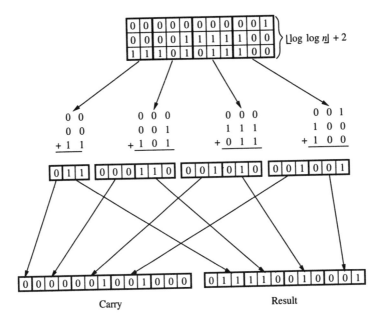

Figure 7.7
Step 5 of the circuit in Theorem 7.2.5.

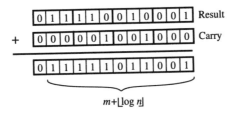

Figure 7.8
Step 6 of the circuit in Theorem 7.2.5.

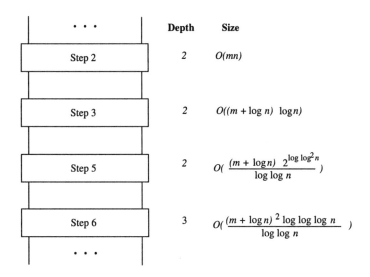

Figure 7.9
Structure of the circuit in Theorem 7.2.5.

The structure of the complete circuit is shown in Figure 7.9. The sizes of each of the crucial steps are shown below:

$$\begin{aligned}
\text{Step 2:} \quad & O(mn) \\
\text{Step 3:} \quad & O((m + \log n) \log n) \\
\text{Step 5:} \quad & O(m + \log n)2^{\log\log^2 n} / \log\log n) \\
\text{Step 6:} \quad & O((m + \log n)^2 \log\log\log n / \log\log n).
\end{aligned}$$

If $m = \Omega(\log n)$, the sizes are:

$$\begin{aligned}
\text{Step 2:} \quad & O(mn) \\
\text{Step 3:} \quad & O(m \log n) \\
\text{Step 5:} \quad & O(m2^{\log\log^2 n} / \log\log n) \\
\text{Step 6:} \quad & O(m^2 \log\log\log n / \log\log n),
\end{aligned}$$

each of which is $O(m^2 \log\log\log n / \log\log n + mn)$. Alternatively, if $m = O(\log n)$, the sizes are:

$$\begin{aligned}
\text{Step 2:} \quad & O(n \log n) \\
\text{Step 3:} \quad & O(\log^2 n) \\
\text{Step 5:} \quad & O(2^{\log\log^2 n} \log n / \log\log n) \\
\text{Step 6:} \quad & O(\log^2 n \log\log\log n / \log\log n),
\end{aligned}$$

each of which is $O(n \log n)$. Both of $O(m^2 \log \log \log n / \log \log n + mn)$ and $O(n \log n)$ are $O(m^2 \log \log \log n / \log \log n + mn + n \log n)$, as required.

The circuits for Steps 2, 3, and 5 each have depth 2, and the circuit for Step 6 has depth 3, giving a total depth of 9. Recall, however, that the circuits for Steps 5 and 6 are alternating circuits. Theorem 5.3.2 has the property that the first layer can be either AND or OR-gates. Therefore, we can choose the circuit for Step 5 to have AND-gates in its first layer and OR-gates in its second layer, and the circuit for Step 6 to have OR-gates in its first layer. Therefore, using compression (Theorem 5.2.2) we can save a single layer of gates between Steps 5 and 6, giving a total depth of 8.

Finally, the circuits for Steps 2 and 3 were constructed using Theorem 7.2.1, and hence have balanced gates in the last layer. Applying Lemma 7.2.3 twice reduces the depth to 6, and reduces the size slightly. □

COROLLARY 7.2.6 The multiplication of two n-bit natural numbers can be performed with a unit-weight threshold circuit of size $O(n^2)$ and depth 7.

PROOF: Suppose we are to multiply two natural numbers x, y to give a result z. Suppose the binary representation of x is $x_1, \ldots, x_n$, and the binary representation of y is $y_1, \ldots, y_n$. Then,

$$z = xy = x \sum_{i=1}^{n} 2^{n-i} y_i = \sum_{i=1}^{n} 2^{n-i} (x \cdot y_i).$$

Since $y_i \in \mathbf{B}$, the products $x \cdot y_i$ can be computed with a single layer of $O(n^2)$ two-input AND-gates. The sum can be computed using Theorem 7.2.5 in size $O(n^2)$ and depth 3. The total size is therefore $O(n^2)$, and the total depth is 7. Figure 7.10 shows the construction for $n = 3$. □

7.3   Small Weight Threshold Circuits

While Theorem 7.2.5 uses threshold-gates with unit weights, it is possible to reduce the depth dramatically using small weights. This can be achieved by using the obvious unrestricted weight circuit for iterated addition, described in the next theorem, on scaled-down subproblems.

THEOREM 7.3.1 The addition of n m-bit natural numbers can be performed with a threshold circuit of size $O(mn + n \log n)$, depth 2, and maximum weight 2^{m-1}.

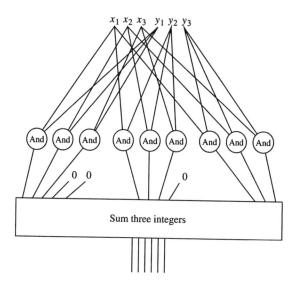

Figure 7.10
Circuit for multiplying two 3-bit natural numbers using Corollary 7.2.6.

PROOF: The proof is very similar to that of Theorem 7.2.1 and Corollary 7.2.2. Suppose the input numbers are $x_1, \ldots, x_n \in \mathbb{N}$, and that for $1 \leq i \leq n$, the binary representation of x_i is $x_{i,1} x_{i,2} \cdots x_{i,m}$. Let the sum y have binary representation $y_1 y_2 \cdots y_{m+\ell+1}$, where for conciseness, ℓ denotes $\lfloor \log n \rfloor$. This situation is depicted in Figure 7.11. We will describe a threshold circuit for computing the kth bit y_k of the sum. Note that y_k depends only on $x_{i,j}$ for $1 \leq i \leq n$ and $k - \ell - 1 \leq j \leq m$ (see Figure 7.12). For the purposes of description, assume for the moment that $k \geq \ell + 2$.

$$
\begin{array}{rccccc}
 & x_{1,1} & x_{1,2} & \cdots & x_{1,m} \\
+ & x_{2,1} & x_{2,2} & \cdots & x_{2,m} \\
 & & \vdots & & \\
+ & x_{n,1} & x_{n,2} & \cdots & x_{n,m} \\
\hline
y_1 \quad \cdots \quad y_{\ell+1} & y_{\ell+2} & y_{\ell+3} & \cdots & y_{m+\ell+1}
\end{array}
$$

Figure 7.11
Adding n m-bit natural numbers.

$$
\begin{array}{rcccccc}
 & & x_{1,k-\ell-1} & x_{1,k-\ell} & \cdots & x_{1,m} \\
+ & & x_{2,k-\ell-1} & x_{2,k-\ell} & \cdots & x_{2,m} \\
 & & & \vdots & & \\
+ & & x_{n,k-\ell-1} & x_{n,k-\ell} & \cdots & x_{n,m} \\
\hline
c_1 \ \cdots \ c_{\ell+1} & \boxed{y_k} & & y_{k+1} & \cdots & y_{m+\ell+1}
\end{array}
$$

Figure 7.12
y_k depends on $x_{i,j}$ for $1 \leq i \leq n$ and $k - \ell - 1 \leq j \leq m$.

It is easy to construct a threshold-gate g with maximum weight $2^{m+\ell+1-k}$ that has excitation level equal to the natural number with binary representation

$$
c_1 c_2 \cdots c_{\ell+1} y_k y_{k+1} \cdots y_{m+\ell+1},
$$

by connecting $x_{i,j}$ to g with weight 2^{m-j} for $1 \leq i \leq n$ and $k - \ell - 1 \leq j \leq m$. For each of the $2^{\ell+1}$ values of the carry bits $c_1, \ldots, c_{\ell+1}$ we have a pair of these threshold-gates, one that becomes active if its excitation level is at least

$$
c_1 c_2 \cdots c_{\ell+1} 1 \underbrace{00 \ldots 0}_{m+\ell+1-k},
$$

and one that becomes active if its excitation level is at most

$$
c_1 c_2 \cdots c_{\ell+1} 1 \underbrace{11 \ldots 1}_{m+\ell+1-k}.
$$

If $x_k = 0$, then exactly one of each pair is active, and hence there are exactly $2^{\ell+1}$ active gates. If $x_k = 1$, then one pair has both gates active, and exactly one of every other pair is active, and hence there are exactly $2^{\ell+1} + 1$ active gates. The gate that computes y_k is therefore a unit-weight linear threshold function with threshold $2^{\ell+1} + 1$.

We have shown how to compute y_k in depth 2 with size $2^{\ell+2} + 1 = O(n)$ and maximum weight $2^{m+\ell+1-k}$, provided $k \geq \ell + 2$. The bits y_k for $1 \leq k \leq \ell + 1$ are computed similarly within the same depth, size, and weight bounds (Problem 8). Therefore, the sum of n natural numbers of m bits can be computed in depth 2, size $O(mn + n \log n)$, and maximum weight 2^{m-1}. $\square$

For example, Figure 7.13 shows the subcircuit for computing y_3, with $n = 3$ and $m = 4$.

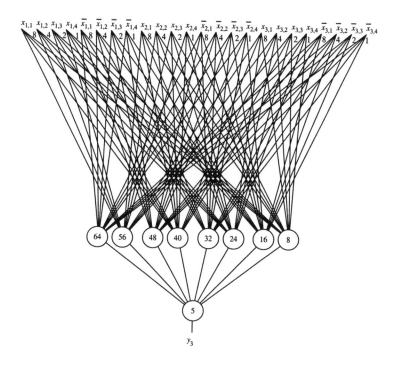

Figure 7.13
A circuit for computing y_3, the third most significant bit of the sum of three four-bit integers using Theorem 7.3.1.

		$x_{1,1}$	$x_{1,2}$	$x_{1,3}$	$x_{1,4}$
	$+$	$x_{2,1}$	$x_{2,2}$	$x_{2,3}$	$x_{2,4}$
	$+$	$x_{3,1}$	$x_{3,2}$	$x_{3,3}$	$x_{3,4}$
y_1	y_2	$\boxed{y_3}$	y_4	y_5	y_6

Note that as in Theorem 7.2.1, the gates in the second layer are balanced threshold-gates.

THEOREM 7.3.2 The addition of n m-bit natural numbers can be performed with a threshold circuit of size $O(m^2 + mn + n \log n)$, depth 3, and maximum weight $O(n)$.

PROOF: The proof is similar in approach to Theorem 7.2.5. As in Step 1 of Theorem 7.2.5, the numbers are first arranged into an $n \times m$ array of bits. The array is divided into blocks with n rows and $\lfloor \log n \rfloor + 1$ columns. The sum of each block has, by

Lemma 7.2.4, $2(\lfloor \log n \rfloor + 1)$ bits. The least significant $\lfloor \log n \rfloor + 1$ bits of each block sum is used to make a result word, and the most significant $\lfloor \log n \rfloor + 1$ bits of each block sum is used to make a carry word, in the manner of Step 5 of Theorem 7.2.5. As in Step 6 of Theorem 7.2.5, these two numbers are then added to give the result. For example, the leftmost part of Figure 7.14 shows the algorithm computing the sum $235+255+178+240$, taking $n = 4$, $m = 8$.

Each block is summed using Theorem 7.3.1 in depth 2, size $O(n \log n)$, and maximum weight $O(n)$. Since there are $O(m/\log n)$ blocks, the total size to this point is $O(mn)$. The result word and carry word are added using Theorem 6.2.2. This part of the circuit has depth 3, size $O((m + \log n)^2)$, and unit weights. Therefore, the circuit has size $O(mn + (m + \log n)^2)$, depth 5, and maximum weight $O(n)$. If $m = O(\log n)$, the size is $O(n \log n)$. If $m = \Omega(\log n)$, the size is $O(m^2 + mn)$. Both of these sizes are $O(m^2 + mn + n \log n)$.

The depth can be reduced from 5 to 4 by observing that the carry-generate and carry-propagate bits of the sum of the result and carry words can be computed at the same time the blocks are summed, using the technique of Theorem 7.3.1, in depth 2 and size $O(mn)$. With the carry-generate and carry-propagate bits provided, it is easy to check that the carry circuit designed in Theorem 6.2.1 has depth 2, which implies that the circuit from Theorem 6.2.2 has depth 2. The task of checking the details is left to the reader (Problem 9).

Finally, the depth can be reduced to 3 by using Lemma 7.2.3, since the second layer of the depth 4 circuit is comprised of balanced threshold-gates. □

COROLLARY 7.3.3 The multiplication of two n-bit natural numbers can be performed with a threshold circuit of size $O(n^2)$ and depth 4, and maximum weight $O(n)$.

PROOF: The proof is identical to that of Corollary 7.2.6, substituting Theorem 7.3.2 for Theorem 7.2.5. □

7.4 Threshold Complexity Classes

Define $\mathcal{UC}^k$, $\mathcal{TC}^k$, and $\mathcal{WC}^k$ to be the class of problems that can be solved respectively by unit-weight, small-weight, and unrestricted weight threshold circuits, of polynomial size and depth $O(\log^k n)$, for $k \geq 0$. Define

$$\mathcal{UC} = \cup_{k \geq 0} \mathcal{UC}^k$$

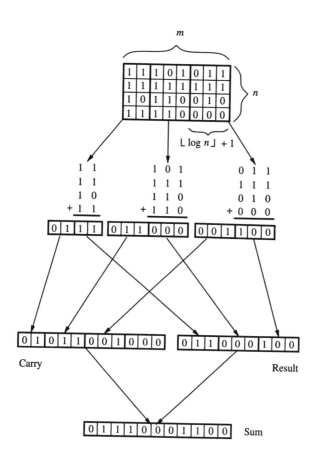

Figure 7.14
The algorithm of Theorem 7.3.2 computing $235 + 255 + 178 + 240 = 908$.

$$\mathcal{TC} \;=\; \cup_{k \geq 0} \mathcal{TC}^k$$
$$\mathcal{WC} \;=\; \cup_{k \geq 0} \mathcal{WC}^k.$$

Obviously, for all $k \geq 0$, $\mathcal{UC}^k \subseteq \mathcal{TC}^k \subseteq \mathcal{WC}^k$.

THEOREM 7.4.1 All Boolean linear threshold functions can be computed by a unit weight threshold circuit of depth 7 and size $O(n^2 \log^2 n)$. All Boolean linear threshold functions can be computed by a small weight threshold circuit of depth 4 and size $O(n^2 \log^2 n)$.

PROOF: Let $f = \theta_n(w_1, \ldots, w_n, h)$ be a Boolean linear threshold function. By Theorem 4.2.1, we can assume without loss of generality that each weight w_i is an integer with $O(n \log n)$ bits, for $1 \leq i \leq n$. By Theorem 3.2.6, we can assume without loss of generality that $h = 0$.

The circuit is constructed as follows (see Figure 7.15). Encode the weights in binary. Select the weights corresponding to **true** inputs using a bank of AND-gates connecting each bit of the encoding of w_i to x_i. Put the result into an iterated addition circuit constructed using either Theorem 7.2.5 (for the first statement claimed) or Theorem 7.3.2 (for the second statement claimed). The sign bit of the output will be **true** iff the Boolean linear threshold function $f(x_1, \ldots, x_n) = 0$. Placing a NOT-gate on the output (and applying Theorem 5.1.1 to move all NOT-gates to the inputs if required) gives the required circuit.

There are $O(n^2 \log n)$ AND-gates used in the selection of the weights, and the iterated addition circuit has size $O(n^2 \log^2 n)$ and depth 6 if unit weights are required, and depth 3 if small weights are required. The total depth is therefore 7 for unit weights and 4 for small weights. $\square$

COROLLARY 7.4.2 $\mathcal{WC}^k = \mathcal{TC}^k = \mathcal{UC}^k$ for all $k \geq 0$.

Since by Corollary 7.4.2, $\mathcal{UC}^0 = \mathcal{TC}^0 = \mathcal{WC}^0$, we will use $\mathcal{TC}^0$ in preference to the $\mathcal{UC}^0$ or $\mathcal{WC}^0$.

Further define $\mathcal{UC}^0_k$, $\mathcal{TC}^0_k$, and $\mathcal{WC}^0_k$ to be the class of problems that can be solved respectively by unit-weight, small-weight, and unrestricted weight threshold circuits, of polynomial size and depth k, for $k \geq 1$. We state the following theorem without proof.

THEOREM 7.4.3 For all $k \geq 1$, $\mathcal{WC}^0_k \subseteq \mathcal{TC}^0_{k+1}$, and $\mathcal{TC}^0_k \subseteq \mathcal{UC}^0_{k+1}$.

The proof of the latter proposition is left to Problem 10. It is interesting to consider the relationships between our threshold complexity classes and those developed in Chapters 2 and 5. First, we consider the relationship between constant depth, polynomial size threshold circuits and alternating circuits.

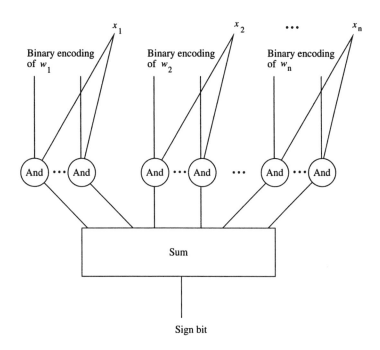

Figure 7.15
A classical circuit for computing a Boolean linear threshold function.

COROLLARY 7.4.4 $\mathcal{TC}^0 \neq \mathcal{AC}^0$.

PROOF: PARITY $\in \mathcal{TC}^0$ by by Theorem 7.2.1, yet PARITY $\notin \mathcal{AC}^0$ by Theorem 6.3.3. Therefore, $\mathcal{TC}^0 \neq \mathcal{AC}^0$. □

Next, we consider the relationship between threshold circuits and classical circuits. While it is obvious that all Boolean linear threshold functions are in $\mathcal{NC}^2$ (by Theorem 6.1.5 and Theorem 6.2.2), we will actually be able to show that they are in $\mathcal{NC}^1$.

LEMMA 7.4.5 There is a classical circuit of size $16n$ and depth 4 that, on input three n-bits natural numbers a, b, c, outputs two natural numbers d, e such that $a+b+c = d+e$.

PROOF: The proof is very similar to that of Theorems 6.2.1 and 6.2.2. The output d is the carry word from Theorem 6.2.1, and e is the result word from Theorem 6.2.2.

$$
\begin{array}{c c c c c c c c}
a &   & 1 & 1 & 1 & 1 & 0 & 1 \\
b & + & 1 & 0 & 0 & 1 & 1 & 1 \\
c & + & 1 & 1 & 0 & 1 & 0 & 1 \\
\hline
d & 1 & 1 & 0 & 1 & 0 & 1 & 0 \\
e &   & 1 & 0 & 1 & 1 & 1 & 1 \\
\end{array}
$$

Figure 7.16
The sum $a + b + c = d + e$ when $a = 61$, $b = 39$, and $c = 53$, using the construction of Lemma 7.4.5.

Suppose the binary representation of a is $a_1 a_2 \cdots a_n$, the binary representation of b is $b_1 b_2 \cdots b_n$, and the binary representation of c is $c_1 c_2 \cdots c_n$. The binary representation of d will be $d_1 d_2 \cdots d_{n+1}$, and the binary representation of e will be $e_1 e_2 \cdots e_n$.

Define d_i to be 1 if there is a carry generated in the ith bit of the operands, for $1 \leq i \leq n$. That is, d_i is 1 if at least two of a_i, b_i, and c_i are 1. Therefore, $d_{n+1} = 0$ and for $1 \leq i \leq n$,

$$d_i = (a_i \vee b_i) \wedge (b_i \vee c_i) \wedge (a_i \vee c_i).$$

The circuit for d thus consists of $3n$ OR-gates and $2n$ AND-gates, arranged in 3 layers.

Define e_i to be 1 if adding the ith bits of the operands results in a 1 in the ith bit of the result, ignoring carry into the ith place. That is, for $1 \leq i \leq n$,

$$e_i = a_i \oplus b_i \oplus c_i.$$

Using Theorem 5.3.1 it is easily seen that

$$a_i \oplus b_i \oplus c_i = (a_i \wedge b_i \wedge c_i) \vee (a_i \wedge \overline{b}_i \wedge \overline{c}_i) \vee (\overline{a}_i \wedge b_i \wedge \overline{c}_i) \vee (\overline{a}_i \wedge \overline{b}_i \wedge c_i).$$

The circuit for e thus consists of $3n$ OR-gates and $8n$ AND-gates, arranged in 4 layers.

It can be proved that $a + b + c = d + e$. The circuit described above for computing d and e uses $6n$ OR-gates and $10n$ AND-gates, in 4 layers. $\square$

As an example of the computation performed by the circuit of Lemma 7.4.5, consider the case in which $a = 61$, $b = 39$, and $c = 53$. Then, $d = 106$ and $e = 47$, and $a + b + c = d + e = 153$. The binary representations of these numbers are shown in Figure 7.16 (note that since we number from left to right, the bits of d appear to be shifted one place to the left).

THEOREM 7.4.6 The addition of n m-bit integers can be performed with a classical circuit of size $O(nm + m^2 + n \log n)$ and depth $O(\log n)$.

PROOF: We will show the required result for the addition of natural numbers. The extension to integers is left to the reader. The sum of n natural numbers can be computed using a tree structure of units built from the circuit of Lemma 7.4.5, somewhat along the lines of the proof of Lemma 6.1.1.

Starting with n numbers, divide them into groups of three and apply the circuit of Lemma 7.4.5 to reduce each group to two numbers. Repeat this until only two numbers remain. After i repetitions we are left with $\lceil (2/3)^i n \rceil$ integers (Problem 13). Therefore, $\log_{3/2} n = O(\log n)$ repetitions suffice. Thus, since the circuit of Lemma 7.4.5 has constant depth, the depth to this point is $O(\log n)$.

A total of $O(n)$ applications of the circuit of Lemma 7.4.5 are used. By Lemma 7.2.4, all partial sums produced by this algorithm have $O(m + \log n)$ bits. Thus, the circuit of Lemma 7.4.5 has size $O(m + \log n)$, and so the size to this point is $O(n(m + \log n))$.

Finally, add the two remaining numbers with a classical circuit of size $O((m + \log n)^2)$ and depth $O(\log n)$ constructed using the alternating circuit from Theorem 6.2.2 and the method of transforming a $\mathcal{AC}^0$ circuit to an $\mathcal{NC}^1$ circuit in Theorem 6.1.5.

If $m = \Omega(\log n)$, the size for the first part of the circuit is $O(nm)$ and the size for the second part of the circuit is $O(m^2)$. If $m = O(\log n)$, the size for the first part of the circuit is $O(n \log n)$ and the size for the second part of the circuit is $O(\log^2 n)$. Therefore, the total size is $O(nm + m^2 + n \log n)$. Since both parts have depth $O(\log n)$, the total depth is $O(\log n)$. $\square$

THEOREM 7.4.7 All Boolean linear threshold functions are in $\mathcal{NC}^1$.

PROOF: The proof is almost identical to Theorem 7.4.1, substituting Theorem 7.4.6 for Theorem 7.2.5. There are $O(n^2 \log n)$ AND-gates used in the selection of the weights, and the iterated addition circuit has size $O(n^2 \log^2 n)$. The depth is clearly $O(\log n)$. $\square$

The relationship between $\mathcal{NC}$, $\mathcal{AC}$, and $\mathcal{TC}$ should now be clear:

COROLLARY 7.4.8 1. For $k \geq 0$, $\mathcal{NC}^k \subseteq \mathcal{AC}^k \subseteq \mathcal{TC}^k$.
2. For $k \geq 0$, $\mathcal{TC}^k \subseteq \mathcal{NC}^{k+1}$.
3. $\mathcal{NC} = \mathcal{AC} = \mathcal{TC}$.

PROOF: The parts of the above statements relating $\mathcal{NC}$ and $\mathcal{AC}$ follow from Corollary 6.1.6. The parts referring to $\mathcal{TC}$ are fairly simple. Part (1) is obvious, since alternating circuits are a special case of threshold circuits. Part (2) is a corollary of Theorem 7.4.7, since polynomial size circuits have polynomial fan-in, and hence weights with a polynomial number of bits. Part (3) follows immediately from part (2). $\square$

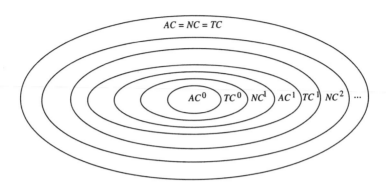

Figure 7.17
The classes $\mathcal{NC}^k$, $\mathcal{TC}^k$, and $\mathcal{AC}^k$.

Figure 7.17 shows the relationships between $\mathcal{NC}^k$ and $\mathcal{AC}^k$ from Corollary 7.4.8. It should now also be clear from Theorem 7.4.6 that the class $\mathcal{P}$ is the same whether we use polynomial size classical, alternating, or weighted threshold circuits.

7.5 The $\mathcal{TC}^0$ Hierarchy

Recall from the previous section that $\mathcal{TC}_k^0$ is the set of functions that can be computed by a polynomial size, small weight threshold circuit of depth k. Note that

$$\mathcal{TC}^0 = \cup_{k \geq 0} \mathcal{TC}_k^0.$$

The $\mathcal{TC}^0$ *hierarchy* is the infinite sequence of sets

$$\mathcal{TC}_0^0 \subseteq \mathcal{TC}_1^0 \subseteq \mathcal{TC}_2^0 \subseteq \mathcal{TC}_3^0 \subseteq \cdots.$$

It is an open problem as to whether the $\mathcal{TC}^0$ hierarchy collapses, that is, whether more than three layers of threshold-gates are needed to compute all functions in $\mathcal{TC}^0$ in polynomial size. It is known that the hierarchy cannot collapse past depth 3, that is, there is a function that is in $\mathcal{TC}_3^0$ that requires exponential size to compute with a depth 2 threshold circuit. That function is the *Boolean inner product* function, defined as follows: $IP: \mathbf{B}^{2n} \to \mathbf{B}$ where

$$IP(x_1, \ldots, x_n, y_1, \ldots, y_n) = \bigoplus_{i=1}^{n} (x_i \wedge y_i).$$

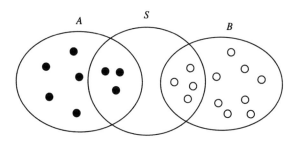

Figure 7.18
S is a 1/24-discriminator of A and B.

We will also follow the convention established in Section 5.3 and use IP to denote the language of the inner product function, that is,

$$IP = \{x_1, \ldots, x_n, y_1, \ldots, y_n \mid IP(x_1, \ldots, x_n, y_1, \ldots, y_n) = 1\}.$$

THEOREM 7.5.1 $IP \in \mathcal{TC}_3^0$.

PROOF: The circuit is constructed as follows. The first layer consists of two-input AND-gates that compute $x_i \wedge y_i$ for each $1 \le i \le n$. The next two layers compute the parity of these conjunctions using Theorem 7.2.1. The resulting circuit has depth 3 and $O(n)$ size. $\square$

Suppose $A, B \subseteq \mathbf{B}^n$, $A \cap B = \emptyset$. A set S is called an ϵ-*discriminator of A over B* if S intersects a larger fraction of A than B.

$$\frac{\|S \cap A\|}{\|A\|} - \frac{\|S \cap B\|}{\|B\|} \ge \epsilon.$$

So, for example, in Figure 7.18, S is a $3/8 - 1/3 = 1/24$-discriminator of A over B. If $A \subseteq \mathbf{B}^n$, let $\overline{A}$ denote $\{x \in \mathbf{B}^n \mid x \notin A\}$. If $A \subseteq \mathbf{B}^n$, a set S is called an ϵ-*discriminator for A* if it is an ϵ-discriminator for A over $\overline{A}$.

If C is a threshold circuit with n inputs and a single output, define the *language* of C, denoted $\mathcal{L}(C)$, as follows:

$$\mathcal{L}(C) = \{x \in \mathbf{B}^n \mid C \text{ outputs 1 on input } x\}.$$

LEMMA 7.5.2 Suppose C is a threshold circuit with a single output gate that has unit weights and inputs from m other subcircuits $C_1, \ldots, C_m$. There exists $1 \le \ell \le m$ such that $\mathcal{L}(C_\ell)$ is a $1/m$-discriminator for $\mathcal{L}(C)$.

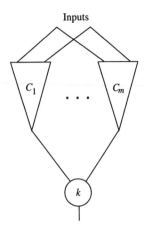

Figure 7.19
The circuit C in Lemma 7.5.2.

PROOF: Suppose C is a threshold circuit with n inputs and a single output, where the output gate has unit weights and threshold k, and inputs from m subcircuits $C_1, \ldots, C_m$, as shown in Figure 7.19. For each $x \in \mathcal{L}(C)$, at least k of the subcircuits output 1. That is, $x \in \mathcal{L}(C_i)$ for at least k choices of i. Therefore,

$$\sum_{i=1}^{m} \|\mathcal{L}(C_i) \cap \mathcal{L}(C)\| \geq k \|\mathcal{L}(C)\|.$$

Similarly, for each $x \in \overline{\mathcal{L}(C)}$, at most $k-1$ of the subcircuits C_i output 1, and hence

$$\sum_{i=1}^{m} \left\| \mathcal{L}(C_i) \cap \overline{\mathcal{L}(C)} \right\| \leq (k-1) \left\| \overline{\mathcal{L}(C)} \right\|.$$

Therefore,

$$\sum_{i=1}^{m} \left(\frac{\|\mathcal{L}(C_i) \cap \mathcal{L}(C)\|}{\|\mathcal{L}(C)\|} - \frac{\left\| \mathcal{L}(C_i) \cap \overline{\mathcal{L}(C)} \right\|}{\left\| \overline{\mathcal{L}(C)} \right\|} \right) \geq 1.$$

Therefore, by the pigeonhole principle, there must be a subcircuit C_ℓ such that

$$\frac{\|\mathcal{L}(C_\ell) \cap \mathcal{L}(C)\|}{\|\mathcal{L}(C)\|} - \frac{\left\| \mathcal{L}(C_\ell) \cap \overline{\mathcal{L}(C)} \right\|}{\left\| \overline{\mathcal{L}(C)} \right\|} \geq 1/m.$$

That is, $\mathcal{L}(C_\ell)$ is a $1/m$-discriminator for $\mathcal{L}(C)$. $\square$

We state the following lemma without proof:

LEMMA 7.5.3 For all $X, Y \subseteq \mathbf{B}^n$,

$$\left| \|(X \times Y) \cap IP\| - \|(X \times Y) \cap \overline{IP}\| \right| \leq \sqrt{\|X\|\|Y\|2^n}.$$

We need one more counting lemma before the main result:

LEMMA 7.5.4 $\left\| IP \cap \mathbf{B}^{2n} \right\| = 2^{n-1}(2^n - 1).$

PROOF: Let

$$
\begin{aligned}
T(n) &= \left\| IP \cap \mathbf{B}^{2n} \right\| \\
F(n) &= \left\| \overline{IP} \cap \mathbf{B}^{2n} \right\|.
\end{aligned}
$$

Then, $T(1) = 1$, $F(1) = 3$, and for all $n > 1$, $T(n) = 3T(n-1) + F(n-1)$. It can be proved by induction on n that $T(n) = 2^{n-1}(2^n - 1)$ and $F(n) = 2^{n-1}(2^n + 1)$. The details are left to the reader (Problem 16). $\square$

We are now ready for the main result of this section:

THEOREM 7.5.5 Any threshold circuit of weight w and depth 2 for $IP\colon \mathbf{B}^{2n} \to \mathbf{B}$ must have size $\Omega(2^{n/2}/w^2)$.

PROOF: Let C' be a threshold circuit of depth 2, weight w, and size z that computes the inner product function $IP(x_1, \ldots, x_n, y_1, \ldots, y_n)$. Then, by Theorem 7.1.1, there is a threshold circuit C of depth 2, weight w, and size z that computes the complement of the inner product function

$$\overline{IP}(x_1, \ldots, x_n, y_1, \ldots, y_n) = \overline{IP(x_1, \ldots, x_n, y_1, \ldots, y_n)}.$$

That is, $\mathcal{L}(C) = \mathcal{L}(\overline{IP}) \cap \mathbf{B}^{2n}$. For the moment, assume that the output gate of C has unit weights. We will return to the general case later. C has the general form illustrated in Figure 7.19, where each subcircuit C_i is a single Boolean threshold-gate with small weights.

Suppose C_i computes $\theta_{2n}(w_1, \ldots, w_{2n}, h)$. For $k \in \mathbf{Z}$, let

$$
\begin{aligned}
X_k &= \{x_1, \ldots, x_n \mid \textstyle\sum_{i=1}^n w_i x_i = k\} \\
Y_k &= \{y_1, \ldots, y_n \mid \textstyle\sum_{i=1}^n w_{i+n} y_i \geq k\}.
\end{aligned}
$$

Then,

$$\mathcal{L}(C_i) = \cup_{j=-w}^{w} X_j \times Y_{h-j}.$$

Therefore, by Lemma 7.5.3 (the absolute value sign in the hypothesis makes sure that it is applicable to $\overline{IP}$ as well as IP), and using the fact that $\|X_k\| \leq 2^n$ and $\|Y_k\| \leq 2^n$ for all $-w \leq k \leq w$,

$$\left| \|\mathcal{L}(C_i) \cap \mathcal{L}(C)\| - \left\|\mathcal{L}(C_i) \cap \overline{\mathcal{L}(C)}\right\| \right|$$

$$\leq \sum_{j=-w}^{w} \sqrt{\|X_j\|\|Y_{h-j}\|2^n}$$

$$\leq (2w+1)2^{3n/2}.$$

By Lemma 7.5.2, one of the threshold-gates C_ℓ is a $1/m$-discriminator for $\mathcal{L}(C)$. Therefore,

$$1/m \quad \leq \quad \frac{\|\mathcal{L}(C_\ell) \cap \mathcal{L}(C)\|}{\|\mathcal{L}(C)\|} - \frac{\left\|\mathcal{L}(C_\ell) \cap \overline{\mathcal{L}(C)}\right\|}{\left\|\overline{\mathcal{L}(C)}\right\|} \quad \text{(by Lemma 7.5.2)}$$

$$= \quad \frac{\|\mathcal{L}(C_\ell) \cap \mathcal{L}(C)\|}{2^{n-1}(2^n+1)} - \frac{\left\|\mathcal{L}(C_\ell) \cap \overline{\mathcal{L}(C)}\right\|}{2^{n-1}(2^n-1)} \quad \text{(by Lemma 7.5.4)}$$

$$\leq \quad \frac{\|\mathcal{L}(C_\ell) \cap \mathcal{L}(C)\| - \left\|\mathcal{L}(C_\ell) \cap \overline{\mathcal{L}(C)}\right\|}{2^{2n-1}}$$

$$\leq \quad \frac{(2w+1)2^{3n/2}}{2^{2n-1}} \quad \text{(by the above)}$$

$$= \quad \frac{(2w+1)}{2^{n/2-1}}.$$

(Note that the second-from-last step of the above sequence of inequalities is valid since Lemma 7.5.2 implies that $\|\mathcal{L}(C_\ell) \cap \mathcal{L}(C)\| - \left\|\mathcal{L}(C_\ell) \cap \overline{\mathcal{L}(C)}\right\| > 0$.) Therefore,

$$m \geq 2^{n/2+1}/(2w+1) = \Omega(2^{n/2}/w).$$

Now, suppose that the output gate does not have unit weights. Simply duplicate each level 1 gate connected to the output gate a number of times equal to the weight of that connection, and make all weights equal to 1. The new circuit has size mw and a unit weight output gate, and hence the above argument can be used to show that $mw = \Omega(2^{n/2}/w)$, and hence $m = \Omega(2^{n/2}/w^2)$. $\square$

COROLLARY 7.5.6 $IP \notin TC_2^0$.

PROOF: By Theorem 7.5.5, any depth 2 circuit of weight n^c for inner product must have size $\Omega(2^{n/2}/n^{2c})$, which is larger than any polynomial. □

Theorem 7.5.5 is actually slightly stronger than strictly necessary to prove Corollary 7.5.6. We can prove something that is slightly better:

COROLLARY 7.5.7 For all $\epsilon < 1/4$, any threshold circuit of weight $2^{\epsilon n}$ and depth 2 for $IP: \mathbf{B}^{2n} \to \mathbf{B}$ must have size $\Omega(2^{(1-4\epsilon)n/2})$.

We can conclude from what we have discovered so far that the TC^0 hierarchy can be separated up to depth 3:

THEOREM 7.5.8 $TC_1^0 \neq TC_2^0 \neq TC_3^0$.

PROOF: By Theorem 4.1.1, PARITY $\notin WC_1^0$, and hence PARITY $\notin TC_1^0$. By Theorem 7.2.1, PARITY $\in TC_2^0$. Hence, $TC_1^0 \neq TC_2^0$.
By Corollary 7.5.6, $IP \notin TC_2^0$. By Theorem 7.5.1, $IP \in TC_3^0$. Hence, $TC_2^0 \neq TC_3^0$. □

The lower bound on inner product can also be used to prove other lower bounds:

COROLLARY 7.5.9 Multiplication of two integers is not in TC_2^0.

PROOF: For a contradiction, suppose multiplication is in TC_2^0. To compute the function $IP(x_1, \ldots, x_n, y_1, \ldots, y_n)$, it is enough to compute the the product of the natural number with binary representation

$$x = x_1 \underbrace{0 \ldots 0}_{\lfloor \log n \rfloor + 1} x_2 \underbrace{0 \ldots 0}_{\lfloor \log n \rfloor + 1} \ldots \underbrace{0 \ldots 0}_{\lfloor \log n \rfloor + 1} x_n$$

times the natural number with binary representation

$$y = y_1 \underbrace{0 \ldots 0}_{\lfloor \log n \rfloor + 1} y_2 \underbrace{0 \ldots 0}_{\lfloor \log n \rfloor + 1} \ldots \underbrace{0 \ldots 0}_{\lfloor \log n \rfloor + 1} y_n.$$

Suppose $a_{i,j} = x_i \wedge y_j$, for $1 \leq i, j \leq n$. The product of x and y can be written as:

				$a_{1,1}$	0	$a_{2,1}$	0	$\ldots$	$a_{n-1,1}$	0	$a_{n,1}$
	$a_{1,2}$		0	$a_{2,2}$	0	$a_{3,2}$	0	$\ldots$	$a_{n,2}$		
				$\vdots$							
$a_{1,n}$	$\ldots$	$a_{n-1,n}$	0	$a_{n,n}$							
? z_1	$\ldots$	z_{n-1}	?	z_n	?	z_{n+1}	?	$\ldots$			z_{2n}

where each 0 denotes a block of $\lfloor \log n \rfloor + 1$ zeros, and "?" denotes a block of arbitrary bits. By Lemma 7.2.4, the carry from each of the nonzero columns fits into the block of zeros to the left, and hence there can never be a carry into a nonzero column. Therefore, each z_i is the parity of the nonzero column appearing above it, and in particular

$$z_n = \bigoplus_{i=1}^{n} a_i = \bigoplus_{i=1}^{n} (x_i \wedge y_i) = IP(x_1, \ldots, x_n, y_1, \ldots, y_n).$$

Therefore, $IP \in \mathcal{TC}_2^0$. But this contradicts Corollary 7.5.6. Therefore, multiplication cannot be in $\mathcal{TC}_2^0$. $\square$

7.6   Problems

1. Improve Theorem 7.2.1 by showing that any symmetric function $f : \mathbf{B}^n \to \mathbf{B}$ can be computed by a unit-weight threshold circuit with size $n + 2$ and depth 2. (Hint: consider the proof of Theorem 5.3.1.)

2. A MOD gate is a gate that outputs 1 iff the number of its inputs equal to 1 is congruent to zero modulo p, for some $p \in \mathbf{N}$. Show that for every language L that can be recognized by a polynomial size circuit of unrestricted-weight threshold-gates and unbounded fan-in MOD-gates of depth k,

   (a) $L \in \mathcal{WC}_{k+1}^0$, and

   (b) if the output gate is not a MOD-gate, then $L \in \mathcal{WC}_k^0$.

   balanced gate.

3. State and prove variants of Problem 2 for small-weight threshold-gates, and for unit-weight threshold-gates.

4. State and prove a version of Lemma 7.2.3 in which g_0 does not have unit weights.

5. State and prove a version of Lemma 7.2.3 in which g_0 does not have unit weights, and for $1 \leq i < j \leq m$, gates g_i and g_j do not necessarily have distinct inputs.

6. Complete the proof of Lemma 7.2.4 by showing (by induction on z) that any natural number z can be written using exactly $\lfloor \log z \rfloor + 1$ bits, and (by induction on m) that a natural number with m bits can be at most $2^m - 1$.

7. Show that the bound of Lemma 7.2.4 is tight in the following sense: there exists a value of n such that for all choices of m, the sum of n natural numbers of m bits has exactly $m + \lfloor \log n \rfloor + 1$ bits.

8. Complete the proof of Theorem 7.3.1 by showing that the carry bits y_k for $1 \leq k \leq \ell+1$ can be computed by a single threshold circuit of depth 2, size $O(n)$ and maximum weight 2^{m-1}.

9. Complete the proof of Theorem 7.3.2.

10. Prove that for all $k \geq 1$, $\mathcal{T}C_k^0 \subseteq \mathcal{U}C_{k+1}^0$ (This is part of Theorem 7.4.3.)

11. Define $\mathcal{M}C^k$ to be the class of problems that can be solved in polynomial size and depth $O(\log^k n)$ by a circuit of MAJORITY-gates, and $\mathcal{M}C_k^0$ to be the class of problems that can be solved in polynomial size and depth k by a circuit of MAJORITY-gates. Show that:

    (a) For all $k \geq 0$, $\mathcal{M}C^k = \mathcal{T}C^k$.

    (b) For all $k \geq 1$, $\mathcal{U}C_k^0 \subseteq \mathcal{M}C_{k+1}^0$.

    (c) For all $k \geq 1$, $\mathcal{T}C_k^0 \subseteq \mathcal{M}C_{k+1}^0$.

12. Show that the fan-in of any unit weight threshold circuit can be reduced from f to $\sqrt{f}$ in return for a polynomial increase in size and a constant-multiple increase in depth.

13. Use the tools from Problem 1 of Section 6.4 to prove the statement in the proof of Theorem 7.4.6 that "after i repetitions we are left with $\lceil (2/3)^i n \rceil$ integers".

14. Prove a weighted version of Lemma 7.5.2, as follows. Suppose C is a threshold circuit of weight w with a single output gate that has inputs from m other subcircuits $C_1, \ldots, C_m$. Prove that there exists $1 \leq i \leq m$ such that $\mathcal{L}(C_i)$ is a $1/w$-discriminator for $\mathcal{L}(C)$.

15. Show that the multiplication of two n-bit natural numbers can be performed by a unit-weight threshold circuit of depth 4 and size $O(n^3)$.

16. Complete the proof of Lemma 7.5.4 by showing that $T(1) = 1$, $F(1) = 3$, and for all $n > 1$, $T(n) = 3T(n-1) + F(n-1)$, and hence deducing that $T(n) = 2^{n-1}(2^n - 1)$ and $F(n) = 2^{n-1}(2^n + 1)$.

17. Prove a variant of Theorem 5.3.4 for threshold circuits. That is, show that there exists a function that requires a threshold circuit of size $\Omega(2^{n/3})$, even if weights are unrestricted.

18. Separate $\mathcal{T}C_1^0$ from $\mathcal{T}C_2^0$ by showing that PARITY $\in \mathcal{T}C_2^0$, but PARITY $\notin \mathcal{T}C_1^0$.

19. Show that the depth bound of Theorem 7.3.1 is tight in the sense that there can be no shallower threshold circuit that computes the same function.

20. Show that no unit-weight threshold function of 2-input ANDs (see Figure 7.20) can be in $\mathcal{T}C_1^0$, regardless of the threshold value. This is an alternate method of separating $\mathcal{T}C_1^0$ from $\mathcal{T}C_2^0$ (see Problem 18).

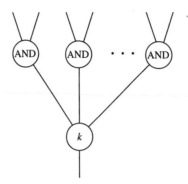

Figure 7.20
The function from Problem 20.

7.7 Bibliographic Notes

Theorem 7.2.1 appears in Hajnal *et. al* [55]. Lemma 7.2.3 is used in Hajnal *et. al* [55] and Hofmeister, Hohberg, and Köhling [62]. The size bound of Theorem 7.2.1 can be reduced by a polynomial amount in exchange for an increase in depth, see Beame, BrissonBrisson, Erik, and Ladner [14], Siu, Roychowdhury, and Kailath [128], and Spielman [132].

A $\mathcal{TC}^0$ circuit for the addition of n natural numbers is implicit in Chandra, Stockmeyer, and Vishkin [27]. An explicit construction for such a circuit was sketched in Parberry [95] from a description that arose with discussions between the author, N. Pippenger and M. S. Paterson on separate occasions in 1986. Theorem 7.2.5 fills in the details in that construction and makes a more serious attempt at optimizing the depth.

Theorem 7.3.1 and Theorem 7.3.2 are due to Hofmeister, Hohberg, and Köhling [62]. In that reference the weights are achieved implicitly by duplicating wires, a method which is not permitted in our model since we defined the interconnections of a circuit using a graph. In their model, although it is not stated explicitly, the interconnections form a graph with multiple edges, commonly known as a *multi-graph*. In their framework it is natural to consider only small-weight circuits, since unrestricted weight circuits could have wires duplicated an exponential number of times, which smacks of intractability. Alon and Bruck [7] have shown how to add two integers in depth 2 with a unit weight threshold circuit. Siu and Roychowdhury [127] present threshold circuits for iterated addition in depth 2 and multiplication in depth 3 with small weight (but larger sizes than Theorem 7.3.2 and Corollary 7.3.3, respectively).

A crude version of Corollary 7.4.2 can be found in Parberry and Schnitger [99, 101].

The proof of the first part of Theorem 7.4.3 (for all $k \geq 1$, $\mathcal{WC}_k^0 \subseteq \mathcal{TC}_{k+1}^0$) can be found in Goldmann, Håstad, and Razborov [48]. Lemma 7.4.5 and Theorem 7.4.6 are due to Hong [63, 64].

Theorem 7.5.1, Lemma 7.5.2, Theorem 7.5.5, and their proofs are from Hajnal *et al.* [55]. The $\mathcal{TC}^0$ hierarchy has not, to date, been separated above depth 3. The corresponding hierarchy for *monotone* $\mathcal{TC}^0$ (that is, $\mathcal{TC}^0$ without Boolean negations) has been separated (Yao [152]). A conjecture slightly weaker than the collapse of the $\mathcal{TC}^0$ hierarchy is that $\mathcal{AC}^0$ is contained in $\mathcal{TC}_3^0$ (Immerman and Landau [67]); however, all that is known is that every function in $\mathcal{AC}^0$ can be computed by threshold circuits of depth 3 and size $n^{\log^c n}$ (Allender [5]). Corollary 7.5.9 is from Hofmeister, Hohberg, and Köhling [62].

Siu, Roychowdhury, Kailath [128] contains a variant of Theorem 5.3.5 for threshold circuits rather than alternating circuits, and prove the result in Problem 17. Lupanov [80, 81] has proved a variant of Theorem 5.3.5 for threshold-gates that achieves size $2^{n/2}/\sqrt{n}$ in depth 4.

8 Cyclic Networks

So far, we have studied only *feedforward circuit*, that is, circuits without feedback loops. This chapter deals with threshold circuits that have feedback loops. Section 8.1 examines the relationship between these *cyclic networks* and feedforward threshold circuits. Section 8.2 considers various problems related to the halting problem for cyclic networks. Perhaps not surprisingly, such questions are generally $\mathcal{NP}$-complete. Section 8.3 is devoted to a special kind of cyclic network called the *Hopfield network*, in which the weights are symmetric.

8.1 Cyclic Networks and Threshold Circuits

A cyclic network is essentially a threshold circuit without the restriction that the interconnection graph be acyclic. Formally, a *cyclic network* is a 6-tuple $M = (V, X, Y, A, w, h)$, where

$$V \text{ is a finite ordered set}$$
$$X, Y, A \subseteq V.$$
$$w : V \times V \to \mathbf{Z}$$
$$h : V \to \mathbf{Z}.$$

The processors of X are *input processors*, and the processors of Y are *output processors*. The processors of A are *initially active processors*. The function w is called a *weight assignment*, and the function h is called a *threshold assignment*. Let $E \subseteq V \times V$ be defined by $E = \{(u, v) \mid w(u, v) \neq 0\}$. E represents the connections between processors. The ordered pair (V, E) forms a graph, which is called the *interconnection graph* of M. The ordered triple (V, E, w) forms a labelled, directed graph. There are three measures of the amount of hardware needed to implement M which we will consider here. The first is the *size*, defined to be $\|V\|$, the second is the *weight*[1], defined to be

$$\sum_{u,v \in V} |w(u, v)|,$$

and the third is the *maximum weight*, defined to be

$$\max_{u,v \in V} |w(u, v)|.$$

Any cyclic network of size z and maximum weight w will have weight at most zw. In a neural network with size z and weight w, we will assume that $w \geq z - 1$. This

---

[1] In the neural networks literature it is customary to add the thresholds into the weight of M. It is clear that our definition differs from this one by at most a factor of two.

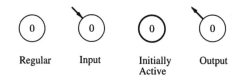

| | Regular | Input | Initially Active | Output |

Regular   Input   Initially   Output
Active

Figure 8.1
Types of processors in a cyclic network.

	v_1	v_2	v_3	v_4
v_1	0	2	-1	0
v_2	0	-1	3	0
v_3	0	0	0	5
v_4	-1	0	0	1

Table 8.1
The weight matrix for a cyclic network. The entry in row i and column j is $w(v_i, v_j)$.

is a reasonable assumption since w is bounded below by the number of edges in the interconnection graph, which is at least $z - 1$ for all connected graphs.

We will depict a cyclic network as a directed graph with thresholds in the nodes and weights on the edges. Input processors will be indicated by an in-pointing arrow, initially active processors will be heavily outlined, and output processors will be indicated by an out-pointing arrow as shown in Figure 8.1. For example, Figure 8.2 shows a cyclic network $M = (V, X, Y, A, w, h)$ with $V = \{v_1, v_2, v_3, v_4\}$, $X = \{v_1, v_2\}$, $Y = \{v_3\}$, $h(v_1) = 0$, $h(v_2) = 2$, $h(v_3) = h(v_4) = 3$, and weights given by the weight matrix shown in Table 8.1.

Each processor can be in one of two states, which we will call *active*, and *inactive*. A neural network computes by having the processors change state according to certain rules. More formally, a *computation* of $M = (V, X, Y, A, w, h)$ on an input $x \in \mathbf{B}^n$ is defined as follows. Initially, the input processors X are placed into states that encode x. That is, if $X = \{u_1, \ldots, u_n\}$, then processor u_i is placed in the active state iff $x_i = 1$. The processors of A are also placed in the active state. All other processors are placed in the inactive state. The computation then begins.

Time is measured by dividing it into discrete intervals. These intervals are numbered consecutively, with time interval 0 denoting the period immediately before the computation begins. We will say "at time t" to denote the period immediately after interval t

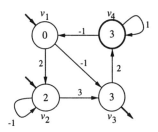

Figure 8.2
A cyclic network.

has ended and immediately before interval $t + 1$ begins. During each interval, some or all of the processors are given the opportunity to update their states.

The state of an individual processor $v \in V$ is updated as follows. Let $S(v, t) \in \mathbf{B}$ denote the state of processor v at time t. We will use the Boolean value 1 to denote the active state and 0 to denote the inactive state. Define the *excitation level* of processor v at time t, denoted $\sigma(v, t)$, by

$$\sigma(v, t) = \sum_{u \in V} w(u, v) S(u, t). \tag{8.1.1}$$

Define the state of processor v at time 0, $S(v, 0)$, as follows. Suppose $X = \{u_1, \ldots, u_n\}$. Then, $S(u_i, 0) = x_i$ for $1 \le i \le n$. For $v \notin X$,

$$S(v, 0) = \begin{cases} 1 & \text{if } v \in A \\ 0 & \text{otherwise.} \end{cases}$$

Suppose $v \in V$. Define the *potential state* of processor v at time $t \ge 0$, $S'(v, t)$ as follows.

$$S'(v, t) = \begin{cases} 1 & \text{if } \sigma(v, t) \ge h(v) \\ 0 & \text{otherwise.} \end{cases}$$

Processor $v \in V$ is said to be *stable* at time t if its state is consistent with its excitation level, that is, $S(v, t) = S'(v, t)$, and *unstable* otherwise. The state of processor v at time $t > 0$, $S(v, t)$, is then defined to be

$$S(v, t) = \begin{cases} S'(v, t - 1) & \text{if } v \text{ is updated during interval } t \\ S(v, t - 1) & \text{otherwise.} \end{cases}$$

Suppose $U \subseteq V$, and $U = \{u_1, \ldots, u_m\}$ for some $m \in \mathbb{N}$. The *state* of processor-set U at time t is defined to be the sequence

$$S(U, t) = (S(u_1, t), S(u_2, t), \ldots, S(u_m, t)).$$

$S(U, t)$ is *stable* if $S(U, t) = S(U, t+1)$. A *configuration* of M at time t is defined to be $S_M(t) = S(V, t)$. A computation is said to be *terminated* by time t if it has reached a stable configuration. that is, $S_M(t) = S_M(t+1)$. Other terminology used to describe termination includes *halting, reaching a stable state*, and *converging*. The *time* required by a computation of M on input x, denoted $\tau(M, x)$, is defined to be the smallest value of t such that the computation of M on input x has terminated by time t. The *output* of M on input x is defined to be $S(Y, \tau(M, x))$.

A cyclic network M_2 is said to be *$f(t)$-equivalent* to M_1 iff for all inputs x, for every computation of M_1 on input x that terminates in time t there is a computation of M_2 on input x that terminates in time $f(t)$ with the same output. A cyclic network M_2 is said to be *equivalent* to M_1 iff it is *t*-equivalent to it.

An alternative mode of computation commonly used in neural network literature involves what is called *clamping* the inputs, that is, physically restraining the input processors from participating in the computation. This is achieved by redefining the states of input processors $X = \{u_1, \ldots, u_n\}$ on input $x_1, \ldots, x_n$ to be $S(u_i, t) = x_i$, and insisting that $w(v, u_i) = 0$, for all $1 \le i \le n$, $t \ge 0$, $v \in V$. The effect of clamping can easily be obtained in our model.

THEOREM 8.1.1 For every clamped cyclic network M_1 of size z and weight w there exists an equivalent unclamped cyclic network M_2 of size z and weight $w + n$.

PROOF: Let $M_1 = (V, X, Y, A, w_1, h_1)$ be a clamped neural network. Define $M_2 = (V, X, Y, A, w_2, h_2)$, where w_2 and h_2 are the same as w_1 and h_1 respectively, except for the fact that $w_2(u, u) = 1$ and $h_2(u) = 1$ for all $u \in X$, and $w_1(v, u) = 0$ for all $v \in V$, $u \in X$. Since the input processors of M_2 are always stable, any computation of M_1 can be duplicated exactly in M_2. $\square$

Figure 8.3 shows a clamped cyclic network (with clamped input processors marked "C") and the equivalent unclamped network constructed using Theorem 8.1.1.

When we gave a formal definition of a cyclic network, we divided time into discrete intervals and stated that *"During each interval, some or all of the processors are given the opportunity to update their states"*. However, we did not specify exactly which processors update their state within any particular interval. Two modes of computation are prevalent in the literature.

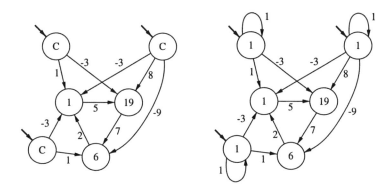

Figure 8.3
A clamped cyclic network (left) and its implementation (right).

1. *Sequential operation*, in which a single processor updates its state within each interval. This processor may be chosen at random, or according to some deterministic rule.
2. *Parallel operation*, in which at least two processors update their state during each interval. For example, each processor could decide randomly and independently whether to update, or all processors could update during every interval. The former is called *random parallel*, and the latter *fully parallel* operation.

A computation is called *productive* if at least one unstable processor is updated in each interval.

Cyclic networks operated in fully parallel mode are very similar to threshold circuits. Every cyclic network that is known to terminate under fully parallel mode within a given time bound can be replaced by a threshold circuit:

THEOREM 8.1.2 For every cyclic network of size z and weight w that halts in time t on all inputs when operated in fully parallel mode, there is an equivalent threshold circuit of size zt, weight wt and depth t.

PROOF: Suppose $M = (V, X, Y, A, w, h)$ is a cyclic network that halts in time t on all inputs in fully parallel mode. Suppose $X = \{v_1, \ldots, v_n\}$, $A = \{v_{n+1}, \ldots, v_m\}$. The corresponding threshold circuit $C = (V', X', Y', E, \ell)$ consists of t "snapshots" of M, one at each point in time:

$$\begin{aligned} V' &= \{(v, i) \mid 1 \le i \le t\} \\ X' &= \{x_1, \ldots, x_n\} \end{aligned}$$

$$Y' = \{(y,t) \mid y \in Y\}$$
$$E = \{((u,i),(v,i+1)) \mid w(u,v) \neq 0, \ 1 \leq i < t\}$$
$$\cup \{(x_i,v) \mid w(x_i,v) \neq 0, \ 1 \leq i \leq n\}.$$

The node function assignment ℓ is defined as follows. If $v \in V$, and $u_1, \ldots, u_k$ are the members of V such that $w(u_i,v) \neq 0$, then for all $2 \leq i \leq t$,

$$\ell((v,i)) = \theta_k(w(u_1,v), \ldots, w(u_k,v), h(v)).$$

For all $v \in V$, define

$$h_1(v) = h(v) - \sum_{i=n+1}^{m} w(v_i,v).$$

If $v \in V$, and $u_1, \ldots, u_k$ are the members of X such that $w(u_i,v) \neq 0$, then

$$\ell((v,1)) = \theta_k(w(u_1,v), \ldots, w(u_k,v), h_1(v)).$$

It can be proved by induction on i that for all inputs $b_1, \ldots, b_n \in \mathbf{B}^n$, for all $v \in V$, and for all $1 \leq i \leq t$, the value of gate (v,i) of C on input $b_1, \ldots, b_n$ (denoted $v_C(b_1, \ldots, b_n)((v,i))$ in Section 2.3) equals the state of processor v of M at time i. The details of the proof are left to the reader (Problem 1).

Since C essentially consists of t copies of M, it has weight at most wt and size zt. Since all edges are from one copy to the next, each copy of M takes up a single level in C. Therefore, C has depth t. $\square$

For example, Figure 8.4 shows the threshold circuit constructed from the cyclic network in Figure 8.2.

Threshold circuits are essentially a special case of cyclic networks, in the sense that for every threshold circuit of size z and depth d there is a cyclic network of size z that terminates in time d in fully parallel mode. This observation together with the partial converse obtained in Theorem 8.1.2 tells us that polynomial size cyclic networks that run in polynomial time in fully parallel mode are very close to threshold circuits: the size is related by a polynomial, and the time requirement is identical in each case.

8.2   Termination of Cyclic Networks

Not all cyclic neural networks will halt on all inputs. For example, the network shown in Figure 8.5 will not converge in any mode of operation, regardless of initial state. Instead, it alternates between two configurations. A cyclic network that repeats the same sequence

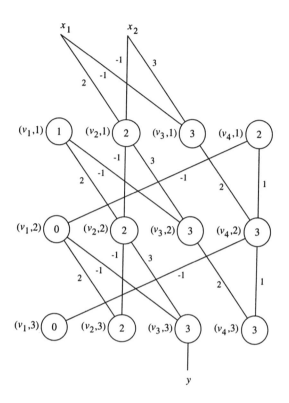

Figure 8.4
A threshold circuit constructed from the cyclic network of Figure 8.2 using Theorem 8.1.2.

of configurations indefinitely is said to be in a *limit cycle*. The *length* of a limit cycle is defined to be the of distinct configurations in it. For example, the network of Figure 8.5 has a limit cycle of length 2 under any mode of operation.

THEOREM 8.2.1 For all $k \in \mathbf{N}$, there is a cyclic neural network that has a limit cycle of length $2k$ under any mode of operation.

PROOF: Suppose $k \in \mathbf{N}$. If $k = 1$, we use the network in Figure 8.5. Now suppose $k \geq 2$. Define $M = (V, X, Y, A, w, h)$ as follows. $V = \{v_1, \ldots, v_k\}$, and $X = Y = A = \emptyset$. All weights are 0 except for the following: $w(v_i, v_{i+1}) = 1$ for $1 \leq i < k$, and $w(v_k, v_1) = -1$. The thresholds are set as follows: $h(v_1) = 0$, and $h(v_i) = 1$ for $1 < i \leq k$. For example, if $k = 6$, M is shown in Figure 8.6.

Figure 8.5
A cyclic network that does not converge in any mode of operation.

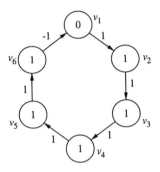

Figure 8.6
A cyclic network that has a limit cycle of length 12.

Suppose M is started with all processors inactive. Then, v_1 is the only unstable node. When it becomes active, v_2 becomes the only unstable node. When v_2 becomes active, v_3 becomes the only unstable node. This continues around the cycle until all nodes become active. At this point, v_1 becomes the only unstable node. The entire process is repeated around the cycle with nodes becoming inactive again. Since only one node is unstable in each configuration, the limit cycle exists regardless of the computation mode.

For example, the limit cycle for the cyclic network illustrated in Figure 8.6 is shown in Table 8.2. ☐

The limit cycle described in the proof of Theorem 8.2.1 is *inherently sequential*, meaning that there is always exactly a single unstable node (see Problem 6).

It is clear that some (but not all) cyclic networks have stable configurations. It would be useful to tell which cyclic networks have stable configurations, and which do not. Unfortunately, the problem of determining whether a given cyclic network has a stable configuration is computationally intractable.

v_1	v_2	v_3	v_4	v_5	v_6	Unstable
0	0	0	0	0	0	v_1
1	0	0	0	0	0	v_2
1	1	0	0	0	0	v_3
1	1	1	0	0	0	v_5
1	1	1	1	0	0	v_5
1	1	1	1	1	0	v_6
1	1	1	1	1	1	v_1
0	1	1	1	1	1	v_2
0	0	1	1	1	1	v_3
0	0	0	1	1	1	v_4
0	0	0	0	1	1	v_5
0	0	0	0	0	1	v_6
0	0	0	0	0	0	v_1

Table 8.2
The limit cycle for the cyclic network of Figure 8.6.

The Stable Configuration Problem (SNN)

INSTANCE: A cyclic network M.

QUESTION: Does M have a stable configuration?

THEOREM 8.2.2 SNN is $\mathcal{NP}$-complete.

PROOF: SNN $\in \mathcal{NP}$ since a stable configuration can be easily verified by a polynomial size circuit (see Problem 7). We will prove that 3SAT $\leq_p$ SNN. This is enough to prove, by Theorem 5.4.5 and Theorem 6.2.4, that SNN is $\mathcal{NP}$-complete.

Suppose we are given an alternating circuit C of depth 2 in which the first layer gates have fan-in 3. We will assume, from the construction used in the proof of Theorem 6.2.4, that the first layer gates are OR-gates and the second layer gate is an AND-gate. The corresponding cyclic network has three parts, or units, called the the *input unit*, the *computation unit*, and the *output unit*. The input unit has the task of receiving the input to C and maintaining it throughout the computation. The computation unit evaluates C on the given input. The output unit is unstable unless the computation unit reports that C is satisfied by input encoded in the input unit.

The input unit consists of n clamped input processors, one for each variable, constructed using Theorem 8.1.1. The computation unit is a two-layer circuit that simulates

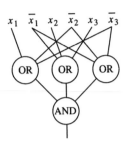

Figure 8.7
An alternating circuit of depth 2 and first-layer fan-in 3.

C on the input stored in the input unit. The first layer simulates the first layer of C, using Lemma 4.1.3 to simulate complementation using negative weights. The third layer simulates the output gate of C. The output unit consists of an unstable processor from Theorem 8.2.1, with an edge of unit weight from the second layer processor of the computation unit.

More formally, let $C = (V, X, Y, E, \ell)$ be an alternating circuit, where $X = \{x_1, \ldots, x_n\}$ and $Y = \{y\}$. The corresponding cyclic network $M = (V', X', Y', A, w, h)$ is constructed as follows.

$$
\begin{aligned}
V' &= V \cup X \cup \{u\} \text{ for some } u \notin V \cup X \\
X' &= X \\
Y' &= \{u\} \\
A &= \emptyset.
\end{aligned}
$$

For all $x_i \in X$, $w(x_i, x_i) = 1$ and $h(x_i) = 1$. For each $v \in V$ in the first level of C, let $x_1[b_1]$, $x_2[b_2]$, $x_3[b_3]$ be the three literals such that $(x_i[b_i], v) \in E$ for all $1 \le i \le 3$, where $b_1, b_2, b_3 \in \mathbf{B}$ (using the notation of Theorem 5.3.1). Then, $w(x_i, v) = 2b_i - 1$ and $h(v) = 1 - b_1 - b_2 - b_3$. For all edges $(v, y) \in E$, $w(v, y) = 1$, and $h(y) = \|\{v \mid (v, y) \in E\}\|$. Finally, $w(y, u) = 1$, $w(u, u) = -1$, and $h(u) = 0$. All unspecified weights are zero. For example, Figure 8.8 shows the cyclic network constructed for the alternating circuit shown in Figure 8.7.

It is simple to design a polynomial time algorithm, and hence (by Theorem 2.3.3) a polynomial size circuit for the transformation given above. The processors of the input unit are all stable. The computation unit is stable iff it simulates C on the input encoded in the input unit. The output unit is stable iff the computation unit outputs one. Therefore, M has a stable configuration iff C is satisfiable. $\square$

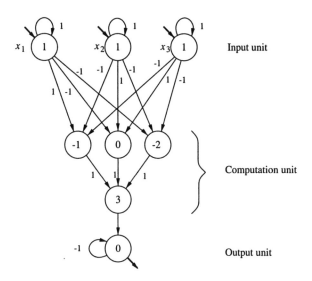

Figure 8.8
The cyclic network corresponding to the alternating circuit of Figure 8.7 in Theorem 8.2.2.

COROLLARY 8.2.3 SNN is $\mathcal{NP}$-complete even for cyclic networks with unit weights under one of the following conditions:

1. All nodes have fan-in 3 and all terminating computations do so in polynomial time.
2. All terminating computations do so in constant time under fully parallel operation.

PROOF: Theorem 8.2.2 uses only unit weights. $\mathcal{NP}$-completeness under condition (1) follows by replacing node y in that construction by a tree of nodes using the technique of Theorem 6.1.5, and noting that all terminating computations of M involve changing the state of each node simulating first-level gates in C only once. $\mathcal{NP}$-completeness under condition (2) is obvious. □

SNN asked whether a given cyclic network has a stable configuration. It is perhaps more important to ask about whether the computation of a cyclic network on a given input ever reaches a stable configuration.

The Halting Problem (HNN)
INSTANCE: A cyclic network M and an input x.
QUESTION: Is there a computation of M that reaches a stable configuration?

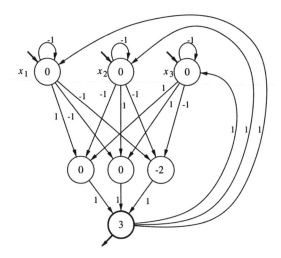

Figure 8.9
The cyclic network corresponding to the alternating circuit of Figure 8.7 in Theorem 8.2.4.

THEOREM 8.2.4 HNN is $\mathcal{NP}$-hard.

PROOF: The proof is almost identical to that of Theorem 8.2.2. HNN is $\mathcal{NP}$-hard rather than $\mathcal{NP}$-complete because a computation that reaches a stable configuration might take time exponential in the number of nodes in the cyclic network.

The essential difference in the proof is that the input unit is left unclamped and allowed to float unless the computation unit is satisfied. There is no longer any need for the output unit u, which can be deleted. That is, we change $h(x_i)$ to 0 and $w(x_i, x_i)$ to -1, and add new weights $w(y, x_i) = 1$, for $1 \leq i \leq n$. For example, Figure 8.9 shows the cyclic network constructed for the alternating circuit shown in Figure 8.7.

Suppose C is satisfiable. A stable configuration for M can be found by setting the states of the nodes in the input unit to the satisfying assignment, and setting the states of all the other nodes to active. Conversely, if M has a stable configuration, then node y must be active, which implies that the input unit encodes a satisfying assignment for C. $\square$

8.3   Hopfield Networks

A Hopfield network is a cyclic network in which the interconnection graph is undirected (that is, $w(u, v) = w(v, u)$ for all $u, v \in V$).

THEOREM 8.3.1 For every clamped Hopfield network M_1 of size z and weight w there exists an equivalent unclamped Hopfield network M_2 of size z and weight $w + n$.

PROOF: The proof is similar to that of Theorem 8.1.1, and is left to the reader (Problem 8). □

A Hopfield network is called *simple* if it has no self-loops (that is, $w(v, v) = 0$ for all $v \in V$), *semisimple* if it has no self-loops of negative weight. It is said to be in *normal form* if the presentations of the linear threshold functions computed by the nodes are decisive, and have a threshold value of 0.

THEOREM 8.3.2 Any productive sequential computation of a simple, normal form Hopfield network with weight w will terminate in time $2w$.

PROOF: Let $M = (V, X, Y, A, w, h)$ be a Hopfield network. Define the *stability* of M at time t to be

$$\beta(t) = \sum_{u \in V} S(u, t)\sigma(u, t)/2. \qquad (8.3.2)$$

We claim that an inactive node contributes 0 to the stability, and an active node v at time t contributes $\sigma(v, t)$. To see this, note that by the definition of σ (Equation (8.1.1)),

$$
\begin{aligned}
\beta(t) &= \sum_{u \in V} S(u, t)\sigma(u, t)/2 \\
&= \sum_{u \in V} \sum_{u' \in V} S(u, t)S(u', t)w(u', u)/2.
\end{aligned}
$$

Vertex v appears in this summation when $u = v$, in which case its contribution is

$$\sum_{u' \in V} S(v, t)S(u', t)w(v, u')/2,$$

and when $u' = v$, in which case its contribution is

$$\sum_{u \in V} S(u, t)S(v, t)w(u, v)/2.$$

Since the weights in a Hopfield network are symmetric, both of these contributions are identical, and sum to

$$\sum_{u \in V} S(u,t)S(v,t)w(u,v).$$

Hence, the contribution of any active node v to the stability is

$$\sum_{u \in V} S(u,t)w(u,v) = \sigma(v,t),$$

and the contribution of any inactive node v to the stability is 0. (Note that we are using the property that $w(v,v) = 0$ for all $v \in V$.)

We claim that for all $t \geq 0$, if some processor $v \in V$ is unstable and is updated at time t, then $\beta(t) \geq \beta(t-1) + 1$. There are two cases to consider. First, consider the case $S(v,t-1) = 0$ and $\sigma(v,t-1) \geq 1$. As was discussed in the previous paragraph, the contribution of vertex v to $\beta(t-1)$ is 0, and the contribution of v to $\beta(t)$ is $\sigma(v,t) = \sigma(v,t-1)$. Therefore, $\beta(t) = \beta(t-1) + \sigma(v,t-1)$, and so $\beta(t) \geq \beta(t-1) + 1$ as claimed. Now suppose $S(v,t-1) = 1$ and $\sigma(v,t-1) \leq -1$. The contribution of v to $\beta(t-1)$ is $\sigma(v,t-1) = \sigma(v,t)$. Therefore, $\beta(t) = \beta(t-1) - \sigma(v,t-1)$, and so $\beta(t) \geq \beta(t-1) + 1$ as claimed.

Suppose M has weight w. Then, for all $t \geq 0$, $-w \leq \beta(t) \leq w$. Since, from the above, $\beta(t) \geq \beta(t-1) + 1$, this implies that the computation must terminate in time $2w$. $\square$

COROLLARY 8.3.3 Any productive sequential computation of a semisimple normal form Hopfield network of weight w will terminate in time $2w$.

PROOF: Let $M = (V, X, Y, A, w, h)$ be a semisimple Hopfield network in normal form. A simple normal form Hopfield network M' can be found with the property that for every productive sequential computation of M, there is a productive sequential computation of M' that emulates M in the sense that M' has a set of processors that undergo the same state changes as their counterparts in M. Since the computation of M' terminates, the computation of M must also terminate. The details are left to Problem 11. $\square$

COROLLARY 8.3.4 Any productive sequential computation of a semisimple Hopfield network of size z and weight w will terminate in time $4w(z+1)$.

PROOF: Let $M = (V, X, Y, A, w, h)$ be a normal form Hopfield network. By Theorem 3.2.6 (using an initially-active processor with a positive-weight self-loop as in Theorem 8.1.1 to give a clamped value that provides the extra weight) we can construct a new Hopfield network M' with all thresholds equal to zero. This can be combined with Theorem 4.1.8 to make all presentations decisive while keeping thresholds equal to 0. Thus, M' is in normal form. Any computation of M can be emulated in M' by updating the processors in exactly the same order. Therefore, by Corollary 8.3.3, any productive sequential computation of M must terminate.

Suppose M has size z and weight w. Theorem 3.2.6 increases the weight of the network by an amount equal to the sum of the thresholds, each of which is bounded above by w. Theorem 4.1.8 doubles all of the weights. Therefore, by Corollary 8.3.3, termination is guaranteed within $4w(z+1)$ steps. $\square$

It is an easy matter to design a Hopfield network with negative-weight self-loops that does not halt when run in any mode. For example, the network shown in Figure 8.10(a) has a productive computation that cycles through all 2^n possible states on n processors. Figure 8.10(a) is slightly unsatisfying since its interconnection graph is *unconnected* (a graph is said to be *connected* if there is a sequence of edges that leads from every vertex to every other vertex). However, connected Hopfield networks with the same property do exist (see Problem 12).

It is also easy to design a Hopfield network without self-loops that does not halt when run in fully parallel mode, for example, the network shown in Figure 8.10(b) started with one node active and the other inactive. The network illustrated in Figure 8.10 alternates between two configurations. This is true of all Hopfield networks in fully parallel operation.

THEOREM 8.3.5 A fully parallel computation of a Hopfield network of weight w and size z will eventually alternate between two configurations within time $16z(w+1)$.

PROOF: Let $M = (V_1, X_1, Y_1, A_1, w_1, h_1)$ be a Hopfield network. Define a second Hopfield network $M_2 = (V_2, X_2, Y_2, A_2, w_2, h_2)$ as follows. This network will have a special property: the interconnection graph will be *bipartite*, that is, $V_2 = V_\ell \cup V_r$, where $V_\ell \cap V_r = \emptyset$, and if $w(u,v) \neq 0$, then either $u \in V_\ell$ and $v \in V_r$, or *vice-versa*. M_2 is defined as follows:

$$V_2 = V_\ell \cup V_r \text{ where}$$
$$V_\ell = \{(v,0) \mid v \in V_1\} \text{ and}$$
$$V_r = \{(v,1) \mid v \in V_1\}$$
$$X_2 = \{(v,0) \mid v \in X_1\}$$
$$Y_2 = \emptyset \ A_2 = \{(v,0) \mid v \in A_1\}.$$

The weights and thresholds are set as follows: For all $u, v \in V_1$, $w_2((u,0),(v,1)) = w_2((v,1),(u,0)) = w_1(u,v)$. All other weights set to zero. For all $v \in V_1$, $h_2((v,0)) =$

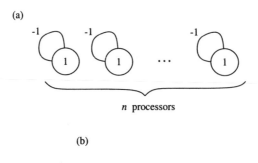

n processors

(b)

Figure 8.10
(a) A Hopfield network that does not converge in sequential mode, and (b) a Hopfield network with positive weights that does not converge in fully parallel mode.

$h_2((v,1)) = h_2(v)$.

For example, let $M_1 = (V_1, X_1, Y_1, A_1, w_1, h_1)$ be defined as follows.

$$V_1 = \{v_1, v_2, v_3, v_4, v_5\}$$
$$X_1 = \{v_1\}$$
$$Y_1 = \{v_4\}$$
$$A_1 = \emptyset,$$

w_1 is given by the weight matrix shown in Table 8.3, and $h_1(v_1) = h_1(v_2) = h_1(v_3) = 1$, $h_1(v_4) = 19$, $h_1(v_5) = 6$. Then, M_2 is given by:

$$V_\ell = \{(v_1, 0), (v_2, 0), (v_3, 0), (v_4, 0), (v_5, 0)\}$$
$$V_r = \{(v_1, 1), (v_2, 1), (v_3, 1), (v_4, 1), (v_5, 1)\}$$
$$X_1 = \{(v_1, 0)\}$$
$$Y_1 = \emptyset$$
$$A_1 = \emptyset,$$

w_2 is given by the weight matrix shown in Table 8.4, and $h_2((v_1, 0)) = h_2((v_2, 0)) = h_2((v_3, 0)) = 1$, $h_2((v_4, 0)) = 19$, $h_2((v_5, 0)) = 6$, and $h_2((v_1, 1)) = h_2((v_2, 1)) = h_2((v_3, 1)) = 1$, $h_2((v_4, 1)) = 19$, $h_2((v_5, 1)) = 6$. M_1 and M_2 are shown in Figure 8.11.

M_2 can be used to simulate M_1 as follows. In time interval 1, update processors $(v, 1)$ for all $v \in V$, sequentially in any order. If $x \in \mathbb{N}$, let $\delta(x) \in \mathbf{B}$ be zero if x is even and one otherwise. In each subsequent time interval t, update processors $(v, \delta(t))$ for all

	v_1	v_2	v_3	v_4	v_5
v_1	-1	0	1	-3	0
v_2	0	0	-3	0	1
v_3	1	-3	0	5	2
v_4	-3	0	5	0	7
v_5	0	1	2	7	0,

Table 8.3
The weight matrix for a cyclic network. The entry in row i and column j is $w_1(v_i, v_j)$.

	$(v_1,0)$	$(v_2,0)$	$(v_3,0)$	$(v_4,0)$	$(v_5,0)$	$(v_1,1)$	$(v_2,1)$	$(v_3,1)$	$(v_4,1)$	$(v_5,1)$
$(v_1,0)$	0	0	0	0	0	-1	0	1	-3	0
$(v_2,0)$	0	0	0	0	0	0	0	-3	0	1
$(v_3,0)$	0	0	0	0	0	1	-3	0	5	2
$(v_4,0)$	0	0	0	0	0	-3	0	5	0	7
$(v_5,0)$	0	0	0	0	0	0	1	2	7	0
$(v_1,1)$	-1	0	1	-3	0	0	0	0	0	0
$(v_2,1)$	0	0	-3	0	1	0	0	0	0	0
$(v_3,1)$	1	-3	0	5	2	0	0	0	0	0
$(v_4,1)$	-3	0	5	0	7	0	0	0	0	0
$(v_5,1)$	0	1	2	7	0	0	0	0	0	0

Table 8.4
The weight matrix for a cyclic network constructed from the one with weight matrix shown in Table 8.3, using Theorem 8.3.5.

$v \in V$, sequentially in any order. Suppose $V = \{v_1, \ldots, v_p\}$. Let $S_1(t)$ denote the state of M_1 at time t. Let $S_2(v,t)$ denote the state of processor $v \in V_2$ of M_2 at time t, and for $i \in \mathbf{B}$,

$$S_2^i(t) = (S_2((v_1, i), t), \ldots, S_2((v_p, i), t)).$$

Then, by induction on t, for all $t \geq 0$, $S_1(t) = S_2^{\delta(t)}(t)$ and for all $t \geq 1$, $S_1(t-1) = S_2^{\delta(t-1)}(t)$.

Since a bipartite graph has no self-loops, and hence no negative weight self-loops, all sequential computations of M_2 halt by Corollary 8.3.4. Hence, there is some termination time τ for which $S_2^0(\tau) = S_2^0(\tau + 2t)$ and $S_2^1(\tau + 1) = S_2^1(\tau + 2t + 1)$ for all $t \geq 1$. Therefore, for all $t \geq 1$, $S_1(\tau) = S_1(\tau + 2t)$ and $S_1(\tau + 1) = S_1(\tau + 2t + 1)$.

Suppose M has weight w and size z, and M_2 has weight w_2 and size z_2. Then, by Corollary 8.3.4, halts in time $4z(w+1)$, and hence M either halts or enters a limit cycle of length 2 in time $2z(w+1)$. Since $w_2 = 2w$ and $z_2 = 2z$, the result follows. $\square$

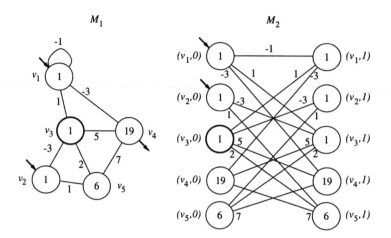

Figure 8.11
The original Hopfield network M_1 and the new Hopfield network M_2 constructed using Theorem 8.3.5.

Hopfield networks can be used to simulate threshold circuits by increasing the weights.

THEOREM 8.3.6 For every threshold circuit of size z, depth d, and maximum weight w, there is a Hopfield network of size z and weight $z^d w^d$ that computes the same function in time d in fully parallel mode.

PROOF: Suppose C is a threshold circuit of size z, depth d, and maximum weight w. A Hopfield network C' is obtained from C as follows. We make each edge of C bidirectional and increase the weights in such a manner that each processor is only affected by those edges which were formerly incoming. The processors at level k have their thresholds multiplied by $(zw)^{d-k}$, and the edges between level $k-1$ and level k have their weights multiplied by the same amount. Thus, the edges that were formally outputs from a processor at level k can have combined weight less than $z^{d-k} w^{d-k-1}$, whereas the presentation of each processor, which was formerly 1-separable, has become $z^{d-k} w^{d-k-1}$-separable, and the function computed is therefore unaffected by the former outputs.

The Hopfield network has size z and maximum weight $z^{d-1} w^d$, and therefore has weight $z^d w^d$. In fully parallel mode, at time t the first t levels of the circuit behave correctly, and hence the computation terminates in time d. $\square$

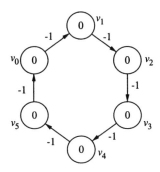

Figure 8.12
The network C_6 from Problem 2.

8.4   Problems

1. Complete the proof of Theorem 8.1.2 by proving by induction on i that for all inputs $b_1, \ldots, b_n \in \mathbf{B}^n$, for all $v \in V$, and for all $1 \leq i \leq t$, $v_C(b_1, \ldots, b_n)((v, i)) = S(v, t)$.

2. A *negative weight cycle* of length n is a cyclic network $C_n = (V, X, Y, A, w, h)$, where $V = \{v_0, \ldots, v_{n-1}\}$, $X = Y = A = \emptyset$, $h(v_i) = 0$ for $0 \leq i < n$, and $w(v_i, v_j) = -1$ if $j = i + 1 \pmod{n}$ (all unspecified weights are 0). For example, C_6 is shown in Figure 8.12. Show that for all odd n, C_n has no stable configuration.

3. Does the network C_n from Problem 2 have stable configurations for all even n?

4. What is the length of the longest limit cycle in the network C_n from Problem 2, as a function of n?

5. Define $M_n = (V, X, Y, A, w, h)$ as follows. $V = \{v_0, \ldots, v_{n-1}\}$, $X = Y = A = \emptyset$, $h(v_i) = 1$ for $0 \leq i < n$, $w(v_i, v_j) = 1$ if $j = i + 1 \pmod{n}$, and $w(v_i, v_j) = -1$ if $j = i + 2 \pmod{n}$, (all unspecified weights are 0). For example, M_6 is shown in Figure 8.13. Prove that for all $n \in \mathbf{N}$, M_n has an inherently sequential limit cycle of length $2n$.

6. Prove that the limit cycle described in Theorem 8.2.1 is inherently sequential for all $n \in \mathbf{N}$.

7. Prove that SNN $\in \mathcal{NP}$. (Hint: use the technique used in Lemma 1 to prove that SAT $\in \mathcal{NP}$.)

8. Prove Theorem 8.3.1, the clamping result for Hopfield networks analogous to Theorem 8.1.1.

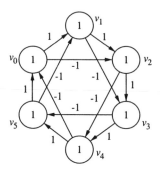

Figure 8.13
The network M_6 from Problem 5.

9. What part of the proof of Theorem 8.3.2 fails when negative weight self-loops are allowed?

10. What part of the proof of Theorem 8.3.2 fails when applied to general cyclic networks?

11. Prove that any productive sequential computation of a normal form Hopfield network of weight w will terminate in time $2w$, by completing the proof of Corollary 8.3.3.

12. Find a connected Hopfield network with n processors that has a productive computation which cycles through all 2^n possible states. (Figure 8.10(a) shows an *unconnected* Hopfield network with this property.)

13. The *evaluation problem* for cyclic neural networks is the problem of determining whether a given cyclic network with a single output has a stable configuration with output 1. Show that the evaluation problem is $\mathcal{NP}$-complete.

14. Show that the evaluation problem for Hopfield networks is $\mathcal{NP}$-complete. Is the same true if the weights are small?

15. Show that for every polynomial size Hopfield network there is a Hopfield network with exponential weights (recall that "exponential" means 2^{n^c} for some $c \in \mathbb{N}$.)

8.5 Bibliographic Notes

Theorem 8.1.2 uses a standard technique that can be traced back to Savage [120] (see also Goldschlager and Parberry [52], and Parberry and Schnitger [100, 102]).

Section 8.2 is based on the work of Porat [109], Godbeer [47], and Lipscomb [79]. More details can be found in those references, and in Parberry [95].

Theorem 8.3.2 is due to Hopfield [65]. Stability is essentially the quantity that Hopfield calls *energy*, and P. Smolensky [131] calls *harmony*. The proof of Theorem 8.3.5 is from Bruck and Goodman [21]. Alternate proofs of Theorem 8.3.5 can be found in Poljak and Sura [108], and Odlyzko and Randall [93] (see also Poljak [107]).

Goles-Chacc *et al.* [53] study the termination properties of cyclic networks in *block parallel mode*, in which the nodes are divided into blocks, each block is updated sequentially, and update of a block is defined to be a parallel update of all nodes in that block. Alon [6] has shown that every positive weight cyclic network has a terminating sequential computation. Lepley and Miller [77] show that a cyclic network can simulate a sequential computer such as a RAM with a polynomial overhead in hardware and time with high probability under random sequential operation. Problem 2 is from Alon [6].

9 Probabilistic Neural Networks

This chapter deals with threshold circuits in which the gates exhibit random behaviour. If the random behaviour is independent (such as a source of white noise), we find that it can actually be used to reduce size and depth. However, if the randomness is malicious (that is, it occurs in the worst possible way), extra resources must be used by the circuit to guard against frequent failure of gates.

Section 9.1 considers a probabilistic neural network model obtained by adding to the threshold circuit model a special kind of gate that changes state at random with a certain fixed probability, and defines a notion of computation on such a circuit model to within a small probability of error. Section 9.2 considers a randomized version of $\mathcal{TC}^0$, called $\mathcal{RTC}^0$, in which the error probability scales with input size. Section 9.3 introduces the *Boltzmann machine*, which has a completely different definition of probabilistic behaviour, yet is very close in resource requirements to threshold circuits. Section 9.4 considers threshold circuits with gates that behave unreliably, and possibly even maliciously. It is found that classical circuits can be simulated reliably and with small overhead by threshold circuits with unreliable gates.

9.1 Probabilistic Threshold Circuits

Suppose we add to our threshold circuit model the ability to make random choices. That is, we add gates that output **true** with probability p for any $0 < p < 1$. We will count these probabilistic gates in the size of the circuit, but since they can be grouped into a single layer, we will not count them in the depth. It is often useful to think of them as extra inputs that are provided values from an external random source. We will depict a probabilistic gate that is active with probability p as shown in Figure 9.1.

How useful is a circuit with probabilistic gates? Its output changes with time, but it is useful if it gives the correct answer *most* of the time. More formally, if $0 < \epsilon < 0.5$, a probabilistic threshold circuit C *ϵ-recognizes* a language L if it can determine whether or not a given input x belongs to L with probability of error ϵ. That is, it recognizes L iff there is a real number $0 < \epsilon < 0.5$ such that:

Figure 9.1
A probabilistic gate that is active with probability p.

1. For all $x \in L$, the probability that C accepts x is at least $1 - \epsilon$.
2. For all $x \notin L$, the probability that C accepts x is at most ϵ.

This is often called *two-sided bounded-error probabilism*. Note that $\epsilon < 0.5$ because a circuit with error probability 0.5 gives an unbiased random output regardless of the input, and is therefore not a useful computational device. (A circuit with error probability $\epsilon > 0.5$ is, however, every bit as useful as a circuit with $\epsilon < 0.5$: simply complement its output.)

A *Bernoulli trial* is a random event having some probability of success. In a sequence of N independent Bernoulli trials each with probability p of failure, the probability that at least m trials fail is denoted $B(m, N, p)$. We will find the following result invaluable:

LEMMA 9.1.1 If $m \geq Np$,

$$B(m, N, p) \leq \left(\frac{Np}{m} \right)^m \left(\frac{N - Np}{N - m} \right)^{N-m}.$$

Two-sided bounded-error probabilism appears at first to be an unnatural choice; for example, a language recognizer with error probability 0.4 cannot be considered very reliable. However, we will see that by repeating the probabilistic computation many times and taking the consensus, the probability of error can be made arbitrarily close to 0. This can be achieved while increasing the depth of the circuit by 1, and increasing the size by a constant multiple.

THEOREM 9.1.2 For every $0 < \lambda < \epsilon < 1/2$, any language that can be ϵ-recognized by a threshold circuit of depth d and size z can be λ-recognized by a threshold circuit of depth $d + 1$ and size

$$\left\lceil \frac{2 \log \lambda}{\log(4\epsilon(1 - \epsilon))} \right\rceil z + 1.$$

PROOF: Suppose C is a threshold circuit of size z and depth d which ϵ-recognizes a language $L \subseteq \mathbf{B}^n$. Suppose we perform N computations of C on the same input. Taking $p = \epsilon$ and $m = N/2$ in Lemma 9.1.1, we learn that the probability of at least half of N trials being in error is given by

$$B(N/2, N, \epsilon) \leq (4\epsilon(1 - \epsilon))^{N/2}.$$

Thus, if we make

$$N \geq \frac{2 \log \lambda}{\log(4\epsilon(1 - \epsilon))},$$

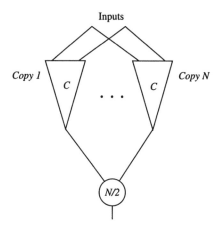

Figure 9.2
The circuit C' from Theorem 9.1.2.

trials and take the majority decision, the probability of failure is reduced to λ, for any $0 \leq \lambda \leq \epsilon$.

A new threshold circuit C' that λ-recognizes L can be obtained by taking N copies of C, and putting the results into a MAJORITY-gate (see Figure 9.2). C' thus has size $zN + 1$ and depth $d + 1$.

$\square$

It is possible to find more exact figures for N for given values of ϵ and λ. It suffices to find the smallest N for which $B(N/2, N, \epsilon) \leq \lambda$, where

$$B(m, N, p) = \sum_{i=m}^{N} \binom{N}{i} p^m (1-p)^{N-m}.$$

For example, the theory states that a probabilistic threshold circuit with only 60% chance of making the correct decision ($\epsilon = 0.4$) can be used to obtain 99.9% certainty ($\lambda = 0.001$) with 339 trials, regardless of the size of the input, but in practice (due to the weakness of Lemma 9.1.1), only 244 trials are necessary. Figures 9.3 and 9.4 give the number trials required in theory and in practice for each value of λ from 0.001 to 0.4, with $\epsilon = 0.4$. It is quite evident from a perusal of Figure 9.3 that the number of trials increases rapidly as the required error λ approaches zero.

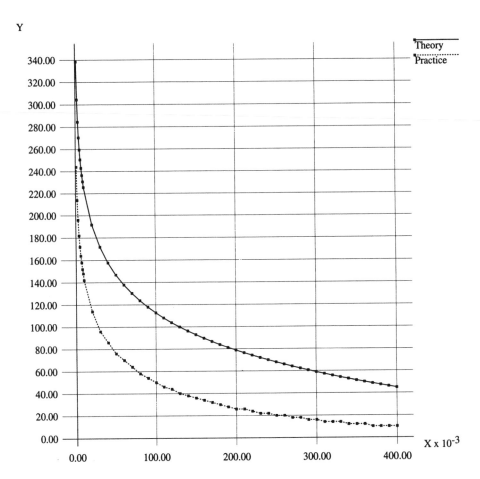

Figure 9.3
Number of trials N versus required error probability λ, with existing error probability $\epsilon = 0.4$ in Theorem 9.1.2. The value of λ is recorded on the X-axis, and N on the Y-axis. The upper line is the theoretical value, and the lower line the one required in practice.

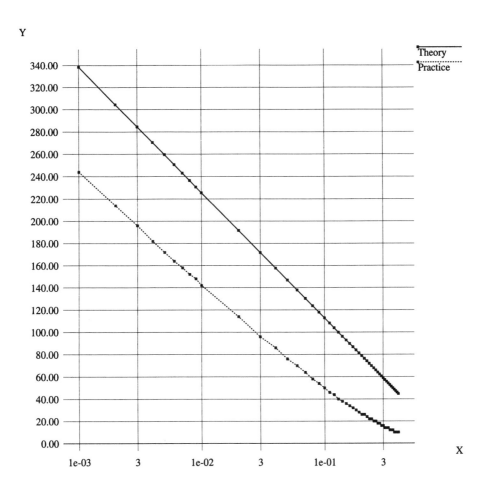

Figure 9.4
Figure 9.3 with log scale on X-axis.

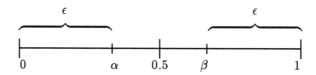

Figure 9.5
ϵ-recognition as (α, β)-separation.

Figure 9.6
The circuit C from Theorem 9.1.3.

There is an interesting alternate definition of computation with probabilistic threshold circuits. More formally, if $0 < \alpha < \beta < 1$, a probabilistic threshold circuit C is said to (α, β)-*separate* a language L if:

1. For all $x \in L$, the probability that C accepts x is at least β.
2. For all $x \notin L$, the probability that C accepts x is at most α.

Recognition can be viewed as a restricted form of separation: a circuit ϵ-recognizes a language L iff it $(\epsilon, 1 - \epsilon)$-separates it (see Figure 9.5). It is interesting that there is a partial converse to this observation, every language that can be separated can also be recognized with a very small increase in size.

THEOREM 9.1.3 For every language $L \subseteq \mathbf{B}^n$ that can be (α, β)-separated by a probabilistic threshold circuit of size z, weight w, and depth d, there is a probabilistic threshold circuit of size $z + 1$, weight $2w$, and depth d that $(1 - \beta)/(2 - \beta - \alpha)$-recognizes L.

PROOF: Suppose $L \subseteq \mathbf{B}^n$ can be (α, β)-separated by a probabilistic threshold circuit C of size z, weight w, and depth d. We will construct a probabilistic threshold circuit C' of size $z + 1$, weight $2w$, and depth d that ϵ-recognizes L, for some choice of ϵ.

Suppose the output gate g of C has threshold k (see Figure 9.6). The new circuit C' is constructed from C by adding a new probabilistic gate that is connected to the output

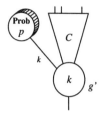

Figure 9.7
The circuit C' from Theorem 9.1.3 in the case $(\beta - \alpha) > 1$.

gate with weight k, and is active with probability

$$p = \frac{1 - \alpha - \beta}{2 - \alpha - \beta}.$$

For C' to output 1, the output gate g' must either receive an amount of excitation from the subcircuit corresponding to C that would have made g output 1, or the new probabilistic gate must output 1. If the input is a member of L, then by the principle of inclusion-exclusion, the probability of this happening is

$$\beta + p - \beta p = \frac{1 - \alpha}{2 - \beta - \alpha}.$$

If the input is not a member of L, the probability of this happening is

$$\alpha + p - \alpha p = \frac{1 - \beta}{2 - \beta - \alpha}.$$

Therefore, C' $(\epsilon, 1 - \epsilon)$-separates L, where $\epsilon = (1 - \beta)/(2 - \beta - \alpha)$. We conclude, by the observation immediately preceding this Theorem, that C' ϵ-recognizes L. $\square$

It is perhaps surprising that probabilistic threshold circuits are not much more powerful than nonuniform threshold circuits. The randomness can be replaced by a nonuniform sample with a small increase in size and depth.

LEMMA 9.1.4 If $k = Np(1 + \beta)$ for some $0 \leq \beta \leq 1$, then $B(k, N, p) \leq e^{-0.5\beta^2 Np}$.

PROOF: The proof follows from Lemma 9.1.1. $\square$

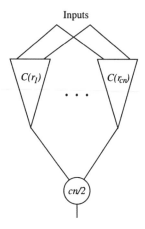

Figure 9.8
The circuit C' from Theorem 9.1.5.

THEOREM 9.1.5 For every $0.25 < \epsilon < 0.5$, any language that can be ϵ-recognized by a probabilistic threshold circuit of depth d and size z can be recognized by a nonuniform threshold circuit of depth $d+1$ and size

$$\left\lceil \frac{8\epsilon \ln 2}{(1 - 2\epsilon)^2} \right\rceil nz.$$

PROOF: Suppose C is a probabilistic threshold circuit that ϵ-recognizes a language L. We will construct a new threshold circuit C' that also recognizes L. Suppose C has m probabilistic gates g_i for $1 \leq i \leq m$, each of which is **true** with probability p_i respectively. If $r = (r_1, \ldots, r_m) \in \mathbf{B}^m$, let $C(r)$ be the machine obtained by replacing each g_i with an r_i-gate (that is, a gate that always outputs the fixed value r_i), for $1 \leq i \leq m$.

Suppose we pick cn strings $r_i = (r_{i,1}, \ldots, r_{i,m}) \in \mathbf{B}^m$ for $1 \leq i \leq cn$ at random, where c is a constant to be determined later, choosing each $r_{i,j}$ independently at random with probability p_j, for $1 \leq i \leq cn$. C' is constructed similarly to the circuit in Theorem 9.1.2, consisting of cn modified copies of the original circuit $C(r_1), \ldots, C(r_{cn})$, with a final layer consisting of a single MAJORITY-gate with inputs from the cn copies of the old output gate (see Figure 9.8).

We claim that there is a choice of $r_1, \ldots, r_{cn}$ such that C' recognizes L. C' consists of a copy of each of $C(r_1), \ldots, C(r_{cn})$. Each of these sub-circuits is a sample of the probabilistic circuit C. C' decides which output to produce by taking the consensus of the outputs of those samples (we assume that c is even).

Let $x \in \mathbf{B}^n$ be an input of size n. Let

$$\text{Failures}(x) = \{(r_1, \ldots, r_{cn}) \mid C' \text{ gives the wrong output on input } x\}$$

If we pick any r_i at random, then for each input x the probability that $C(r_i)$ gives the wrong output on input x is ϵ. Without loss of generality, assume that $\epsilon \geq 1/4$. If we perform cn independent Bernoulli trials to pick $(r_1, \ldots, r_{cn})$, where

$$c > 8\epsilon \ln 2 / (1 - 2\epsilon)^2,$$

and take $N = cn$, $p = \epsilon$, $\beta = 1/2\epsilon - 1$, $k = cn/2$, then by Lemma 9.1.4, the probability that there are at least $cn/2$ failures out of cn trials is

$$B(cn/2, cn, \epsilon) \leq e^{-c\epsilon n(1/2\epsilon - 1)^2/2} < 2^{-n}.$$

Therefore, if we pick $(r_1, \ldots, r_{cn})$ at random, the probability that it is in $\cup_x \text{Failures}(x)$ is less than one (since there are only 2^n choices for $x \in \mathbf{B}^n$). Hence, there must be at least one choice of cn strings $r_1, \ldots, r_{cn}$ that make C' work correctly for all inputs of size n. Therefore, C' recognizes the same language as C. $\square$

The constant multiple c in Theorem 9.1.5 is quite small for reasonable values of error probability ϵ, and increases rapidly as ϵ approaches 0.5 (see Figure 9.9).

9.2   Randomized $\mathcal{TC}^0$

Section 9.1 dealt with finite probabilistic threshold circuits. Suppose we allow the error probability of a threshold circuit family to increase slowly with the number of inputs. We say that a family of probabilistic threshold circuits $C = (C_1, C_2, \ldots)$ $E(n)$-*recognizes* a language L if for all $n \in \mathbf{N}$, C_n $E(n)$-recognizes $L \cap \mathbf{B}^n$. Define $\mathcal{RTC}^0$ to be the class of languages recognized by a circuit family $C = (C_1, C_2, \ldots)$ of size $Z(n)$, depth $D(n)$, maximum weight $W(n)$, and error probability $E(n)$, where

- $D(n) = O(1)$,
- $Z(n) = n^{O(1)}$,
- $W(n) = n^{O(1)}$,
- $E(n) = 0.5 - 1/n^{O(1)}$.

That is, C is a $\mathcal{TC}^0$ circuit family with probabilistic gates and an error probability that approaches 0.5 (recall that an error of 0.5 is intolerable) no faster than the inverse of a polynomial in n. We will call this type of error probability *small*, even though our use of the term is conservative.

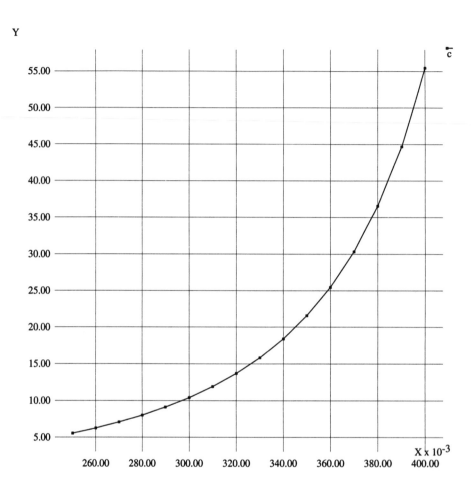

Figure 9.9
Number of trials versus error probability ϵ for Theorem 9.1.5. The value of ϵ is recorded on the X-axis, and the constant c on the Y-axis.

LEMMA 9.2.1 (Stirling's Approximation) For all $n \in \mathbb{N}$,

$$n! \sim \sqrt{2\pi n} \left(\frac{n}{e}\right)^n$$

LEMMA 9.2.2 For all $n \in \mathbb{N}$,

$$\binom{n}{n/2} \sim 2^n \sqrt{\frac{2}{\pi n}}.$$

PROOF: By Lemma 9.2.1,

$$\binom{n}{n/2} = \frac{n!}{(n/2)!^2} \sim 2^n \sqrt{\frac{2}{\pi n}}.$$

□

A sequence of Bernoulli trials is said to be *unbiased* if the probability of success of each trial is 0.5. If $0 \le k \le n$, let $P(n, k)$ be the probability of getting exactly k successes out of a sequence of n unbiased Bernoulli trials.

LEMMA 9.2.3 If n is even,

$$P(n, n/2) \sim \sqrt{\frac{2}{\pi n}}.$$

PROOF: Since the probability of exactly m ones out of n trials is

$$P(n, m) = \binom{n}{m} 0.5^m 0.5^{n-m},$$

we conclude, by Lemma 9.2.2, that if n is even,

$$P(n, n/2) = \binom{n}{n/2} 0.5^n \sim \sqrt{\frac{2}{\pi n}}.$$

□

LEMMA 9.2.4 For all $n \in \mathbb{N}$,

$$B(n/2, n, 0.5) = \begin{cases} 0.5 & \text{if } n \text{ is odd} \\ 0.5 + \sqrt{\frac{1}{2\pi n}} & \text{if } n \text{ is even} \end{cases}$$

PROOF: Suppose we perform n independent unbiased Bernoulli trials. If n is odd, there are an even number of outcomes (i successes, where $0 \le i \le n$). Therefore, the probability of more than $n/2$ successes is exactly 0.5 (see, for example Figure 9.10, which shows the probability distribution with $n = 9$). If n is even, there are an odd number of outcomes. Therefore, the probability of at least $n/2$ successes is $0.5 + P(n, n/2)/2$. (see, for example Figure 9.11, which shows the probability distribution with $n = 10$). By Lemma 9.2.4,

$$0.5 + P(n, n/2)/2 = 0.5 + \frac{1}{\sqrt{2\pi n}},$$

as required.   □

Sometimes probabilism helps to compute a function in smaller depth. For example, consider the function IP from Section 7.5.

THEOREM 9.2.5 $IP \in \mathcal{RTC}_2^0$.

PROOF: Consider the probabilistic threshold circuit C_n shown in Figure 9.12. Let $k = \{i \mid x_i = y_i = 1\}$. The task of the circuit is to compute the parity of k. For all $1 \le i \le n$, if $x_i = y_i = 1$, then gates c_i and d_i both output the same random value, otherwise c_i outputs 0 and d_i outputs 1. Therefore, g receives $n - k$ ones, and two copies each of k random bits. For g to output 1, at least $k/2$ of the k random bits must be one. Therefore, the probability of g having output 1 is $B(k/2, k, 0.5)$, and so by Lemma 9.2.4, C_n $(0.5, 0.5 + 1/\sqrt{2\pi n})$-separates $\overline{IP}$. C_n has unit weights, and size $O(n)$. Hence, by Theorem 9.1.3, there is a probabilistic threshold circuit of size $O(n)$ and maximum weight $O(n)$ that $1/2\sqrt{2\pi n}$-recognizes $\overline{IP}$. Therefore, by Theorem 7.1.1, there is a probabilistic threshold circuit of size $O(n)$ and maximum weight $O(n)$ that $1/2\sqrt{2\pi n}$-recognizes IP. That is, $IP \in \mathcal{RTC}_2^0$ as required.   □

We can conclude from Theorem 9.2.5 that small-weight probabilistic threshold circuits are more powerful than small-weight deterministic threshold circuits, since the former can compute IP in depth 2 and polynomial size, whereas the latter need exponential size to compute it (Corollary 7.5.7). That is $IP \in \mathcal{RTC}_2^0$ but $IP \notin \mathcal{TC}_2^0$. We know already that $IP \in \mathcal{TC}_3^0$. Therefore, probabilism saved us one layer in computing IP. Can probabilism ever save us more than one layer? The answer is no:

THEOREM 9.2.6   For all $d \in \mathbb{N}$, $\mathcal{RTC}_d^0 \subseteq \mathcal{TC}_{d+1}^0$.

PROOF: Let $d \in \mathbb{N}$. Suppose $C = (C_1, C_2, \ldots)$ is a probabilistic threshold circuit family of depth d, maximum weight $W(n)$, size $Z(n)$, and error probability $E(n)$. By

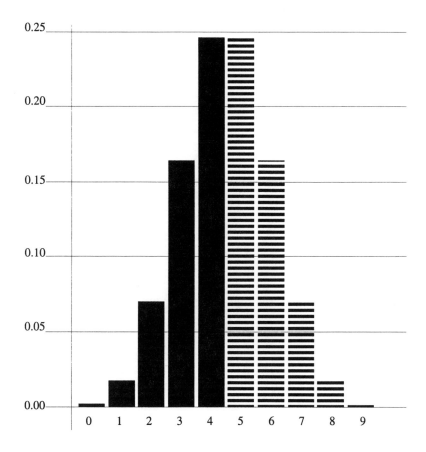

Figure 9.10
The probability of m successes out of $n = 9$ independent unbiased Bernoulli trials, with m on the X-axis and the probability on the Y-axis. $B(n/2, n, 0.5)$ is shown shaded horizontally on the right, and can easily be seen to be exactly 0.5.

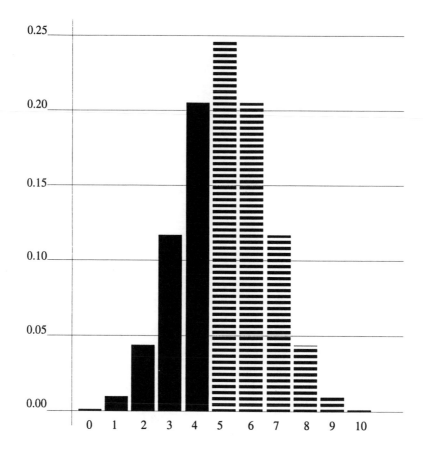

Figure 9.11
The probability of m successes out of $n = 10$ independent unbiased Bernoulli trials, with m on the
X-axis and the probability on the Y-axis. $B(n/2, n, 0.5)$ is shown shaded horizontally on the right, and
can easily be seen to be greater than 0.5 by exactly $P(n, n/2)/2$.

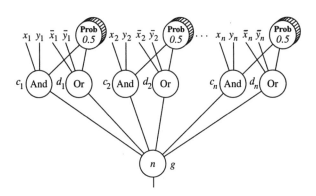

Figure 9.12
A probabilistic threshold circuit that separates IP.

Theorem 9.1.5, for each $n \in \mathbb{N}$ there is a threshold circuit C'_n that recognizes the same language as C_n. Therefore, $C' = (C'_1, C'_2, \ldots)$ recognizes the same language as C.

Also by Theorem 9.1.5, C' has depth $d + 1$, maximum weight $W(n)$, and size

$$Z'(n) = \left\lceil \frac{8E(n)\ln 2}{(1 - 2E(n))^2} \right\rceil nZ(n).$$

Suppose $Z(n) \leq n^c$ and $E(n) = 0.5 - n^{-d}$. Then, $Z'(n) = \ln 2 \cdot n^{c+d+1}(n^d - 2)$.

Therefore, if C is an $\mathcal{RTC}^0_d$ circuit, C' is a $\mathcal{TC}^0_{d+1}$ circuit that recognizes the same language. We conclude that $\mathcal{RTC}^0_d \subseteq \mathcal{TC}^0_{d+1}$. $\square$

Thus, we see the true reason for not counting probabilistic gates in the depth bound of probabilistic threshold circuits: they can be replaced by constant values, which are cheap to supply.

9.3   Boltzmann Machines

The type of probabilistic gate used in Sections 9.1 and 9.2 is not typical of neural network models seen in the literature. More typically, a probabilistic threshold gate becomes active with probability depending on the difference between its excitation level and its threshold, with that probability being 0.5 when the excitation level equals the threshold, tending to zero when it is below the threshold, and tending to one when it is above the threshold. We will call this type of threshold-gate a *Boltzmann gate*.

More precisely, if a Boltzmann gate has threshold h and n inputs $x_1, \ldots, x_n$ of weights $w_1, \ldots, w_n$ respectively, then it becomes active with probability $p(\sum_{i=1}^{n} w_i x_i - h)$, for some *activation probability function* p that has the following properties:

- $p: \mathbf{R} \rightarrow (0, 1)$
- p is continuous and monotone increasing
- $p(0) = 0.5$
- $\lim_{x \to \infty} p(x) = 1$, and
- $\lim_{x \to -\infty} p(x) = 0$.

A *family of activation probability functions* P is a set of such functions with the additional property that:

- for all $x \in \mathbf{R}$ and all $y \in (0, 1)$, there exists $p \in P$ such that $p(x) = y$.

One popular candidate for P is the set of *sigmoid functions* $p(x) = 1/(1 + e^{-cx})$ for $c \in \mathbf{R}$ (see Figure 9.13 and Problem 3).

Suppose we define a *Boltzmann circuit* to be a threshold circuit constructed from Boltzmann gates. We will assume that all weights are integers. Boltzmann circuits are not much more complicated than probabilistic threshold circuits:

THEOREM 9.3.1 Every Boolean function that can be ϵ-recognized by a Boltzmann circuit of depth d, size z, and weight w can be ϵ-recognized by a probabilistic threshold circuit of depth $d + 1$, size $(8w + 5)z$ and weight $4w^2 + 10w + 4$.

PROOF: Let C be a finite Boltzmann circuit. Consider a Boltzmann gate g with weights $w_1, \ldots, w_n$ and threshold h that has activation probability function p. We will assume that C has integer weights. Suppose g has weight w. For each v with $|v| \leq w$, it is easy to construct a probabilistic threshold circuit $C(v)$ that on input $x_1, \ldots, x_n$ outputs 1 with probability $p(v - h)$ if the excitation level of g on inputs $x_1, \ldots, x_n$ is exactly v, and outputs 0 otherwise. $C(v)$ consists of two threshold-gates, an AND-gate, and a probabilistic gate (see Figure 9.14).

A probabilistic threshold circuit $T(g)$ with behaviour identical to that of g can be constructed from a copy of $C(v)$ for each $-w \leq v \leq w$ and an OR-gate as depicted in Figure 9.15. Clearly, whenever g has excitation level v, $C(v)$ outputs 1 with probability $p(v - h)$, and for all $u \neq v$, $-w \leq u \leq w$, $C(u)$ outputs 0, and hence the OR-gate outputs 1 with probability $p(v - h)$.

A probabilistic threshold circuit C' can be constructed from C by replacing each Boltzmann gate g by the equivalent circuit $T(g)$. C' has the same behaviour as C, and hence will ϵ-recognize the same language that C does. Suppose C has depth d,

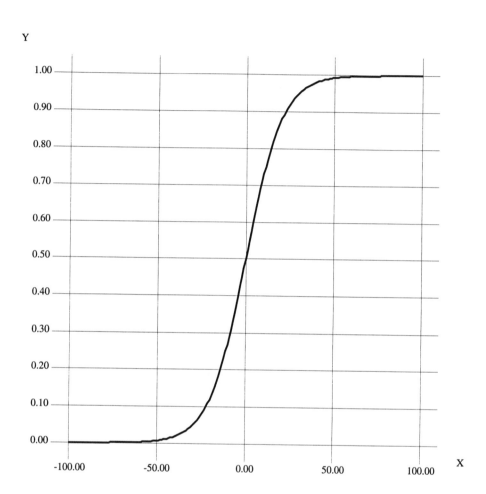

Figure 9.13
The sigmoid function $1/(1 + e^{-x/10})$.

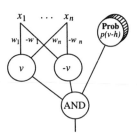

Figure 9.14
The probabilistic threshold circuit $C(v)$ from Theorem 9.3.1.

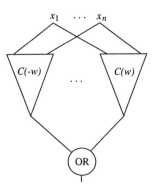

Figure 9.15
The probabilistic threshold circuit $T(g)$ from Theorem 9.3.1.

size z, and weight w. Since each gate in C is replaced by a circuit of depth 3, size $3(2w + 1) + 1 = 6w + 4$, and weight $(2w + 1)(2w + 4)$, C' will have depth $3d$, size $2z(3w + 2)$, and weight $2z(w + 1)(2w + 1)$. The depth can be reduced to $d + 1$ using the techniques of Theorem 7.2.1 and Lemma 7.2.3 (Problem 5). $\square$

THEOREM 9.3.2 For all $0 < \delta < 1$, every Boolean function that can be ϵ-recognized by a probabilistic threshold circuit of depth d, size z, and weight w can be $\epsilon + \delta$-recognized by a Boltzmann circuit of depth d, size z and weight $2w$.

PROOF: Let C be a probabilistic threshold circuit of depth d, size z, weight w, and error probability ϵ. Suppose P is a family of activation probability functions. Let $0 <$

$\delta < 1$. We will construct a Boltzmann circuit C' by replacing each gate of C with a suitable Boltzmann gate. There are two types of gates in a probabilistic threshold circuit: probabilistic gates, and deterministic threshold-gates.

The probabilistic gates are replaced as follows. For each $r \in \mathbf{R}$, it is possible to construct a Boltzmann gate that outputs 1 with probability exactly r: simply take a Boltzmann gate with no inputs, threshold -1, and activation probability function p such that $p(1) = r$.

The deterministic threshold-gates are replaced as follows. Suppose g is a threshold-gate with presentation $(w_1, \ldots, w_n, h)$. We can assume (by Theorem 4.1.8) that this is a decisive presentation, at most doubling the weight of C. Gate g is replaced by a Boltzmann gate g' with weights $w_1, \ldots, w_n$, threshold h, and an activation probability function $p \in P$ such that $p(1) \geq 1 - \delta/z$, and $p(-1) \leq \delta/z$. By construction, g' computes the same function as g with error probability at most δ/z.

A Boltzmann circuit C' can be constructed from C by replacing every gate of C in this fashion. C' will fail to behave like C exactly when one of the gates that simulate deterministic threshold-gates fails to behave properly, which happens only with probability δ/z for each gate. The probability of this happening is thus less than δ, and hence the probability of C' making an error is less than $\epsilon + \delta$. $\square$

Theorem 9.3.1 and Theorem 9.3.2 show that Boltzmann circuits are very similar to probabilistic threshold circuits. For example, Boltzmann circuits of constant depth, polynomial size, small weights, and small error probability recognize exactly the languages in $\mathcal{RTC}^0$, as do probabilistic threshold circuits under the same resource bounds.

Boltzmann circuits are a feedforward version of the cyclic *Boltzmann machine* that is popular in the neural networks literature. One can also add probabilistic gates to cyclic networks to obtain *probabilistic networks*. Boltzmann machines and probabilistic networks operating in fully parallel mode can be unwound into circuits using Theorem 8.1.2, and then the above results apply. Similar results also hold for random parallel and random sequential operation (Problems 6 and 7).

9.4   Reliable Simulation of Classical Circuits

One advantage that the brain has over conventional computers is its ability to perform reliable computations with unreliable hardware. Carver Mead has been quoted as saying (perhaps somewhat optimistically):

> "The brain has this wonderful property — you can go through and shoot out every tenth neuron and never miss them".

A plausible interpretation of this observation is that correct computations can be carried out with high probability when neurons malfunction with probability one in ten. As we shall see, threshold circuits have such a fault-tolerant ability for language recognition. In particular, they can reliably simulate fault-free classical circuits with not much increase in size or depth.

Suppose $f: \mathbf{B}^n \to \mathbf{B}$ is a Boolean function, and C is a Boolean circuit. We say that C *fails to compute* f *on input* x if the output of C on input x is not $f(x)$, and that C *fails to compute* f if it fails to compute $f(x)$ for some input x. C is (μ, ϵ)-*resilient* on f for some $0 \le \mu + \epsilon \le 1$ if, when each of the gates of C is damaged independently with probability at most ϵ (or equivalently, each gate is unreliable, with error probability ϵ), the probability that C fails to compute f is at most $\mu + \epsilon$. Note that $\mu \ge 0$, since the output gate will be damaged with probability ϵ. Intuitively, the ϵ term in the $\mu + \epsilon$ is the probability of harming the output gate, and μ is the probability of harming the rest of the circuit. Our aim is to minimize μ.

We wish to be able to deal with a worst-case scenario in which damage to a gate may cause adversarial behaviour. That is, a damaged gate may behave in the worst possible fashion. We will assume no bound on the fan-in and fan-out of C, and that reliable inputs are available. The latter assumption is not crucial, and can be replaced by an assumption that the inputs can be repeatedly sampled with independent failure probability at most ϵ.

THEOREM 9.4.1 Every function computed by a threshold circuit of fan-in f, size z, and depth d can be computed by a (μ, ϵ)-resilient threshold circuit with size

$$\frac{4z}{\epsilon \beta^2} (\ln z + \ln \frac{2}{\mu}) + 1$$

and depth $2d+1$, for all $1/4(f+1) \le \epsilon < 1/2(f+1)$ and $\mu > 0$, where $\beta = 1/2\epsilon(f+1)-1$.

PROOF: Let C be a circuit of fan-in f, size z, and depth d. We construct a new circuit C' as follows. Each wire in C is replaced by a *cable*, which consists of m wires (m will be given explicitly later). Each gate in C will be replaced by a circuit that has two input cables and an output cable. A wire w in one of these cables will be called *correct* if it always carries the same value as the wire in C that the cable replaces. A cable will be called *correct* if at most θm of its wires are incorrect ($\theta \in \mathbf{R}^+$ will be given explicitly later).

Let g be a gate in C with inputs $x_1, \ldots, x_f$, and output z. The circuit corresponding to g consists of two levels of gates. The first level consists of m copies of g, with the ith copy taking as input the ith wire from each of the f input cables. The second level

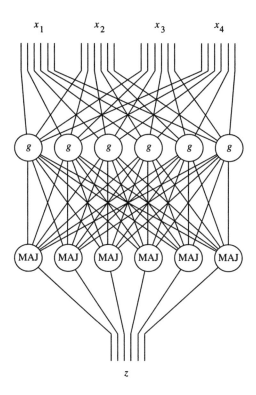

Figure 9.16
The reliable subcircuit corresponding to g.

of the circuit consists of m MAJORITY-gates, each of which has m inputs, one from
each of the copies of g. The outputs of these gates form the output cable for the circuit.
Figure 9.16 shows the construction with $f = 4$ and $m = 6$.

Suppose that we damage each gate in C' independently with probability ϵ, where
$1/4(f + 1) \leq \epsilon < 1/2(f + 1)$. We will analyze the probability that the output cable of
a circuit corresponding to a gate is incorrect, assuming that its input cables are correct.
Consider a circuit in C' corresponding to gate g in C. Since its input cables are correct,
at most $f\theta m$ of the copies of g will be incorrect due to receiving a faulty input. In
the worst case, it will take only a further $(0.5 - f\theta)m$ faults in the copies of g to make
at least half of them incorrect. Therefore, the probability that more than half of the
copies of g are incorrect is $B((0.5 - f\theta)m, m, \epsilon)$. The probability that the output cable
is incorrect given that less than half of the first-level gates are incorrect is $B(\theta m, m, \epsilon)$.

Therefore, the probability that the output cable is incorrect given that the input cables are correct is $B((0.5 - f\theta)m, m, \epsilon) + B(\theta m, m, \epsilon)$. Therefore, taking $\theta = 1/2(f + 1)$, the probability that the output cable being incorrect given that the input cables are correct is, by Lemma 9.1.4, $2B(m/2(f+1), m, \epsilon) \leq 2e^{-\beta^2 \epsilon m/2}$ where $\beta = 1/2\epsilon(f+1) - 1$, provided $1/4(f + 1) \leq \epsilon < 1/2(f + 1)$.

Since there are z cables which may independently fail, and in the worst case the failure of a cable may result in the failure of the whole circuit, the probability that the cable representing the output of C is incorrect is bounded above by $2ze^{-\beta^2 \epsilon m/2}$. This is at most μ when

$$m = \frac{2}{\epsilon\beta^2}(\ln z + \ln \frac{2}{\mu}).$$

Thus, the output cable of the new circuit is incorrect with probability at most μ. The circuit is completed by placing an m-input MAJORITY-gate on the output cable. The probability that the output of this gate is incorrect is less than $\mu + \epsilon$. The total number of gates is $2mz + 1$, and the depth is $2d + 1$. $\square$

We can draw two conclusions from Theorem 9.4.1. Suppose we call the value $\mu^{-1} \in \mathbf{R}$ the *accuracy* of the circuit. Firstly, an arbitrary circuit can be made reliable under malicious faults with a log-linear increase in size. Secondly, accuracy can be increased to an arbitrary constant with a further increase linear in the original size.

Theorem 9.4.1 is only interesting when $\mu + \epsilon < 0.5$. Suppose we call a circuit ϵ-*resilient* if it is (μ, ϵ)-resilient for some $\mu \in \mathbf{R}^+$ such that $\mu + \epsilon < 0.5$. Taking $f = 2$ and Carver Mead's example of $\epsilon = 0.1$, we have:

COROLLARY 9.4.2 Every function computed by a classical circuit of size z, and depth d can be computed by a 0.1-resilient threshold circuit of size $63z \log z + 145z + 1$ and depth $2d + 1$.

If $\epsilon \leq 1/12$, our construction becomes even more practical.

COROLLARY 9.4.3 Every function computed by a classical circuit of size z, and depth d can be computed by an ϵ-resilient threshold circuit of size $48z \log z + 76z + 1$ and depth $2d + 1$, where $\epsilon \leq 1/12$.

Unfortunately, the general construction of Theorem 9.4.1 can only be used for Carver Mead's test case of $\epsilon = 1/10$ provided $f \leq 4$.

9.5   Problems

1. What is the weight increase in Theorem 9.1.2?

2. State and prove a variant of Theorem 9.1.3 that uses only unbiased probabilistic gates, that is, gates that are active with probability 0.5. You many assume that the depth of the original circuit is at least 2.

3. Prove that the set of sigmoid functions have the properties listed in Section 9.3 that make them suitable for use as activation probability functions.

4. Prove a variant of Theorem 7.1.1 for Boltzmann circuits. That is, show that for every Boltzmann circuit of depth d, size s and maximum weight w, there exists an equivalent Boltzmann circuit in which all weights are positive, of depth at most d, size at most $2s$, and maximum weight w.

5. Show that the depth of the circuit constructed in the proof of Theorem 9.3.1 can be reduced from $3d$ to $d + 1$.

6. State and prove a version of Theorem 8.1.2 for random sequential operation.

7. State and prove a version of Theorem 8.1.2 for random parallel operation.

9.6   Bibliographic Notes

Lemma 9.1.1 is from Chernoff [28]. Lemma 9.1.1 can be found in Valiant and Angluin [10], and Valiant and Brebner [140]. Theorem 9.1.5, which uses a standard proof technique due to Adleman [2], is from Parberry and Schnitger [100, 102]. It is also stated without proof in Parberry and Schnitger [99]. Theorem 9.1.3, Problem 2, Theorem 9.2.5, and Theorem 9.2.6 are due to Hajnal *et al.* [55]. Theorem 9.3.1 is an improved version of a result from Parberry and Schnitger [100, 102]. Boltzmann machines were introduced in Ackley, Hinton, and Sejnowski [1], Hintonn, Sejnowski, and Ackley [61], and Hintonn and Sejnowski [60].

Section 9.4 is based on Berman, Parberry, and Schnitger [16]. Theorem 9.4.1 uses the techniques of Pippenger [105, 106], which builds on earlier work by von Neumann [144] and Dobrushin and Ortyukov [39]. The results of that section are a little unsatisfying because they work only for the simulation of classical circuits, and they do not appear to work when the fan-in is allowed to scale. Hajnal *et al.* [55] have some results for the simulation of unreliable threshold circuits, but their results have two undesirable features: the increase in size is exponential in depth (and is therefore only usable when depth is a very small constant), and all gates must have equal probability of failure. Berman, Parberry, and Schnitger [16] have a result that does not share these weaknesses, but it works only on a threshold circuit model in which the summation and thresholding parts of the threshold-gates are independent units that can be put together arbitrarily, and it requires large weights.

10 Learning

This chapter deals with the question of how neural networks can efficiently learn from experience. Section 10.1 considers the *loading problem*, in which a neural network with a fixed architecture must learn a sequence of input-output pairs. It is found that this problem is $\mathcal{NP}$-complete even for quite simple architectures. Section 10.2 considers the running time of the *perceptron learning algorithm*. Section 10.3 considers the problem of learning a Boolean function over a large domain in which input-output pairs are presented at random according to an unknown probability distribution. An approximation to the function to be learned must be computed with high probability, regardless of the probability distribution. This is called *PAC learning*. It is proved that if the sample size is large enough, it is sufficient to construct hypotheses that are consistent with the data seen so far.

10.1   The Loading Problem

An *architecture* is a neural network with the node functions left unspecified, that is, a 4-tuple $A = (V, X, Y, E)$, where

V is a finite ordered set
$X \cap V = \emptyset$
$Y \subseteq V$
$(V \cup X, E)$ is a directed, acyclic graph.

The following is an attractive formalization of the learning problem. Suppose $A = (V, X, Y, E)$ is an architecture with $\|X\| = n$ and $\|Y\| = m$. A *task* for A is an element of $\mathbf{B}^n \times \mathbf{B}^m$, and a *task set* is a set of tasks. If $\mathcal{F}$ is a node function set and $\ell : V \to \mathcal{F}$, the *neural network* corresponding to A and ℓ is given by $A(\ell) = (V, X, Y, E, \ell)$. A neural network $A(\ell)$ is said to *support* task $(x_1 \cdots x_n, y_1 \cdots y_m)$ if the output of $A(\ell)$ on input $(x_1, \ldots, x_n)$ is $(y_1, \ldots, y_m)$, and is said to *support* a task set if it supports every task in it. The *loading problem* for node function set $\mathcal{F}$ is the following problem: given an architecture A and a task set T, find a node function assignment $\ell : V \to \mathcal{F}$ such that $A(\ell)$ supports T.

The loading problem is clearly computable (simply try all combinations of functions from the node function set), but is it feasibly computable? That is, is there a polynomial time algorithm (or equivalently, a polynomial size circuit) that solves it? Clearly, if there were, then there would be one for the following decision problem:

The Loading Problem (LOADING)

INSTANCE: An architecture A and a task set T

QUESTION: Is there a node function assignment ℓ such that $A(\ell)$ supports T?

There are many variations of the loading problem obtained by placing restrictions on the architecture A (the size, depth, fan-in, interconnection graph, or the number of outputs), or on the node function set. For the moment, let us take the node function set to be unrestricted.

THEOREM 10.1.1 The loading problem for neural networks of depth 2 and fan-in 3 is $\mathcal{NP}$-complete.

PROOF: It is clear that the loading problem is a member of $\mathcal{NP}$. That is, it is possible to devise a polynomial time algorithm (or equivalently, by Theorem 2.3.3, a polynomial size circuit) that verifies whether a given architecture and node function assignment can support a given task set (that is, polynomial in the number of gates and the number of tasks). It remains to show that LOADING is $\mathcal{NP}$-hard. We will show that 3SAT $\leq_p$ LOADING. Since 3SAT is $\mathcal{NP}$-complete (by Theorem 6.2.4), this will imply that LOADING is $\mathcal{NP}$-complete.

Suppose we are given an instance of 3SAT, that is, an n-input alternating circuit of depth 2 with OR-gates of fan-in 3 at the first level. This circuit computes

$$C = C_1 \wedge C_2 \wedge \cdots \wedge C_m$$

for some $m \in \mathbf{N}$, where each *clause* C_i is the disjunction of at most three literals over the variables $x_1, \ldots, x_n$. Suppose for all $1 \leq j \leq m$, that clause C_j uses variables x_{j_k} for $1 \leq k \leq 3$. In particular, suppose clause $C_j = (x_{j_1}[\alpha_j] \vee x_{j_2}[\beta_j] \vee x_{j_3}[\gamma_j])$ for $\alpha_j, \beta_j, \gamma_j \in \mathbf{B}$ (using the notation from the proof of Theorem 5.3.1).

The architecture A is constructed as follows. There is a special *training input* e. For every variable x_i, $1 \leq i \leq n$ there is a *variable component* consisting of an input x_i and a gate v_i. For every clause C_j, $1 \leq i \leq m$, there is a *clause component* consisting of a gate c_j. Each v_i is connected to x_i and e, and each c_j is connected to v_{j_k}, for $1 \leq i \leq n$, $1 \leq j \leq m$, and $1 \leq k \leq 3$. There is an output from every clause component. More formally, $A = (V, X, Y, E)$ is defined as follows.

$$
\begin{aligned}
V &= \{v_i \mid 1 \leq i \leq n\} \cup \{c_i \mid 1 \leq i \leq m\} \\
X &= \{x_i \mid 1 \leq i \leq n\} \cup \{e\} \\
Y &= \{c_i \mid 1 \leq i \leq m\} \\
E &= \{(x_i, v_i), (e, v_i) \mid 1 \leq i \leq n\} \cup \{(v_{j_k}, c_j) \mid 1 \leq j \leq m,\ 1 \leq k \leq 3\}.
\end{aligned}
$$

We will devise a set of tasks that force A to behave as follows. When $e = 0$, v_i will compute either x_i or its complement, for $1 \leq i \leq n$. When $e = 0$, x_i will be free to output any value, which will be interpreted as a truth assignment for x_i, for $1 \leq i \leq n$. Each gate c_j will evaluate clause C_j on the truth assignment to x_{j_1}, x_{j_2}, x_{j_3} output from v_{j_1}, v_{j_2}, v_{j_3}, respectively.

Define $\delta : \mathbf{N} \times \mathbf{B}^3 \rightarrow \mathbf{B}^n$ as follows:

$$\delta(j, \alpha\beta\gamma) = b_1 \cdots b_n$$

where $b_{j_1} = \alpha$, $b_{j_2} = \beta$, $b_{j_3} = \gamma$, and $b_i = 0$ for $i \neq j_1, j_2, j_3$. Let $v(j, \alpha\beta\gamma)(i)$ be the value of clause j when all variables are assigned zero except for $x_{j_1}, x_{j_2}, x_{j_3}$ which are assigned the values $\alpha, \beta, \gamma \in \mathbf{B}$, respectively. For each clause C_j, $1 \leq j \leq m$, we have eight *enforcer tasks* $t(j, \alpha\beta\gamma)$, for $\alpha\beta\gamma \in \{000, 001, 010, 011, 100, 101, 110, 111\}$, defined as follows:

$$t(j, \alpha\beta\gamma) = (v(j, \alpha\beta\gamma)(0), v(j, \alpha\beta\gamma)(1) \cdots v(j, \alpha\beta\gamma)(m)).$$

There is also a single *computation task*:

$$(\underbrace{0 \cdots 0}_{n} 1, \underbrace{1 \cdots 1}_{m}).$$

It is easy to devise a polynomial time algorithm or polynomial size circuit that constructs A and the task set from any given instance of 3SAT C. It remains to show that C is satisfiable iff A supports the tasks.

Suppose C is satisfiable. It can be verified by inspection that A supports the enforcer tasks and the computation task with the following node function assignments. Suppose $b_1, \ldots, b_n \in \mathbf{B}^n$ is a satisfying assignment for C. For $1 \leq i \leq n$, when $e = 0$, v_i outputs x_i, and when $e = 1$, v_i outputs b_i. For $1 \leq j \leq m$, c_j computes $(v_{j_1}[\alpha_j] \vee v_{j_2}[\beta_j] \vee v_{j_3}[\gamma_j])$.

Conversely, suppose architecture A can support the tasks listed above. The enforcer tasks for clause C_j force gate c_j to correctly evaluate C_j on inputs $x_{j_1}, x_{j_2}, x_{j_3}$ provided to the first layer of gates. Since C_j has value 0 on exactly one of the eight possible inputs (specifically, $x_{j_1} = \overline{\alpha}_j$, $x_{j_2} = \overline{\beta}_j$, $x_{j_3} = \overline{\gamma}_j$), we can deduce that when $e = 0$, gate v_i computes either x_i or its complement (since the only other possibility is a constant function). Define $\text{value}(v_i)$ to be x_i in the former case and $\overline{x}_i$ in the latter. Then, it is clear that the enforcer tasks force gate c_j to compute

$$\text{value}(v_{j_1})[\alpha_j] \vee \text{value}(v_{j_2})[\beta_j] \vee \text{value}(v_{j_3})[\gamma_j].$$

That is, if we interpret the outputs of gates $v_1, \ldots, v_n$ as a truth assignment for the variables $x_1, \ldots, x_n$ of C in the obvious manner (modulo the reservation that the values

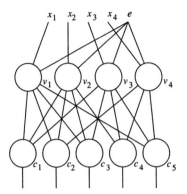

Figure 10.1
The architecture corresponding to 3SAT instance
$(x_1 \vee x_2 \vee \overline{x}_3) \wedge (x_1 \vee x_2 \vee \overline{x}_4) \wedge (\overline{x}_1 \vee \overline{x}_2 \vee x_3) \wedge (x_2 \vee \overline{x}_3 \vee x_4) \wedge (\overline{x}_1 \vee x_3 \vee x_4)$.

for some variables may be listed as the complement of how they really appear), then c_j computes the value of C_j under that truth assignment. The computation task requires that there be an output of $v_1, \ldots, v_n$ that makes all clauses output 1. Therefore, the computation task requires that there be a truth assignment that satisfies C. $\square$

For example, the architecture corresponding to the instance of 3SAT

$$(x_1 \vee x_2 \vee \overline{x}_3) \wedge (x_1 \vee x_2 \vee \overline{x}_4) \wedge (\overline{x}_1 \vee \overline{x}_2 \vee x_3) \wedge (x_2 \vee \overline{x}_3 \vee x_4) \wedge (\overline{x}_1 \vee x_3 \vee x_4)$$

is shown in Figure 10.1, and the tasks are shown in Table 10.1. The starred values in the outputs are of secondary importance only, and can be filled in by the interested reader.

If we extend our definition of a *task* for an architecture $A = (V, X, Y, E)$ with $\|X\| = n$ and $\|Y\| = m$ to be an element of $\mathbf{B}^n \times (\mathbf{B} \cup *)^m$, and modify our definition of *support* to say that starred outputs can carry any value, then we would have the following:

THEOREM 10.1.2 The loading problem for neural networks of size 4 is $\mathcal{NP}$-complete.

PROOF: It is clear that the loading problem for neural networks of size 4 is a member of $\mathcal{NP}$. It remains to show that it is $\mathcal{NP}$-hard. As in Theorem 10.1.1, we will show that 3SAT reduces in polynomial size to the loading problem for neural networks of size 4.

Suppose we are given an instance of 3SAT, that is, an n-input alternating circuit of depth 2 with OR-gates of fan-in 3 at the first level. This circuit computes

$$C = C_1 \wedge C_2 \wedge \cdots \wedge C_m$$

Type	Tasks	
Enforcer for C_1	$(0000\ 0\ ,\ 1****)$	$(1000\ 0\ ,\ 1****)$
	$(0010\ 0\ ,\ 0****)$	$(1010\ 0\ ,\ 1****)$
	$(0100\ 0\ ,\ 1****)$	$(1100\ 0\ ,\ 1****)$
	$(0110\ 0\ ,\ 1****)$	$(1110\ 0\ ,\ 1****)$
Enforcer for C_2	$(0000\ 0\ ,\ *1***)$	$(1000\ 0\ ,\ *1***)$
	$(0001\ 0\ ,\ *0***)$	$(1001\ 0\ ,\ *1***)$
	$(0100\ 0\ ,\ *1***)$	$(1100\ 0\ ,\ *1***)$
	$(0101\ 0\ ,\ *1***)$	$(1101\ 0\ ,\ *1***)$
Enforcer for C_3	$(0000\ 0\ ,\ **1**)$	$(1000\ 0\ ,\ **1**)$
	$(0010\ 0\ ,\ **1**)$	$(1010\ 0\ ,\ **1**)$
	$(0100\ 0\ ,\ **1**)$	$(1100\ 0\ ,\ **0**)$
	$(0110\ 0\ ,\ **1**)$	$(1110\ 0\ ,\ **1**)$
Enforcer for C_4	$(0000\ 0\ ,\ ***1*)$	$(0100\ 0\ ,\ ***1*)$
	$(0001\ 0\ ,\ ***1*)$	$(0101\ 0\ ,\ ***1*)$
	$(0010\ 0\ ,\ ***0*)$	$(0110\ 0\ ,\ ***1*)$
	$(0011\ 0\ ,\ ***1*)$	$(0111\ 0\ ,\ ***1*)$
Enforcer for C_5	$(0000\ 0\ ,\ ****1)$	$(1000\ 0\ ,\ ****0)$
	$(0001\ 0\ ,\ ****1)$	$(1100\ 0\ ,\ ****1)$
	$(0010\ 0\ ,\ ****1)$	$(1010\ 0\ ,\ ****1)$
	$(0110\ 0\ ,\ ****1)$	$(1110\ 0\ ,\ ****1)$
Computation	$(0000\ 1\ ,\ 11111)$	

Table 10.1
Tasks for the architecture shown in Figure 10.1 and 3SAT instance
$(x_1 \vee x_2 \vee \overline{x}_3) \wedge (x_1 \vee x_2 \vee \overline{x}_4) \wedge (\overline{x}_1 \vee \overline{x}_2 \vee x_3) \wedge (x_2 \vee \overline{x}_3 \vee x_4) \wedge (\overline{x}_1 \vee x_3 \vee x_4)$.

for some $m \in \mathbb{N}$, where each C_i is the disjunction of at most three literals over the variables $x_1, \ldots, x_n$. Suppose for all $1 \leq j \leq m$, that clause C_j uses variables x_{j_k} for $1 \leq k \leq 3$. In particular, suppose clause $C_j = (x_{j_1}[\alpha_j] \vee x_{j_2}[\beta_j] \vee x_{j_3}[\gamma_j])$ for $\alpha_j, \beta_j, \gamma_j \in \mathbf{B}$ (using the notation from the proof of Theorem 5.3.1).

The architecture corresponding to an instance of 3SAT with n inputs and m clauses is $A = (V, X, Y, E)$, where (see Figure 10.2)

$$V = \{v_1, v_2, v_3, c\}$$
$$X = \{c_j \mid 1 \leq j \leq m\} \cup \{x_j \mid 1 \leq i \leq n\} \cup$$
$$\{y_j \mid 1 \leq i \leq n\} \cup \{z_j \mid 1 \leq i \leq n\} \cup \{e\}$$

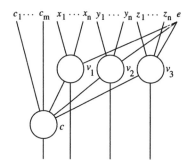

Figure 10.2
The architecture corresponding to an instance of 3SAT with n variables and m clauses.

$$Y = V$$
$$E = \{(c_i, c) \mid 1 \le i \le m\} \cup \{(x_i, v_1), (y_i, v_2), (z_i, v_3) \mid 1 \le i \le n\} \cup$$
$$\{(e, v_i), (v_i, c) \mid 1 \le i \le 3\}.$$

We will construct a set of tasks that force A to behave as follows. Inputs $(c_1, \ldots, c_m)$ will encode a clause number in unary, and inputs $(x_1, \ldots, x_n)$, $(y_1, \ldots, y_n)$, and $(z_1, \ldots, z_n)$ will each encode a variable number in unary. Input e will be used to distinguish between two types of training sets. We will use tasks with $e = 0$ to enforce proper behaviour by all of the gates. When $e = 1$, gates v_1, v_2, and v_3 will be free to choose values for the variables whose indices are given to them as input. When this happens, c will evaluate the clauses whose index is given to it as input. Let $\delta_n : \mathbf{N} \to \mathbf{B}^n$ be defined as follows: $\delta_n(i)$ is a string of $n - i$ zeros followed by a 1 followed by $i - 1$ zeros. That is,

$$\delta_n(i) = \underbrace{0 \cdots 0}_{n-i} 1 \underbrace{0 \cdots 0}_{i-1}.$$

We will use 0^n as a shorthand for the string of n zeros, and 1^n as a shorthand for the string of n ones.

The first set of tasks are called *equality enforcers*, and when $c_j = 0$ for all $1 \le j \le m$ will force c to output 1 iff the outputs from v_1, v_2, and v_3 are identical.

$$(0^m 0^n 0^n 0^n 0, 1000) \quad (0^m 1^n 0^n 0^n 0, 0100)$$
$$(0^m 0^n 0^n 1^n 0, 0001) \quad (0^m 1^n 0^n 1^n 0, 0101)$$
$$(0^m 0^n 1^n 0^n 0, 0010) \quad (0^m 1^n 0^n 0^n 0, 0110)$$
$$(0^m 0^n 1^n 1^n 0, 0011) \quad (0^m 1^n 0^n 1^n 0, 1111).$$

(00000 0000 0000 0000 0 , 1 000)	(00000 1111 0000 0000 0 , 0 100)
(00000 0000 0000 1111 0 , 0 001)	(00000 1111 0000 1111 0 , 0 101)
(00000 0000 1111 0000 0 , 0 010)	(00000 1111 1111 0000 0 , 0 110)
(00000 0000 1111 1111 0 , 0 011)	(00000 1111 1111 1111 0 , 1 111)

Table 10.2
Equality tasks for the architecture shown in Figure 10.2 and 3SAT instance
$(x_1 \vee x_2 \vee \overline{x}_3) \wedge (x_1 \vee x_2 \vee \overline{x}_4) \wedge (\overline{x}_1 \vee \overline{x}_2 \vee x_3) \wedge (x_2 \vee \overline{x}_3 \vee x_4) \wedge (\overline{x}_1 \vee x_3 \vee x_4)$.

The second set of tasks are called *consistency enforcers*, and ensure that the value chosen for each variable by v_1, v_2, and v_3 are the same for each gate. This is achieved with a task of the following form, for $1 \leq i \leq n$:

$$(0^m \delta_n(i)\delta_n(i)\delta_n(i)1, 1***).$$

The third set of tasks are called *computation tasks*, and ensure that c evaluates the clauses of C. For $1 \leq i \leq m$,

$$(\delta_m(j)\overline{\alpha}_j^n\overline{\beta}_j^n\overline{\gamma}_j^n 0, 0\overline{\alpha}_j\overline{\beta}_j\overline{\gamma}_j),$$

and for $\alpha, \beta, \gamma \in \mathbf{B}$, $\alpha\beta\gamma \neq \overline{\alpha}_j\overline{\beta}_j\overline{\gamma}_j$,

$$(\delta_m(j)\alpha^n \beta^n \gamma^n 0, 1\alpha\beta\gamma).$$

It is easy to devise a polynomial time algorithm or polynomial size circuit that constructs A and the task set from any given instance of 3SAT C. It remains to show that C is satisfiable iff A supports the tasks.

Suppose $b_1, \ldots, b_n$ is a satisfying assignment for C. It can be verified by inspection that A supports the equality and consistency enforcer tasks and the computation tasks with the following node function assignments. When $e = 0$, v_1, v_2, and v_3 all compute the conjunction of their remaining inputs. When $e = 1$ and their remaining inputs are $\delta_n(i)$, each of v_1, v_2, and v_3 output b_i. When $c_1 = \cdots = c_m = 0$, c outputs 1 iff v_1, v_2, and v_3 output the same value. If $c_1 \cdots c_m = \delta_m(j)$, c computes $(v_1[\alpha_j] \vee v_2[\beta_j] \vee v_3[\gamma_j])$.

Conversely, if A supports the tasks above, then by construction C is satisfied by setting x_i to the output of v_1 when $e = 1$ and $x_1 \cdots x_n = \delta_n(i)$. $\square$

For example, the task set for the instance of 3SAT used before,

$$(x_1 \vee x_2 \vee \overline{x}_3) \wedge (x_1 \vee x_2 \vee \overline{x}_4) \wedge (\overline{x}_1 \vee \overline{x}_2 \vee x_3) \wedge (x_2 \vee \overline{x}_3 \vee x_4) \wedge (\overline{x}_1 \vee x_3 \vee x_4),$$

Variable	Task
x_1	(00000 0001 0001 0001 1 , 1 ***)
x_2	(00000 0010 0010 0010 1 , 1 ***)
x_3	(00000 0100 0100 0100 1 , 1 ***)
x_4	(00000 1000 1000 1000 1 , 1 ***)

Table 10.3
Consistency tasks for the architecture shown in Figure 10.2 and 3SAT instance used in Table 10.2.

Clause	Tasks	
C_1	(00001 0000 0000 0000 0 , 1 000)	(00001 1111 0000 0000 0 , 1 100)
	(00001 0000 0000 1111 0 , 0 001)	(00001 1111 0000 1111 0 , 1 101)
	(00001 0000 1111 0000 0 , 1 010)	(00001 1111 1111 0000 0 , 1 110)
	(00001 0000 1111 1111 0 , 1 011)	(00001 1111 1111 1111 0 , 1 111)
C_2	(00010 0000 0000 0000 0 , 1 000)	(00010 1111 0000 0000 0 , 1 100)
	(00010 0000 0000 1111 0 , 0 001)	(00010 1111 0000 1111 0 , 1 101)
	(00010 0000 1111 0000 0 , 1 010)	(00010 1111 1111 0000 0 , 1 110)
	(00010 0000 1111 1111 0 , 1 011)	(00010 1111 1111 1111 0 , 1 111)
C_3	(00100 0000 0000 0000 0 , 1 000)	(00100 1111 0000 0000 0 , 1 100)
	(00100 0000 0000 1111 0 , 1 001)	(00100 1111 0000 1111 0 , 1 101)
	(00100 0000 1111 0000 0 , 1 010)	(00100 1111 1111 0000 0 , 0 110)
	(00100 0000 1111 1111 0 , 1 011)	(00100 1111 1111 1111 0 , 1 111)
C_4	(01000 0000 0000 0000 0 , 1 000)	(01000 1111 0000 0000 0 , 1 100)
	(01000 0000 0000 1111 0 , 1 001)	(01000 1111 0000 1111 0 , 1 101)
	(01000 0000 1111 0000 0 , 0 010)	(01000 1111 1111 0000 0 , 1 110)
	(01000 0000 1111 1111 0 , 1 011)	(01000 1111 1111 1111 0 , 1 111)
C_5	(10000 0000 0000 0000 0 , 1 000)	(10000 1111 0000 0000 0 , 1 100)
	(10000 0000 0000 1111 0 , 1 001)	(10000 1111 0000 1111 0 , 1 101)
	(10000 0000 1111 0000 0 , 1 010)	(10000 1111 1111 0000 0 , 1 110)
	(10000 0000 1111 1111 0 , 0 011)	(10000 1111 1111 1111 0 , 1 111)

Table 10.4
Computation tasks for the architecture shown in Figure 10.2 and 3SAT instance used in Table 10.2.

is shown in Tables 10.2, 10.3, and 10.4.

Up to now, we have placed no restriction on the node function set $\mathcal{F}$. It is clear from close inspection of the proof of Theorem 10.1.1 that the argument still holds when we let $\mathcal{F}$ be $\mathcal{AC}_1^0$. Therefore, the result holds when $\mathcal{F}$ is the set of Boolean linear threshold functions, the set of unit-weight linear threshold functions, or $\mathcal{AC}_1^0$ (since the first is a superset of the second, which is a superset of the third). The weakest node function set for which Theorem 10.1.2 still holds is $\mathcal{AC}_3^0$.

What do Theorems 10.1.1 and 10.1.2 mean? They imply that any learning algorithm that takes as input a set of tasks and a fixed architecture runs the risk of taking exponential time in the worst case even for architectures drawn from quite innocuous architecture classes. This can be avoided by limiting the node function set and choosing specific architectures for which the loading problem is not intractable, or perhaps more realistically by only loading task sets that do not cunningly encode $\mathcal{NP}$-complete problems.

10.2   The Perceptron Learning Algorithm

One way of avoiding the intractability of learning demonstrated in Section 10.1 is to learn only limited task sets on simple architectures with limited node function sets. In this section we will consider the problem of learning linear threshold functions on the simplest architecture of all — a single threshold-gate. More precisely, we consider the problem of learning presentations for linear threshold functions on a finite domain, that is, given a finite domain $X \subset [0,1]^n$ and the values $f(x)$ for all $x \in X$ for some linear threshold function $f : \mathbf{R}^n \to \mathbf{B}$, find a presentation $(w_1, \ldots, w_n, h)$ such that for all $x \in X$, $f(x) = \vartheta_n(w_1, \ldots, w_n, h)(x)$.

One obvious method is to set up the problem as a linear programming problem (as was done in the proof of Theorem 3.3.8). Suppose elements of X can be expressed in binary using a finite number of bits. More precisely, suppose that there exists $b \in \mathbf{N}$ such that for each $(x_1, \ldots, x_n) \in X$,

$$x_i = \sum_{j=1}^{b} 2^{-j} x_{i,j},$$

where $x_{i,j} \in \mathbf{B}$ for all $1 \le i \le n$, $1 \le j \le b$. Let $m = \|X\|$. Then, the linear programming problem can be solved in time $O(b(m+n)^5)$ with word size $O(b(m+n)^2)$. Therefore, the problem of learning a linear threshold function over a domain of polynomial size and polynomial precision can be solved in polynomial time. This is true also for the Boolean domain. Unfortunately, if the precision is unbounded, then there is no polynomial time algorithm known for the linear programming problem even when arithmetic operations on arbitrary reals can be performed in constant time.

If $x \in X$ has the property that $f(x) = 1$, then x is called a *positive example*, and if $f(x) = 0$, then x is called a *negative example*. It is sufficient to consider algorithms for learning linear threshold functions from negative examples:

THEOREM 10.2.1 For every domain $X \subset [0,1]^n$ and linear threshold function f, there is a domain $Y \subseteq [-1,1]^n$ of negative examples such that every presentation of a linear threshold function over Y is also the presentation of a linear threshold function over X.

PROOF: Construct Y from X as follows: replace every positive example $(x_1, \ldots, x_n) \in X$ by $(-x_1, \ldots, -x_n)$. The proof that this Y satisfies the hypothesis is left to Problem 1.
$\square$

The following algorithm for learning a linear threshold function from negative examples is called the *perceptron learning algorithm*.

```
1.    procedure perceptron(n, X)
2.    for i := 1 to n do w_i := 0
3.    repeat
4.        finished:=true
5.        for each (x_1, ..., x_n) ∈ X do
6.            if ϑ_n(w_1, ..., w_n, 0)(x_1, ..., x_n) ≠ 0 then
7.                finished:=false
8.                for i := 1 to n do w_i := w_i − x_i
9.    until finished
```

All weights are initially set to zero in line 2. The for-loop in lines 5–8 cycles through the elements of the domain. In line 6, the threshold function defined by the current weights $\vartheta_n(w_1, \ldots, w_n, 0)$ is compared with f on the current domain element. If they are different, then the weights are modified in line 8. The Boolean variable "finished" on lines 4, 7, and 9 is used to ensure that the algorithm terminates when f and $\vartheta_n(w_1, \ldots, w_n, 0)$ agree on all of the domain elements. Each iteration of the repeat-loop in lines 3–9 is called an *epoch*. When $\vartheta_n(w_1, \ldots, w_n, 0)(x_1, \ldots, x_n) \neq f(x_1, \ldots, x_n)$ on line 6, a *mistake* is said to have been made.

THEOREM 10.2.2 Let $X \subset [-1,1]^n$ be a finite domain with $\|X\| = m$, and f a linear threshold function over X of weight w. If X consists of negative examples, then the perceptron learning algorithm for f over X makes $O(n^2 w^2)$ mistakes and runs in time $O(n^2(n+m)w^2)$.

PROOF: Let $X \subset [-1,1]^n$ be a finite domain, and f a linear threshold function over X of weight w. By Theorem 10.2.1, we can assume that X consists of negative examples.

Since every linear threshold function over a finite domain is separable, by Corollary 3.3.6 f has an integer presentation of weight w. Apply Lemma 3.3.1 to this presentation to get an n-separable integer presentation $(v_1, \ldots, v_n, 0)$ of weight nw for f over X. Note that we can assume a zero threshold by Theorem 3.2.6. Since $(v_1, \ldots, v_n, 0)$ is n-separable, for all $(x_1, \ldots, x_n) \in X$,

$$\sum_{i=1}^{n} v_i x_i \leq -n. \qquad (10.2.1)$$

Suppose $c = (c_1, \ldots, c_n)$ is the list of current weights in the perceptron learning algorithm, and that input $x = (x_1, \ldots, x_n)$ is inconsistent with these weights, that is,

$$\sum_{i=1}^{n} c_i x_i \geq 0. \qquad (10.2.2)$$

Let $(c'_1, \ldots, c'_n)$ be the new set of weights obtained from the old set by executing line 8 of the perceptron learning algorithm, that is, $c'_i = c_i - x_i$ for $1 \leq i \leq n$. Define $d: \mathbf{R}^n \times \mathbf{R}^n \to \mathbf{R}$ as follows. For all $r = (r_1, \ldots, r_n), s = (s_1, \ldots, s_n) \in \mathbf{R}^n$,

$$d(r, s) = \sum_{i=1}^{n} (r_i - s_i)^2.$$

Then,

$$
\begin{aligned}
d(c', v) &= \sum_{i=1}^{n} (c'_i - v_i)^2 \\
&= \sum_{i=1}^{n} ((c_i - x_i) - v_i)^2 \\
&= \sum_{i=1}^{n} ((c_i - v_i) - x_i)^2 \\
&= \sum_{i=1}^{n} (c_i - v_i)^2 - 2\sum_{i=1}^{n} (c_i - v_i)x_i + \sum_{i=1}^{n} x_i^2 \\
&= \sum_{i=1}^{n} (c_i - v_i)^2 - 2\sum_{i=1}^{n} c_i x_i + 2\sum_{i=1}^{n} v_i x_i + \sum_{i=1}^{n} x_i^2 \\
&\leq \sum_{i=1}^{n} (c_i - v_i)^2 + 2\sum_{i=1}^{n} v_i x_i + \sum_{i=1}^{n} x_i^2 \quad \text{(by (10.2.2))} \\
&\leq \sum_{i=1}^{n} (c_i - v_i)^2 + 2\sum_{i=1}^{n} v_i x_i + n
\end{aligned}
$$

$$\leq \sum_{i=1}^{n}(c_i - v_i)^2 - n \quad \text{(by (10.2.1))}$$
$$= d(c, v) - n.$$

Therefore, each time a mistake is made, $d(c, v)$ is reduced by at least n. Since $0 \leq d(c, v) \leq n^3 w^2$, this implies that at most $n^2 w^2$ mistakes are made. There is an overhead of $O(n)$ arithmetic and logical operations for each correction, and a mistake may occur only once in each epoch in the worst case, incurring an extra overhead of $O(m)$ time per mistake. The running time is thus $O(m + n)$ times the mistake bound. $\square$

The problem of learning linear threshold functions can be scaled in the obvious way. The domain becomes a sequence $X_1, X_2, \ldots$ of domains, where for all $n \in \mathbb{N}$, each $X_n \subseteq \mathbb{R}^n$, and the function to be learned becomes a sequence of functions $f_1, f_2, \ldots$, where for all $n \in \mathbb{N}$, $f_n : X_n \to \mathbb{B}$. A sequence of domains is said to have *polynomial size* if there exists $c, d \in \mathbb{N}$ such that for all $n \in \mathbb{N}$, $X_n \subset [-n^c, n^c]$, where $\|X_n\| \leq n^d$. The learning problem is then the following: for all $n \in \mathbb{N}$, find a presentation $(w_1, \ldots, w_n, h)$ such that $f_n = \vartheta_n(w_1, \ldots, w_n, h)$ over domain X_n. From Theorem 10.2.2 we can conclude the following (the proof is left to Problem 3):

COROLLARY 10.2.3 The perceptron learning algorithm runs in polynomial time for linear threshold functions with polynomial weights over domains of polynomial size.

However, the perceptron learning algorithm must take exponential time to learn linear threshold functions of large weight, such as those encountered in Sections 4.2–4.4 (see Problem 4).

10.3 PAC Learning

Up to this point, we have considered only the complexity of *exact* learning of a Boolean function over a finite domain when all of the members of the domain are classified as either positive or negative examples. There is a problem with this definition of learning. In practice, not all members of the domain are available for analysis, and the learner must *generalize* from the available positive and negative examples. Naturally, exact learning is not possible in this model, but it may be equally desirable to learn a good approximation to the desired function.

For example, consider the mouse shown in Figure 10.3. The mouse wishes to learn to distinguish predators from other animals. It observes other animals and determines from their behaviour whether they are positive or negative examples. The mouse only

Figure 10.3
Positive and negative examples drawn from the environment.

has access to animals in the immediate environment, which occur at random according to some unknown probability distribution. The mouse's survival will be enhanced if it can learn an pproximation to the concept of "predator" that neither undergeneralizes (identifies a predator as being harmless, with dire consequences), nor overgeneralizes (identifies a harmless, and possible beneficial animal as a predator) by more than a small amount. The *error* of a hypothesis made by the mouse is the probability that it is wrong on a single observation drawn from the probability distribution of the observed animals. A successful learning algorithm is one that given a random sample of positive and negative examples from the unknown probability distribution, with high probability arrives at a hypothesis with small error.

The accepted terminology for the mouse's problem is *probably-approximately correct* learning (abbreviated PAC learning), or *distribution-independent* learning. Given a *problem domain* $X \subseteq \mathbf{B}^n$ and a hypothesis set H that consists of a set of functions $h : X \rightarrow \mathbf{B}$, the aim of the learning algorithm A is to learn some *target function* $f \in H$. For some $m \in \mathbf{N}$, a *sample* of m instances are drawn at random from X according to some unknown probability distribution P. A is given the chosen elements of X, and told whether f classifies them as positive or negative examples. A then constructs some hypothesis function $h \in H$. The *error* of h is the probability that $h(x) \neq f(x)$, where x is chosen from X according to probability distribution P. The hypothesis h is said to be (ϵ, δ)-*consistent* with f, where $0 < \epsilon, \delta < 0.5$, if for all probability distributions P, the probability that h has error at most ϵ is at least $1 - \delta$.

A hypothesis function $h \in H$ is said to be *consistent* with target function f on sample $x_1, \ldots, x_m \in X$ if for all $1 \leq i \leq m$, $h(x_i) = f(x_i)$. The following result states that for all $0 < \epsilon, \delta < 0.5$, if m is large enough, then any hypothesis that is consistent with a sample of size m is (ϵ, δ)-consistent with f.

LEMMA 10.3.1 Any hypothesis drawn from a finite hypothesis set H of size r that is consistent with a sample of size m is (ϵ, δ)-consistent with $f \in H$ when

$$m \geq \frac{\log r - \log \delta}{-\log(1 - \epsilon)}.$$

PROOF: Suppose the target function is f, and the hypothesis is h. Let $S = (x_1, \ldots, x_m)$ be a sample of m elements chosen from X according to an arbitrary probability distribution P. Let E_h be the event that $h(x) = f(x)$ for some x chosen at random from the domain X according to P. Let E_h^S be the event that $h(x_i) = f(x_i)$ for all $1 \leq i \leq m$. Let $R \subseteq H$ be the set of hypotheses that have error greater than ϵ. Then, by the principle of inclusion-exclusion, the probability that there exists a hypothesis with error larger than

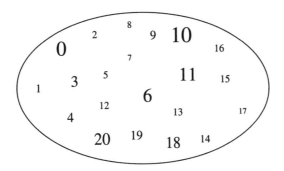

Figure 10.4
A problem domain.

ϵ that is consistent with S is

$$\Pr(\bigvee_{h \in R} E_h^S) < \sum_{h \in R} \Pr(E_h^S) = \sum_{h \in R}(1 - \epsilon)^m \leq (1 - \epsilon)^m r.$$

Hence, the probability that all hypotheses consistent with the sample have error at most ϵ is larger than $1 - (1 - \epsilon)^m r$. Therefore, all hypotheses consistent with the sample have error at most ϵ with probability larger than $1 - \delta$ provided $(1 - \epsilon)^m r \leq \delta$, that is,

$$m \geq \frac{\log r - \log \delta}{-\log(1 - \epsilon)}.$$

$\square$

For example, Figure 10.4 shows the domain $X = \{0, 1, 2, \ldots, 20\}$, with the size of the domain members indicating their relative probability of occurrence according to an unknown probability distribution P. Figure 10.5 shows a hypothesis set H of Boolean functions over domain X. Each function $h \in H$ is represented by an ellipse. Within each ellipse the shaded area indicates those domain elements x for which $h(x) = 1$. Figure 10.6 shows a target function from the hypothesis set H. Figure 10.7 shows a random sample of 9 domain elements drawn from X according to the probability distribution P. Figure 10.8(a) shows the information that is given to the learning algorithm, that is, the classification of the sample as positive or negative examples according to the target function. Figure 10.8(b) shows the members of the hypothesis set H that are consistent with this classification of the sample. Figure 10.9 shows that the first member of the hypothesis set shown in Figure 10.8(b) has error 5/21. Lemma 10.3.1 states that if the

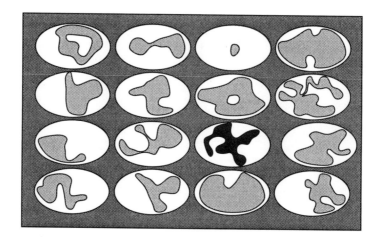

Figure 10.5
A hypothesis set.

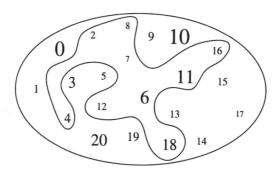

Figure 10.6
A target function.

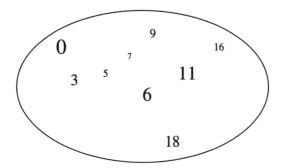

Figure 10.7
A sample drawn at random from the problem domain.

random sample is large enough, then any member of the hypothesis set that is consistent with the sample will have error at most ϵ with probability $1 - \delta$.

Lemma 10.3.1 is good news for our mouse. All it needs to do is construct a hypothesis that is consistent with the sample seen so far, and adjust this hypothesis as new data is encountered. Eventually, after a large enough sample has been obtained, it will have PAC-learned the concept of "predator" to within an arbitrarily small value of ϵ and δ.

THEOREM 10.3.2 Let H be a hypothesis set of size r, and $f \in H$ a target function that can be exactly learned on a domain of size n in time $T(n)$. Then, for all $0 < \epsilon, \delta \leq 0.5$, a hypothesis $h \in H$ that is (ϵ, δ)-consistent with f can be learned in time

$$O\left(T\left(\left\lceil \frac{\log r - \log \delta}{-\log(1 - \epsilon)} \right\rceil\right)\right).$$

PROOF: The algorithm computes

$$m = \left\lceil \frac{\log r - \log \delta}{-\log(1 - \epsilon)} \right\rceil$$

in time $O(m)$, collects a sample of size m, and then constructs a hypothesis that is consistent with that sample in time $T(m)$. By Lemma 10.3.1, that hypothesis is (ϵ, δ)-consistent with the target function. $\square$

We will say that a hypothesis set H of functions with domain $X \subseteq \mathbf{B}^n$ is *PAC learnable* if there is a learning algorithm that for every target function $f \in H$ and every $0 < \epsilon, \delta < 0.5$, produces a hypothesis that is (ϵ, δ)-consistent with f. The *running time* of this learning algorithm will be expressed as a function of n, ϵ, and δ.

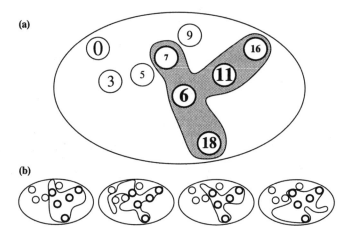

Figure 10.8
(a) The sample elements classified as positive (shaded area) or negative examples. (b) The members of the hypothesis set that are consistent with the sample.

COROLLARY 10.3.3 The class of linear threshold functions of weight w can be PAC-learned in time

$$O\left(\frac{nw^2(n^2 - \log \delta)}{-\log(1 - \epsilon)}\right).$$

PROOF: By Theorem 4.2.3, using the perceptron learning algorithm (Theorem 10.2.2), and Theorem 10.3.2. □

We will say that a problem class C can be *PAC-learned in polynomial time* if for all $n \in \mathbb{N}$, $\{h \in C \mid h : \mathbf{B}^n \to \mathbf{B}\}$ can be PAC-learned in time polynomial in n, $\log \delta$, and $\log(1-\epsilon)$. Then, for example, linear threshold functions with small weights can be learned in polynomial time (see Problem 8). Theorem 10.3.2 can also be used to construct polynomial time PAC-learning algorithms for other hypothesis sets (see Problems 9 and 10).

10.4   Problems

1. Complete the proof of Theorem 10.2.1.

2. Use Theorem 10.2.1 and the perceptron learning algorithm for negative examples in Section section.perceptron to design a perceptron learning algorithm for mixed positive

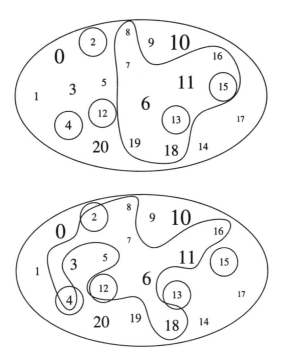

Figure 10.9
A member of the hypothesis set (shown above) that is consistent with the sample, and is
5/21-consistent with the target function (shown below). The circled domain elements are misclassified.

and negative examples.

3. Prove that the perceptron learning algorithm runs in polynomial time for linear threshold functions with polynomial weights over domains of polynomial size.

4. Prove that there exist linear threshold functions over a bounded domain for which the
   perceptron learning algorithm must take an exponential number of epochs to learn.

5. Prove a variant of Theorem 10.2.2 in which f is a linear threshold function that has
   a presentation in which the sum of the weights is w. Show that, in this case, the
   perceptron learning algorithm for f over X makes $O(nw^2)$ mistakes.

6. Complete the proof of Theorem 10.3.2 by showing that m can be computed within
   the stated time bound.

7. Fill in the details of Corollary 10.3.3.

8. Use the technique of Corollary 10.3.3 to show that the class of linear threshold functions of weight n^c can be PAC-learned in time

$$O\left(\frac{n^{2c+1}(n\log n - \log \delta)}{-\log(1-\epsilon)}\right).$$

9. Show that for all $k \in \mathbb{N}$, the class of languages that can be recognized by an alternating circuit of depth 2 the gates on the first level are AND-gates and have fan-in k can be PAC-learned in polynomial time.

10. Show that for all $k \in \mathbb{N}$, the class of languages that can be recognized by an alternating circuit of depth 2 the gates on the first level are OR-gates and have fan-in k can be PAC-learned in polynomial time.

10.5   Bibliographic Notes

Theorem 10.1.1 is from Judd [70]. Theorem 10.1.2 is from Parberry [97]. For more information on the complexity of variants of the loading problem, consult also Judd [68, 69, 71], and Lin and Vitter [78]. Surprisingly, the loading problem is $\mathcal{NP}$-complete for networks of size 3 if the node function set is the set of Boolean linear threshold functions (Blum and Rivest [17, 18]).

Karmarkar's polynomial time linear programming algorithm (Karmarkar [72]) can be used to learn linear threshold functions over a bounded domain as described in Section 10.2. The analysis used in that section is from Schrijver [121]. The perceptron learning algorithm is due to Rosenblatt [116]. The proof of Theorem 10.2.2 is based upon the standard argument that the perceptron learning algorithm terminates, which can be found in Novikoff [92] and Minsky and Papert [86]. Gallant [45] states without proof a version of Theorem 10.2.2 for the Boolean domain. Venkatesh [143] has shown that the perceptron learning algorithm runs in polynomial time for unit-weight linear threshold functions over the bipolar domain. Siu, Dembo, and Kailath [129] have shown that the perceptron learning algorithm runs in polynomial time with high probability over the bipolar domain.

The concept of probably-approximately correct learning was first studied in the seminal paper of Valiant [139]. Valiant used the generic term "learning", and the terms "probably-approximately correct learning" and "PAC learning" were coined by Dana Angluin (see Angluin [8], and Angluin and Laird [9]). Theorem 10.3.1 is from Blumer *et al.* [19], and Rivest [113]. Blumer *et al.* also report that a similar result can be derived from Pearl [103].

Bibliography

[1] D. H. Ackley, G. E. Hinton, and T. J. Sejnowski. A learning algorithm for Boltzmann machines. *Cognitive Science*, 9:147–169, 1985.

[2] L. Adleman. Two theorems on random polynomial time. In *19th Annual Symposium on Foundations of Computer Science*, pages 75–83. IEEE Computer Society Press, 1978.

[3] A. V. Aho, J. E. Hopcroft, and J. D. Ullman. *The Design and Analysis of Computer Algorithms*. Addison-Wesley, 1974.

[4] A. V. Aho, J. E. Hopcroft, and J. D. Ullman. *Data Structures and Algorithms*. Addison-Wesley, 1983.

[5] E. Allender. A note on the power of threshold circuits. In *30th Annual Symposium on Foundations of Computer Science*, pages 580–584. IEEE Computer Society Press, 1989.

[6] N. Alon. Asynchronous threshold networks. *Graphs and Combinatorics*, 1:305–310, 1985.

[7] N. Alon and J. Bruck. Explicit constructions of depth-2 majority circuits for comparison and addition. Research Report RJ 8300, IBM Research Division, 1991.

[8] D. Angluin. Queries and concept learning. *Machine Learning*, 2:319–342, 1988.

[9] D. Angluin and P. Laird. Learning from noisy examples. *Machine Learning*, 2:343–370, 1988.

[10] D. Angluin and L. Valiant. Fast probabilistic algorithms for Hamiltonian circuits and matchings. In *Proceedings of the Ninth Annual ACM Symposium on Theory of Computing*. ACM Press, 1977.

[11] J. L. Balcázar, J. Díaz, and J. Gabarró. *Structural Complexity I*. EATCS Monographs on Theoretical Computer Science. Springer-Verlag, 1988.

[12] J. L. Balcázar, J. Díaz, and J. Gabarró. *Structural Complexity II*. EATCS Monographs on Theoretical Computer Science. Springer-Verlag, 1990.

[13] D. A. Barrington. Bounded width polynomial size branching programs recognize exactly those languages in NC^1. In *Proceedings of the Eighteenth Annual ACM Symposium on Theory of Computing*, pages 1–5. ACM Press, 1986.

[14] P. Beame, E. Brisson, and R. Ladner. The complexity of computing symmetric functions using threshold circuits. Technical Report No. 90–01–01, Dept. of Computer Science and Engineering, University of Washington, 1990.

[15] G. Bell. The future of high performance computers in science and engineering. *Communications of the ACM*, 32(9):1091–1101, 1989.

[16] P. Berman, I. Parberry, and G. Schnitger. A note on the complexity of reliability in neural networks. Technical Report CRPDC-91-3, Center for Research in Parallel and Distributed Computing, University of North Texas, 1991.

[17] A. Blum and R. L. Rivest. Training a 3-node neural network is NP-complete. In *Neural Information Processing Systems 1*, pages 494–501. Morgan Kaufmann, 1989.

[18] A. Blum and R. L. Rivest. Training a 3-node neural network is NP-complete. *Neural Networks*, 5(1):117–127, 1992.

[19] A. Blumer, A. Ehrenfeucht, D. Haussler, and M. K. Warmuth. Occam's razor. *Information Processing Letters*, 24:377–380, 1987.

[20] A. Borodin. On relating time and space to size and depth. *SIAM Journal on Computing*, 6(4):733–744, December 1977.

[21] J. Bruck and J. W. Goodman. A generalized convergence theorem for neural networks and its applications in combinatorial optimization. In *Proc. IEEE First International Conference on Neural Networks*, volume III, pages 649–656, San Diego, CA, June 1987.

[22] J. Campbell. *The Improbable Machine*. Simon and Schuster, 1989.

[23] M. Caudill and C. Butler. *Advanced Networks*, volume 2 of *Understanding Neural Networks: Computer Explorations*. MIT Press, 1991.

[24] M. Caudill and C. Butler. *Basic Networks*, volume 1 of *Understanding Neural Networks: Computer Explorations*. MIT Press, 1991.

[25] A. K. Chandra, S. Fortune, and R. Lipton. Lower bounds for constant depth circuits for prefix problems. In *Proc. 10th International Colloquium on Automata, Languages, and Programming*, in Series *Lecture Notes in Computer Science*, volume 154, pages 109–117. Springer-Verlag, 1983.

[26] A. K. Chandra, S. J. Fortune, and R. Lipton. Unbounded fan-in circuits and associative functions. In *Proceedings of the Fifteenth Annual ACM Symposium on Theory of Computing*, pages 52–60. ACM Press, 1983.

[27] A. K. Chandra, L. J. Stockmeyer, and U. Vishkin. Constant depth reducibility. *SIAM Journal on Computing*, 13(2):423–439, May 1984.

[28] H. Chernoff. A measure of asymptotic efficiency for tests of a hypothesis based on the sum of observations. *Annals of Mathematical Statistics*, 23:493–507, 1952.

[29] N. Chomsky. On certain formal properties of grammars. *Information and Control*, 2(2):137–167, 1959.

[30] A. Church. The calculi of lambda-conversion. *Annals of Mathematical Studies*, 6, 1941.

[31] P. M. Churchland and P. S. Churchland. Could a machine think? *Scientific American*, 262(1):32–37, 1990.

[32] S. Cook. A taxonomy of problems with fast parallel algorithms. *Information and Control*, 64(1–3):2–22, 1985.

[33] S. A. Cook. The complexity of theorem proving procedures. In *Proceedings of the Third Annual ACM Symposium on Theory of Computing*, pages 151–158. ACM Press, 1971.

[34] S. A. Cook. Towards a complexity theory of synchronous parallel computation. *L'Enseignement Mathématique*, XXVII(1–2):75–100, 1980.

[35] T. H. Cormen, C. E. Leiserson, and R. L. Rivest. *Introduction to Algorithms*. MIT Press, 1990.

[36] *DARPA Neural Network Study*. AFCEA International Press, 1988.

[37] J. Diederich, editor. *Artificial Neural Networks — Concept Learning*. IEEE Computer Society Press, 1988.

[38] D. Dingzhu. A new lower bound for parity circuits. In *Combinatorics, Computing, and Complexity*, pages 132–141. Kluwer Academic Publishers, 1989.

[39] R. L. Dobrushin and S. I. Ortyukov. Upper bounds for the redundancy of self-correcting arrangements of unreliable functional elements. *Problems of Information Transmission*, 13:203–218, 1977.

[40] F. I. Dretske. *Explaining Behavior: Reasons in a World of Causes*. MIT Press, 1988.

[41] P. W. Dymond. Simultaneous resource bounds and parallel computations. Ph. D. Thesis, Technical Report TR145, Dept. of Computer Science, Univ. of Toronto, August 1980.

[42] P. W. Dymond and S. A. Cook. Hardware complexity and parallel computation. In *21st Annual Symposium on Foundations of Computer Science*, pages 360–372. IEEE Computer Society Press, 1980.

[43] G. D. Fischbach. Mind and brain. *Scientific American*, 267(3):48–57, 1992.

[44] M. Furst, J. B. Saxe, and M. Sipser. Parity, circuits and the polynomial time hierarchy. *Mathematical Systems Theory*, 17(1):13–27, 1984.

[45] S. I. Gallant. A connectionist learning algorithm with provable generalization and scaling bounds. *Neural Networks*, 3:191–201, 1990.

[46] M. R. Garey and D. S. Johnson. *Computers and Intractability: A Guide to the Theory of NP-Completeness*. W. H. Freeman, 1979.

[47] G. Godbeer. The computational complexity of the stable state problem for connectionist models. Master's thesis, Dept. of Computer Science, Univ. of Toronto, September 1987.

[48] M. Goldmann, J. Håstad, and A. Razborov. Majority gates vs. general weighted threshold gates. In *Proc. 7th Annual Structure in Complexity Theory Conference*, pages 2–13. IEEE Computer Society Press, 1992.

[49] L. M. Goldschlager. Synchronous parallel computation. Ph. D. Thesis, Technical Report TR114, Dept. of Computer Science, Univ. of Toronto, December 1977.

[50] L. M. Goldschlager. A universal interconnection pattern for parallel computers. *Journal of the ACM*, 29(4):1073–1086, October 1982.

[51] L. M. Goldschlager and A. M. Lister. *Computer Science: A Modern Introduction*. Prentice-Hall, 1983.

[52] L. M. Goldschlager and I. Parberry. On the construction of parallel computers from various bases of Boolean functions. *Theoretical Computer Science*, 43(1):43–58, May 1986.

[53] E. Goles-Chacc and F. Fogelman-Soulie. Decreasing energy functions as a tool for studying threshold networks. *Discrete Applied Mathematics*, 12:261–277, 1985.

[54] R. L. Graham, D. E. Knuth, and O. Patashnik. *Concrete Mathematics: A Foundation for Computer Science*. Addison-Wesley, 1989.

[55] A. Hajnal, W. Maass, P. Pudlák, M. Szegedy, and G. Turán. Threshold circuits of bounded depth. In *28th Annual Symposium on Foundations of Computer Science*, pages 99–110. IEEE Computer Society Press, October 1987.

[56] S. E. Hampson and D. J. Volper. Linear function neurons: Structure and training. *Biological Cybernetics*, 53:203–217, 1986.

[57] D. Harel. *Algorithmics: The Spirit of Computing*. Addison-Wesley, 1987.

[58] J. Hartmanis and R. E. Stearns. On the computational complexity of algorithms. *Transactions of the American Mathematical Society*, 117(5):285–306, 1965.

[59] J. Hertz, A. Krogh, and R. Palmer. *Introduction to the Theory of Neural Computation*. Addison-Wesley, 1991.

[60] G. E. Hinton and T. J. Sejnowski. Learning and relearning in Boltzmann machines. In *Parallel Distributed Processing: Explorations in the Microstructure of Cognition*, volume 1, pages 282–317. MIT Press, 1986.

[61] G. E. Hinton, T. J. Sejnowski, and D. H. Ackley. Boltzmann machines: Constraint satisfaction networks that learn. Technical Report CMU-CS-84-119, Dept. of Computer Science, Carnegie-Mellon Univ., May 1984.

[62] T. Hofmeister, W. Hohberg, and S. Köhling. Some notes on threshold circuits and multiplication in depth 4. *Information Processing Letters*, 39(4):219–226, 1991.

[63] J. Hong. *Computation: Computability, Similarity and Duality*. Pitman Publishing, London, 1986.

[64] J. Hong. On connectionist models. Technical Report 87-012, Dept. of Computer Science, Univ. of Chicago, June 1987.

[65] J. J. Hopfield. Neural networks and physical systems with emergent collective computational abilities. *Proc. National Academy of Sciences*, 79:2554–2558, April 1982.

[66] S.-T. Hu. *Threshold Logic*. University of California Press, 1965.

[67] N. Immerman and S. Landau. The complexity of iterated multiplication. *Proc. 4th IEEE Structure in Complexity Theory Conference*, pages 104–111, 1989.

[68] J. S. Judd. Learning in networks is hard. In *Proc. of the First International Conference on Neural Networks*, pages 685–692. IEEE Computer Society Press, 1987.

[69] J. S. Judd. *Neural Network Design and the Complexity of Learning*. PhD thesis, University of Massachusetts, Amherst, MA, 1988.

[70] J. S. Judd. On the complexity of loading shallow neural networks. *Journal of Complexity*, 4:177–192, 1988.

[71] J. S. Judd. *Neural Network Design and the Complexity of Learning*. MIT Press, 1990.

[72] N. Karmarkar. A new polynomial-time algorithm for linear programming. *Combinatorica*, 4:373–395, 1984.

[73] R. M. Karp and R. J. Lipton. Turing machines that take advice. *L'Enseignment Mathematique*, 30, February 1980.

[74] S. C. Kleene. *Introduction to Metamathematics*. D. Van Nostrand, Princeton, NJ, 1952.

[75] R. E. Ladner. The circuit value problem is log space complete for P. *SIGACT News*, 7(1):18–20, 1975.

[76] D. T. Langendoen and P. M. Postal. *The Vastness of Natural Languages*. Basil Blackwell, 1984.

[77] M. Lepley and G. Miller. Computational power for networks of threshold devices in an asynchronous environment. Dept. of Mathematics, MIT, 1983.

[78] J.-H. Lin and J. S. Vitter. Complexity results on learning by neural nets. *Machine Learning*, 6:211–230, 1991.

[79] J. Lipscomb. On the computational complexity of finding a connectionist model's stable state vectors. Master's thesis, Dept. of Computer Science, Univ. of Toronto, October 1987.

[80] O. Lupanov. Implementing the algebra of logic functions in terms of bounded depth formulas in the basis +, *, −. *Soviet Physics Doklady*, 6(2), 1961.

[81] O. Lupanov. Implementing the algebra of logic functions in terms of bounded depth formulas in the basis +, *, −. *Doklady Akad. Nauk SSR*, 166(5), 1961.

[82] W. S. McCulloch and W. Pitts. A logical calculus of ideas immanent in nervous activity. *Bulletin of Mathematical Biophysics*, 5:115–133, 1943.

[83] C. Mead and L. Conway. *An Introduction to VLSI Systems*. Addison-Wesley, 1981.

[84] P. Mehra and B. W. Wah, editors. *Artificial Neural Networks: Concepts and Theory*. IEEE Computer Society Press, 1992.

[85] G. A. Miller. The magic number seven, plus or minus two: Some limits on our capacity for processing information. *The Psychological Review*, 63(2), 1956.

[86] M. Minsky and S. Papert. *Perceptrons*. MIT Press, 1969.

[87] S. Muroga. Lower bounds of the number of threshold functions and a maximum weight. *IEEE Transactions on Electronic Computers*, EC–14(2):136–148, 1965.

[88] S. Muroga. *Threshold Logic and its Applications*. Wiley-Interscience, New York, 1971.

[89] S. Muroga, I. Toda, and S. Takasu. Theory of majority decision elements. *J. Franklin Inst.*, 271:376–418, May 1961.

[90] S. Muroga, T. Tsuboi, and C. R. Baugh. Enumeration of threshold functions of eight variables. *IEEE Transactions on Computers*, C–19(9):818–825, September 1970.

[91] B. K. Natarajan. *Machine Learning: A Theoretical Approach*. Morgan Kaufmann, 1991.

[92] A. Novikoff. On convergence proofs for perceptrons. In *Proc. Symposium on Mathematical Theory of Automata*, pages 615–622, New York, NY, 1962.

[93] A. M. Odlyzko and D. J. Randall. On the periods of some graph transformations. *Complex Systems*, 1:203–210, 1987.

[94] I. Parberry. *Parallel Complexity Theory*. Research Notes in Theoretical Computer Science. Pitman Publishing, London, 1987.

[95] I. Parberry. A primer on the complexity theory of neural networks. In R. Banerji, editor, *Formal Techniques in Artificial Intelligence: A Sourcebook*, volume 6 of *Studies in Computer Science and Artificial Intelligence*, pages 217–268. North-Holland, 1990.

[96] I. Parberry. Knowledge, understanding, and computational complexity. Technical Report CRPDC-92-2, Center for Research in Parallel and Distributed Computing, Dept. of Computer Sciences, University of North Texas, February 1992.

[97] I. Parberry. On the complexity of learning with a small number of nodes. In *Proc. 1992 International Joint Conference on Neural Networks*, volume 3, pages 893–898, 1992.

[98] I. Parberry. On linear threshold functions with real inputs. Technical Report CRPDC–93–9, Center for Research in Parallel and Distributed Computing, Dept. of Computer Sciences, University of North Texas, 1993.

[99] I. Parberry and G. Schnitger. Parallel computation with threshold functions (preliminary version). In *Proc. Structure in Complexity Theory Conference*, volume 223, pages 272–290, Berkeley, California, June 1986.

[100] I. Parberry and G. Schnitger. Relating Boltzmann machines to conventional models of computation. In *Proc. 2nd International Symposium on Methodologies for Intelligent Systems*, pages 347–354. North-Holland, October 1987.

[101] I. Parberry and G. Schnitger. Parallel computation with threshold functions. *Journal of Computer and System Sciences*, 36(3):278–302, 1988.

[102] I. Parberry and G. Schnitger. Relating Boltzmann machines to conventional models of computation. *Neural Networks*, 2(1):59–67, 1989.

[103] J. Pearl. On the connection between the complexity and credibility of inferred models. *International Journal of General Systems*, 4:255–264, 1978.

[104] N. Pippenger. On simultaneous resource bounds. In *20th Annual Symposium on Foundations of Computer Science*, pages 307–311. IEEE Computer Society Press, 1979.

[105] N. Pippenger. On networks of noisy gates. In *26th Annual Symposium on Foundations of Computer Science*, pages 30–38. IEEE Computer Society Press, 1985.

[106] N. Pippenger. Invariance of complexity measures for networks with unreliable gates. *Journal of the ACM*, 36(3):531–539, July 1989.

[107] S. Poljak. Transformations on graphs and convexity. *Complex Systems*, 1:1021–1033, 1987.

[108] S. Poljak and M. Sura. On periodical behaviour in societies with symmetric influences. *Combinatorica*, 3(1):119–121, 1983.

[109] S. Porat. Stability and looping in connectionist models with asymmetric weights. Technical Report TR 210, Dept. of Computer Science, Univ. of Rochester, March 1987.

[110] E. Post. Formal reductions of the general combinatorial decision problem. *Amer. J. Math.*, 65:197–215, 1943.

[111] P. Raghavan. Learning in threshold networks. In *Proceedings of the 1988 Workshop on Computational Learning Theory*, pages 19–27, Cambridge, MA, August 1988.

[112] N. P. Redkin. Synthesis of threshold element networks for certain classes of Boolean functions. *Kibernetika*, (5):6–9, 1970.

[113] R. L. Rivest. Learning decision lists. *Machine Learning*, 2:229–246, 1988.

[114] A. J. Rockell, R. W. Hiorns, and T. P. S. Powell. The basic uniformity in structure of the neocortex. *Brain*, 103:221–244, 1980.

[115] K. H. Rosen. *Discrete Mathematics and its Applications*. Random House, 1988.

[116] F. Rosenblatt. The perceptron: A probabilistic model for information storage and organization in the brain. *Psychological Review*, 65:386–408, 1958.

[117] D. E. Rumelhart, J. L. McClelland, and The PDP Research Group. *Foundations*, volume 1 of *Parallel Distributed Processing: Explorations in the Microstructure of Cognition*. MIT Press, 1986.

[118] D. E. Rumelhart, J. L. McClelland, and The PDP Research Group. *Psychological and Biological Models*, volume 2 of *Parallel Distributed Processing: Explorations in the Microstructure of Cognition*. MIT Press, 1986.

[119] W. L. Ruzzo. On uniform circuit complexity. *Journal of Computer and System Sciences*, 22(3):365–383, June 1981.

[120] J. E. Savage. Computational work and time on finite machines. *Journal of the ACM*, 19(4):660–674, 1972.

[121] A. Schrijver. *Theory of Linear and Integer Programming*. John Wiley & Sons, 1986.

[122] J. R. Searle. *Minds, Brains and Science*. Harvard University Press, 1984.

[123] J. R. Searle. Is the brain's mind a computer program? *Scientific American*, 262(1):26–31, 1990.

[124] J. C. Sheperdson and H. E. Sturgis. Computability of recursive functions. *Journal of the ACM*, 10(2):217–255, 1963.

[125] G. M. Shepherd. *Neurobiology*. Oxford University Press, second edition, 1988.

[126] M. Sipser. Borel sets and circuit complexity. In *Proceedings of the Fifteenth Annual ACM Symposium on Theory of Computing*, pages 61–69. ACM Press, 1983.

[127] K.-S. Siu and V. Roychowdhury. On optimal depth threshold circuits for multiplication and related problems. *SIAM Journal on Discrete Mathematics*, To Appear.

[128] K.-S. Siu, V. P. Roychowdhury, and T. Kailath. Depth-size tradeoffs for neural computation. *IEEE Transactions on Computers*, 40(12):1402–1412, 1991.

[129] K.-Y. Siu, A. Dembo, and T. Kailath. A note on the perceptron learning algorithm on data with high precision. *Journal of Computer and System Sciences*, To Appear.

[130] D. R. Smith. Bounds on the number of threshold functions. *IEEE Transactions on Electronic Computers*, EC–15(6):368–369, 1966.

[131] P. Smolensky. Information processing in dynamical systems: Foundations of harmony theory. In *Parallel Distributed Processing: Explorations in the Microstructure of Cognition*, volume 1, pages 194–281. MIT Press, 1986.

[132] D. A. Spielman. Computing arbitrary symmetric functions. Technical Report TR–906, Dept. of Computer Science, Yale University, May 1992.

[133] J. Håstad. Improved lower bounds for small depth circuits. In *Proceedings of the Eighteenth Annual ACM Symposium on Theory of Computing*, pages 6–20. ACM Press, 1986.

[134] J. Håstad. On the size of weights for threshold gates. Unpublished Manuscript, 1992.

[135] C. F. Stevens. The neuron. *Scientific American*, 241(3):54–65, 1979.

[136] D. Tam. *Methods for the Analysis of Neural Spike Train Signals*. In Preparation.

[137] A. M. Turing. On computable numbers with an application to the Entscheidungsproblem. *Proc. London Math. Soc.*, 2(42):230–265, 1936.

[138] A. M. Turing. Computing machinery and intelligence. *Mind*, 59:433–460, 1950.

[139] L. G. Valiant. A theory of the learnable. *Communications of the ACM*, 27(11):1134–1142, 1984.

[140] L. G. Valiant and G. J. Brebner. A scheme for fast parallel communication. *SIAM Journal on Computing*, 11(2):350–361, 1982.

[141] V. Vemuri, editor. *Artificial Neural Networks: Theoretical Concepts*. IEEE Computer Society Press, 1988.

[142] V. R. Vemuri, editor. *Artificial Neural Networks: Concepts and Control Applications*. IEEE Computer Society Press, 1992.

[143] S. S. Venkatesh. Directed drift: A new linear threshold algorithm for learning binary weights on-line. *Journal of Computer and System Sciences*, 46(2):198–217, 1993.

[144] J. von Neumann. Probabilistic logics and the synthesis of reliable organisms from unreliable components. In C. E. Shannon and J. McCarthy, editors, *Automata Studies*, pages 43–98. Princeton University Press, 1956.

[145] K. Wagner and G. Wechsung. *Computational Complexity*. D. Reidel Publishing Company, 1986.

[146] I. Wegener. *The Complexity of Boolean Functions*. Wiley-Teubner, 1987.

[147] I. Wegener. Unbounded fan-in circuits. In *Advances in the Theory of Computation and Computational Mathematics*. 1990.

[148] A. N. Whitehead and B. A. W. Russell. *Principia Mathematica*. Cambridge University Press, 1910–1913.

[149] R. O. Winder. *Threshold Logic*. PhD thesis, Mathematics Dept., Princeton University, 1962.

[150] S. Yajima and T. Ibaraki. A lower bound on the number of threshold functions. *IEEE Transactions on Electronic Computers*, EC–14(6):926–929, 1965.

[151] A. C. Yao. Separating the polynomial-time hierarchy by oracles. In *26th Annual Symposium on Foundations of Computer Science*, pages 1–10. IEEE Computer Society Press, 1985.

[152] A. C. Yao. Circuits and local computation. In *Proceedings of the Twenty First Annual ACM Symposium on Theory of Computing*, pages 186–196. ACM Press, 1989.

[153] J. M. Zurada. *Introduction to Artificial Neural Systems*. West Publishing Company, 1992.

Index